ANTI-KISSING IN AMERICA, 1876-1922

by

Kerry Segrave

Contents.

Introduction.

This book looks at the movements that arose in America during the period of 1876 until 1922 and did battle against the kiss. The practice of kissing, or osculation, was frowned upon and even punished to some extent in colonial America but from the late 1600s onward had slowly been rehabilitated until it had almost taken its place as a respected member of society, by the late 1800s. Public kissing by anybody, especially between women, continued to be viewed in a negative light but things were looking up for the kiss. Then in 1876 it was proven that microorganisms could transfer disease from an ailing creature to a healthy creature. Specifically Robert Koch proven anthrax could be passed that way from anthrax-sickened cows to healthy cows, through an injection of infected blood. And within a few years the microbe craze was sweeping the United States. It was a great fear of a bacterial planet. Many items and practices were singled out for attack as America tried desperately, and futilely, to keep itself save from being overrun by disease-laden bacteria, and bacteria were everywhere, from the pen and holder fastened to the bank branch counter, to the common drinking cup found all over the place, and even to the kiss. Especially to the kiss.

The kiss had never quite made it to the point of respectability with a force of puritans always on its heels. Thus the reaction to the kiss, in the face of its bacteria-laden lips, made the kiss an easy target during the microbe wars and fears. That battle against, say, the common drinking cup was strictly unemotional and based solely on health concerns, whether they were correct or not. Morality and the puritan ethic played no part in the war on that item. However, the battle against the kiss was highly emotional and puritanical and based only slightly on health concerns, with the battle against the kiss often carried out under the guise of a health initiative. More off than not if you scratched one of those health fanatics you likely found a puritan fanatic. It is that war against the kiss, both futile and bizarre, that this book is about.

Research for this book was conducted using online databases with the Library of Congress "Chronicling America" database and newspaperarchive.com being the most important and useful ones.

Chapter one looks very briefly at the state of the kiss before Koch's seminal discovery. Just as osculation was beginning to be seen in an increasingly positive light Koch and his microbes turned up. It still was, though, not something to be done very much in public. Especially irritating to certain men was the sight of women kissing each other in public. The arrival of Koch's bugs ensured the kiss would not move that last little way into respectability, at least not for a time.

Chapter two outlines responses to the kiss that really were, for the most part, taken out of concern for issues of health. Doctors often made anti-kissing pronouncements. Various cities and states had their own health departments and officials in those agencies were in the forefront of people battling osculation. Health warnings were regularly issued from such agencies and sometimes odd and bizarre measures were suggested or even undertaken. A major focus of those who fought osculation in the name of health was on babies. That is, a major effort was undertaken to get people to stop kissing babies, particularly on the lips; it was an effort that even was applied to the mothers of the babies.

In chapter three is discussed the sanitary kiss. That is, it was a method that allowed people to kiss away whenever they wanted to, provided that they used some device or implement that had to be placed between the lips of the kissers. It had to have a germicide of some type applied to it and then, of course, since the germicide had a foul taste the device had to also be perfumed. But, if science had caused all the fuss, then science stood ready to solve the problem. The "kissinette" as one of the devices was called, and its brethren, were bizarre indeed.

Chapter four details the crusades against the kiss that were undertaken mainly from a morality standpoint. In some cases it was a lone individual who waged the war while in other instances it was an existing organization that took up the fight. For example the WCTU (Woman's Christian

Temperance Union) added the war on kissing to its fairly lengthy list of targets.

Organizations that came into being as single-issue associations solely to fight the kiss are the subject

of chapter five. Most of these had seemingly brief lives and got little more attention that a brief article

or two in the press. However, some of them were fairly long-lived, or at least got a good deal of media

coverage.

Chapter six looks at rules, regulations and laws in America that dealt with the practice of kissing;

rules from official public or private agencies that had the power to impose those edicts. Such items

ranged from school boards imposing a no-kissing rule on its pupils, to railroads banning osculation on

its platforms between passengers who were coming and going, to city park boards that banned kissing

in the parks, and to hapless people who were taken to court on disorderly conduct charges, after being

found kissing in public, and actually fined.

Ch. 1. Prior to 1876.

When one writer looked at kissing in ancient times he remarked, in 1902, that the ancient Greeks were in the habit of kissing the lips, hands, knees or feet in the way of salutations, with the degree of such greeting being a function of how much or how little respect the greeter thought the person of their attentions merited. He noted that kissing was mentioned numerous times in the Bible and that kissing was a religious ceremonial. It was also stated that kissing was an act of religion in ancient Rome. The nearest friend of a dying person performed the rite of receiving his soul by a kiss, supposing that it escaped through his lips at the moment of his expiration. Later, in Rome, near relatives were allowed to kiss their female kindred on the mouth, but that was done in order to know whether they smelt if wine, because the Roman women, in spite of the prohibition, were sometimes found to have made too free with the wine. According to this account kissing was first introduced into England by royalty. The British monarch Vortigen, a 5th century warlord, gave a banquet in honor of his Scandinavian allies, at which Rowena, the beautiful daughter of Hengist was present. During the proceedings Rowena, after pressing a brimming beaker to her lips, saluted the surprised monarch with a little kiss, after the manner of her people. This writer went on to briefly mention the treacherous kiss – the Judas kiss. He also outlined some of the "serious" kisses of history, notably those and Antony and Cleopatra and of Henry VIII and Anne Boleyn. Both of those, it was said, shook an empire and destroyed a religion. In some quarters of the planet the practice of kissing was not favored if, indeed, it was known. The writer of this piece declared that; "Africa is the largest non-kissing area on the face of the earth."[1]

On July 16, 1439 an act was passed in England forbidding kissing, owing to the pestilence then raging over England and France. That was said to have been the only measure enacted against kissing in England.[2]

Under the Blue Laws of Connecticut in the late 1600s no woman was allowed to kiss even her child

on the Sabbath, or fasting day, under heavy penalties. English author John Bunyan, around the same

time, denounced kissing very forcefully while the Puritans looked upon the practice with extreme

disfavor. Bunyan condemned kissing by saying; "The common salutation of women I abhor, it is

odious to me. When I have seen good men salute women I have made my objection against it. I have

told them that it was not a comely sight." The New Englanders of the late 1600s seemed to have been

very much opposed to the practice. Kissing without the consent of parents was punishable by a fine of

40 shillings. Under that law, at a court in New Haven, Connecticut in May 1660 Jacob Murline and

Sarah Tuttle were prosecuted for "sitting down on a cheste together, his arme around her waiste, and

her arme upon his shoulder, or about his neck, and continuing in that sinful posture about half an hour,

in the which time he kyssed her and she kyssed him and they kyssed one another, as ye witnesses

testified" Another account said the whole affair started when Sarah dropped her gloves and Jacob

found them. When Sarah asked for them back Jacob demanded a kiss as his reward. She agreed and

complied with the request. According to this account each was fined 20 shillings.[3]

One account declared that the New England Blue Laws with respect to kissing were passed during the

reign of King Charles II, who ruled from 1660 to 1685. Under those famous blue laws, it was reported,

many men were fined or put in the stocks for kissing their wives in public on Sundays, such conduct

being, according to the morals of those days, lewd and unseemly behavior."[4]

Over the following 200 or so years animosity toward the kiss seemed to have largely vanished. One

journalist, writing in 1860, depicted the kiss as having entered almost a golden age of acceptance. He

began his piece by stating; "One of the most extensive and dearly cherished institutions of the day is

kissing. From small beginnings and exceedingly strict limitations it has grown and extended until all

classes and ages of people claim its indulgence, and it permeates every possible place where men and

women congregate." He added that; "It is but a few generations since the so-called 'blue laws' of

Connecticut and Massachusetts forbade men from kissing even their wives on Sunday, under severe penalties. Within the remembrance of all middle-aged people kissing was limited by propriety to that which might be indulged in between husband and wife, parents and children, brothers and sisters. The rule was in a few years so much relaxed, it is said, that anxious lovers could seal their engagement with one kiss, the next to be taken only after the meeting at the altar." A few years after that "and a moderate indulgence between cousins was not deemed improper; then, when cousins were not convenient other folks' cousins did just as well. And so it has gone on until kissing between males and females without any reference to relationship or marriage is almost universal." He went on to add that; "Again, it was once believed, and that belief was acted upon, that kissing should be enjoyed only in private or within the domestic circle, but this old fogy notion has for some time been abandoned, as too squeamish for this fast age." In conclusion the journalist declared; "Now kissing is indulged in the most public places, in the street, railway stations and cars, school-houses and churches…And so it has gone on until kissing is a recognized institution, in which all who desire may freely indulge." Undoubtedly this article exaggerated the degree to which kissing had become accepted and acceptable but the practice no longer faced the hostility in had in the recent past.[5]

Kissing in public between opposite sex partners was not nearly as acceptable as the above account would have the reader believe. In an 1873 editorial a newsman wrote a short piece on kissing in public. His piece was partly tongue-in-cheek, and partly serious. He gave advice to the young man who had taken his girl out on an afternoon a few days previous and had been seen hugging and kissing her. The editor advised him "not to kiss and hug her again…unless he is sure there are no lookers on. It is very aggravating to young men to see such a game going on and have no chance to take a part in the enjoyment."[6]

Kissing in public between women also never reached the sort of level of acceptance the above journalist suggested. An editor remarked, also in 1860; "Women kiss each other, because they haven't the courage to ask a man to kiss them. It is a very disagreeable business, doubtless, but vastly suggestive, and rarely happens save in the presence of the opposite sex."[7]

A lengthy article appeared in 1866 that discussed the friendship of women. A small section of that piece stated; "No man likes to see two women kiss one another; he wishes they would put off the caressing till they are safe by the bedroom fire, till their dressing gown is on and their back hair down. And, indeed, no man wishes the existence of this last privilege to be in any way ostentatiously paraded in his sight and hearing. Except in the case of a married man whose wife goes off to chatter with her friend or sister, it does him no harm, but still he does not like it." Continued the journalist; "If a man dislikes to see two women kiss one another, it does not imply that he would like to take the place of one of them, and kiss the other himself. No doubt if such be the case, the feeling is heightened; but it exists even though both women are totally indifferent to him. In no case do people like to see an ostentatious display of privileges from which they are debarred, even though they do not feel the being debarred to be any kind of loss."[8]

Writing in 1870 a newspaper editor stated that he had noticed that when former students and graduates met there was a warmth of greeting and handshaking that made him "almost afraid" that men would take to kissing each other when they meet "as the women now do. It is unnatural enough to see women kiss each other. It is natural enough to see men and women kiss…"[9]

For an editor who was writing in 1876 a conundrum often asked was why was it that women kissed each other in the street when they met. Men shook hands, he observed but the women, old and young, "while shaking hands frantically kiss each other through veils or other head-gear obstructions. Many of the street salutations make a report like a pistol, and must certainly be a tiresome labial exercise. At least so the men think without knowing anything about it, yet we opine they would not object to be included in the custom, which now results in a waste of sweetness on the desert air."[10]

Women kissing in public provoked enough of a hostile reaction that it was the catalyst for a poem that was published in a newspaper on June 4, 1869. It was titled, "Kissing in the Street."

Did you ever notice mortals –

Now I'll bet you did –

Now the ladies – pretty creatures –

Can't keep their feelings hid!

But they are kissing out in public;

Kissing everywhere they meet;

Kiss – kiss at church, at shopping,

And – kissing – in the street!

Behold a charming maiden,

Arrayed in fashion bright,

She meets upon the sidewalk

A friend she saw last night:

"How are you darling Nellie?

How glad I am to meet,"

Then a dainty shake of fingers

And a – kissing – in the street!

A bachelor beside us

Says, "pity this is done

So much, for I am certain

It can't be any fun;

This kissing out in public:

Kissing everywhere they meet;

Kiss, kiss, at church and shopping,

And – kissing – in the street!"

"But the secret great, is this, sir!

The maiden has no beau –

No gentleman to kiss her –

She must her feelings show

By kissing out in public;

Kissing all she may meet:

Kiss, kiss, at church and shopping;

And – kissing – in the street!"

Now merry hearted maidens,

And women most discreet,

Give over this bad habit

Of kissing in the street;

Remember that false traitor

Who knelt at Jesus' feet

And don't become a greeter

By kissing in the street.

Be noble minded women

With hearts attend the right;

Then shall each see the other

As those who dwell in light;

But never for an instant –

Whoever you may meet –

Be caught like silly noodles,

A kissing in the street.[11]

At the start of the period covered by this book kissing was still frowned upon in certain quarters and under certain conditions. However, that opposition likely would have remained minor and limited to something of a fringe activity for a small number of zealots. Then, in 1876 the microorganism and its ability to spread disease from one person to another was proven and that set off a microbe frenzy in America. Many things came under fire such as the use of common drinking cups, handshaking, and so on. Singled out for special attention and attack was the kiss. Many who attacked the practice of kissing did so on purely health grounds but a probably larger number, who opposed the practice on morality grounds, were emboldened to step out of the shadows and add their voices to those attacking osculation. Health scares allowed the moralists to cloak their attacks under the guise their attacks were health-driven and not puritan-driven. Thus, thanks to microbes the attacks on osculation were more widespread and longer lasting than they would have been in the absence of the germ-carrying and germ-spreading bacteria discovery. Ultimately those attacks all failed but they got a lot of attention for a lengthy period of time. By the time the 1920s arrived the anti-kissing forces were spent and the movement to control or regulate osculation quickly and quietly faded away.

Ch. 2. Health.

The war on kissing in America had its roots in the discovery of microbes and the dangers that lay therein. It meant that much of the crusading against osculation was based solely on the supposedly terrible things that could happen to the health of a person who engaged in kissing, however bizarre, irrational and far-fetched those fears might have been. It also allowed the puritans to join in to launch their own attacks on the practice. Sometimes they tried to disguise their agenda under the cloak of a health campaign; they were attacking kissing simply because it was a dangerous health practice. Sometimes their campaigns were openly morally based with health concerns a distant second or non-existent. As kissing received more negative publicity in the press that also gave an impetus to crusaders to enter the fray; that is, as osculation became more and more a "bad" or questionable practice it became easier and easier for moral puritans to attack the habit. Everybody loved to beat up a villain.

The discovery of microorganisms, or microbes as they were known in this era, went back to the 1600s. In 1876 Robert Koch established that microorganisms could cause disease. He found that the blood of cattle that were infected with anthrax always contained large numbers of bacillus anthracis. Koch found he could transmit anthrax from one animal to another by taking a small sample of blood from the infected cow and injecting it into a healthy animal, thus causing the healthy cow to quickly become sick with anthrax. He also discovered he could culture the blood from an infected animal and when a healthy animal received an injection from the cultured material that cow also quickly sickened with anthrax.

That set off a huge amount of media coverage, within a few years of Koch's discovery. The Library of Congress has a database called "Chronicling America" which contains over 10 million newspaper pages from all over America and covers the period 1836 to 1922. Under copyright law anything published in the United States prior to 1923 is in the public domain. When that database was searched using the word "microbe*" it produced, for the 10-year period 1870-1879, a total of 15 hits (3 in the five years from 1870 to 1874, and 12 hits for the last five years of that decade). The figures for 1880 to 1889 were 3,461 hits (367, 3,094); for 1890 to 1899, 20,513 (9,529, 10,984); for 1900-1909, 26,882 (15,055, 11,827) and for 1910 to 1919, 14,261 (9,597, 4,664). The craze for all things microbial had swept America, and no small number of them related to osculation.

Health warnings about the dangers of kissing started to appear regularly from about 1890 onward but some turned up earlier. One of the earliest appeared in January 1875 when an article remarked; "Don't kiss the baby" and went on to show "that adults with a cold may cause an infant to have diphtheria by a mere kiss." Young ladies were warned that they should remember that fact and refrain from exhibiting the customary affection: "Woman spare that baby; touch not its little lips."[1]

About six weeks later a newspaper editor pronounced the promiscuous kissing of children to be a "pestilent practice. We use the word advisedly, and it is mild for the occasion. Murderess would be the proper word did the kissers know the mischief they do." He then stated how children easily got diphtheria from adults and asserted; "It would be absurd to charge the spread of diphtheria entirely to the practice of child-kissing. There are other modes of propagation, yet it is hard to conceive of any more directly suited to the spread of the infection or more generally in its operation. It stands to diphtheria in about the same relation that promiscuous hand-shaking formerly did to the itch." Concluded the editor, with respect to the kissing of children; "It is better to avoid the practice. The children will not suffer if they go unkissed; and their friends ought for their sake to forego the luxury for a season. A single kiss has been known to infect a family; and the most careful may be in condition to communicate the disease without knowing it. Beware, then, of playing Judas, and let the babies alone."[2]

A newspaper editor remarked, in January 1883 that the doctors and medical journals were preaching a crusade against kissing. One "learned" writer, he said, asserted the "promiscuous kissing has been infinitely more productive* of disease of various kinds than the public ever dream of, and it is a practice that should be discountenanced. The people should confine their kissing propensities to members of their own families and even then it is not always safe." That caused the editor to conclude; "If this will have a tendency to check osculatory exercises on the streets and in the streetcars some good will be accomplished."[3]

 Just one year later, in February 1884, the Reverend Mr. Deems of New York delivered a sermon in which he denounced "the purely American habit of kissing," stating that "while it is bad enough for adults to kiss, it is criminal for a lot of dirty-mouthed people to kiss an innocent baby."[4]

 "With the establishment of the recent scientific theory that osculation is a death-dealing practice," remarked a reporter in March 1885, the boys and girls of this country are going to have a dull time of it. He also mentioned that the Minnesota Legislature was then trying to "throttle co-skating." However, the newsman speculated; "But things cannot last this way. Nature's laws are supreme over man's judgment…And just so long as Nature moulds the touching face and plants juicy kisses on ruby lips, young men will osculate, law or no law."[5]

 A writer in a Toronto Ontario newspaper declared, in September 1886; "If I was a woman, and could see the faults of my fellows as well as the average observant man can, I would form a society for the abolition of kissing. It must come to that anyway within the next ten years." He then quoted a medical man, whose opinion of kissing he sought, as saying; "An elegant dissemination of disease. Fever is spread by it; so are lung troubles, and such physical scythes as diphtheria and other contagious diseases. I would abolish kissing and thus save one-tenth of 1 per cent. of human lives every year – if life-saving is the end and aim of science which you know I doubt."[6]

 All the controversy over kissing prompted some wit to write a poem, "The Hygiene of Kisses," which was published on August 9, 1885.

Chawley, dear, said a lovely maid,

As they sat in the house one night,

It's unhealthy to kiss the doctors say,

So, of course, it cannot be right, not right.

"Well darling, spoke the noble youth,

As the color mantled high,

I never thought being kissed to death

Such a horrible death to die. Let's try.[7]

An article that appeared originally in a magazine called *Health and Home* was reprinted in various newspapers in March 1887 and began by stating; "An evil habit existing among women is promiscuous kissing. Undoubtedly many diseases are caught this way. Women are not content, as men are, to shake each other cordially by the hand, but if Jane hasn't been seen for two days she must be kissed." The piece continued by declaring; "But if this practice were only confined to women themselves. Ah, no – the little babes and children must be made the victims as well." In conclusion the writer asserted; "The laws of common sense and hygiene should tell us that the pernicious habit must be curbed. Colds, sore-throat, diphtheria, fevers and many other contagious diseases can be taken by the simple act of kissing."[8]

A news story that appeared in August 1889 took as its topic the decline of the kiss; "Of late kissing has fallen into a state of desuetude. It was not always thus, as a glance at the poets, ancient and modern will show….The fact of the matter is, it is not good form to kiss anymore, The bridal kiss was tabooed long ago, much against ministerial protest, and weddings are as un-osculatory as funerals." According to this newsman; "The medical profession is credited with the decline of the practice, and it is said there is ample evidence in its literature to prove that promiscuous kissing is an admirable means of spreading disease."[9]

An unlikely "expert" whose opinion was sought out was General William Tecumseh Sherman, of American Civil War fame, who was approached by a reporter in November 1890 when Sherman was 70 years old. He was sought out at that time, when he had just turned seventy, to elicit his opinion on various topics. The journalist went to him and told him that "one of the bulwarks of our liberty is in danger." When Sherman asked him which one was in peril the reporter told him there was a crusade on against kissing. Reportedly Sherman was greatly distressed and said; "It's not a subject that admits of any discussion whatever. People have kissed since the world began. The mother kisses her child – the husband his wife." The reporter replied to the military man; "But the doctors say it breeds disease." Sherman replied; "Nonsense. Are you going to believe all that the doctors tell you?..If you listen to them you won't know whether you are alive or a corpse. I guess as long as the girls like it, the men won't hold back."[10]

Also in November 1890 a New York City newspaper made a brief mention of a woman who was beginning a crusade against kissing because the woman believed the habit to be unsanitary. Largely it was a mocking article with the newsman retorting; "no story of microbes has any effect upon me…it strikes me that these advanced women tell too much."[11]

An article that was published in June 1891 dealt with the topic of hygiene for the home by beginning; "The spread of many diseases through contact of the lips is especially noticeable in those countries where kissing is a common custom of greeting. The disease may be communicated from one person to another through the breath, which is full of tiny microbes, or by the lips, on which linger small bacteria, ready to change from one person to another." Especially singled out was; "The promiscuous habit of ladies to kiss every chance acquaintance that they meet is especially to be deplored. They kiss the sick, the well, the dead and everybody who appeals to them in any way. Not infrequently they stop on the street and kiss a blue-eyed child whose appealing face attracts them, and this impulsive act may be the means of spreading some dangerous diseases among all of their friends…There is no telling how much harm may be done by such a simple kindly act." The reader was advised that when a person had a cold, the grippe, tonsillitis or other similar diseases all kissing, even between sweethearts, should be avoided; "Disease knows no respect, and the coral lips of the handsomest girl may carry the deadly bacteria to her lover as well as the roughest mouth of an outcast." This article concluded by warning;

"Young lovers cannot be too careful in this respect, if they wish to show their affection for each other, for it is not a proof of love to communicate a deadly disease to each other."[12]

Boards of health in various states and cities sometimes got involved in the war on kissing by issuing warnings or advice, or even issuing regulations. One of the first of such events took place in Ohio in February 1893. Dr. C. O. Probst, secretary of the Ohio Board of Health appeared before the Pastors' Union of Columbus Ohio on February 12th to urge their cooperation in two sanitary reforms. The second reform was to abolish the use of the same cup in the administration of the sacrament in churches. The same cup was often used in that instance by several hundred people. However, the first reform in Probst's agenda was to stop the custom of indiscriminate kissing. Probst explained that the most certain and most dangerous transmission of the germs of disease was by the mouth-to-mouth method. He cited "the almost universal habit among ladies of kissing friends on greeting then on bidding them good-bye, of kissing babies and children and urging babies and children to kiss each other." Pastors also, he told his audience, normally considered it part of their duties to kiss the babies of their parishioners; "And this was well meant, but it was as dangerous as it was perfunctory in many cases." At the end of the medical man's lecture "a resolution to do all possible to bring about these reforms was adopted," by the pastors.[13]

One day later an editor with a New York City newspaper commented on Probst and his lecture. First though, the editor delivered a little background; "Now sanitary science pushes itself forward to degrade the kiss to the level of sewer gas and the many agencies of which noxious and infectious disease is propagated. It is demanding the abolition of the practice as a remnant of barbarous ignorance of the laws of health. It would subordinate romantic sentiment to cautious prudence and forbid the lover the embrace of his sweetheart, even as a seal of their betrothal until they are able to produce medical certificates that they are free from the transmissible germs of disease." He declared that for several years past prudent parents, under the instructions of their doctors, have guarded their young children jealousy against the indiscriminate kiss which was once in vogue, to prevent germ transmission. The editor thought that was a reasonable precaution; "If then, it is a risk for children then it must also be a risk that older propel also must avoid. So says science." Accordingly Probst urged the Pastors' Union to stop the practice. Concluded the editor; "Thus cold and prudential science is invading the realm of tender and romantic, poetic and religious sentiment, and destroying as a pest house the very temple in which the love of all ages has offered up its worship. It is an appalling resolution."[14]

A different newspaper editor commenting on the Probst campaign observed that; "Persistence in this course will more probably abolish the state board [of health]. Many states have lived and prospered without any board of health, but none ever without kissing." And, he added; "Probably it may transmit disease, but the remedy is worse than the disease. We are confident that the voters of America will rise up as one man and say bring on your transmitter."[15]

Yet another editor felt compelled to discuss Probst and his campaign against kissing. He began his piece by observing that according to the testimony of an old-time Puritan divine "kissing has done by far more harm in the world than cursing." The editor responded by noting that curses injured only the man who uttered them while kissing, on the other hand, was liable "to injure the innocent, to transfer disease and create no end of trouble in whole communities." He then said; "And yet nobody would propose seriously to go back to Puritan asceticism and abolish kissing altogether." Therefore, he asked; "What is true temperance in kissing?" At that point he mentioned Probst and his idea and remarked, facetiously; "perhaps it is time to appoint a committee on osculation on Beacon Hill [Boston] and to move Congress for suitable legislation in the matter…Let us have some regulating in the matter of kissing, and establish it on a purely scientific basis, even if we have to 'nationalize' the whole business."[16]

City of San Francisco Health Officer Keeney addressed a communication, on November 28, 1893, as follows to the stores in that city where a Santa Claus was on exhibition during the Christmas season. It declared; "I respectfully request you to prohibit in your establishment the kissing of children by your representative of Santa Claus. This action is taken to prevent any possible danger from the spread of diphtheria or other sicknesses among the thousands of children who will visit your place during the next few weeks. Respectfully, James W. Keeney, Health Officer." Speaking of his reasons for issuing that communication, Keeney said that in the previous year he traced 23 cases of diphtheria to that cause, and about 10 of those cases ended with a fatality. Dr. Keeney declared that when a child afflicted with diphtheria kissed Santa Claus the germs of diphtheria lingered in the beard of Santa and communicated the disease to others. He believed it was a practice that should be stopped. A representative of the retail store Davis Brothers, of the Golden Rule Bazaar, said that as the Bazaar was the only place with a Santa Claus the communication was meant for his place. He stated; "We wish it understood that our Santa Claus does not kiss the children. In possibly six instances children have kissed him at the request of their parents. The beard, or fringe of white hair, is new and thoroughly clean." That Davis Brothers spokesman said he did not believe the story of 23 cases and 10 deaths from diphtheria as he had heard nothing about it; "We pronounce that statement untrue and instigated by someone whose motive is apparent. The health of the children is jeopardized far more by the condition of the sewers, cesspools, closets, restaurant kitchens, etc., than by a moment's contact with Santa Claus."[17]

An editor on a Texas newspaper commented in November 1893 that he had "grave but futile anxiety" for the public health because; "In these days of bacteria there is no more foolish and dangerous habit than that of kissing…and there is no more certain way of sowing and spreading disease than that of osculation." However, the editor then went on to admit it was "talking through its hat and against the cyclone because people will kiss or die."[18]

A brief editorial that appeared in a Kentucky paper in July 1894, before women had the vote, declared that; "When women get control of the municipal government, they will doubtless make mistakes, but they will never abolish kissing in order to promote heath."[19]

An extreme editorial response to microbes could be found in the remarks from a newsman in Pennsylvania in September 1894. "It is beginning to appear to the judgment of the public at large that the task of discovering the bacteria of disease, in everything calculated to carry on human life so as to make it worth living, has reached the limits beyond which endurance ceases to be a virtue," he fumed. "The street cars are full of them, as well as the woods. At Rochester, N.Y., the bacteriologists have found that the common communion cup must be abolished. Kissing has been lately denounced by health authorities as spreading bacteria. Medicated muzzles for mankind are urged because when a tuberculous person sneezes he fills the air with the germs of consumption." In conclusion he despaired; "The ultimate goal is found by a person who built a germ-proof house from which he never emerges, because he believes that the rest of mankind, and even the circumambient atmosphere, are arsenals loaded with venomous bacteria."[20]

An article that originated in *Good Housekeeping* in the fall of 1894 was reprinted in several newspapers. It argued that tourists to foreign lands during the current year had noticed several "radical departures" in social usage. One item found was that the shaking of hands had gone out of style abroad and that ladies no longer took the arms of gentlemen when walking with them outdoors in the evening. Reportedly no one knew for sure what caused such changes in behavior but that it "may be fear of 'the deadly microbe' which figures so extensively." At home in the United States, declared the article; "Some modern reformers have recently undertaken on its account to abolish the kiss – at least the merely social kind: but the effort has not been an entire success."[21]

An account from San Francisco in March 1895 observed that; "Anti-kissing societies grow and multiply in the land, and for this the babes have the greatest reason to be thankful." As far as this journalist was concerned; "It is at least a breach of etiquette to offer a babe the unpleasant compliment of a kiss, unless you are his near relative. In that case you are still permitted to kiss the little unfortunate, but if you are thoughtful and wise you will at least refrain from encroaching upon the child's comfort and endangering his health by kissing him upon the mouth."[22]

Summarizing what he found to be in the kiss situation in August 1895 a Kansas newspaperman wrote that; "Dr. Reilly of Chicago, warns all young ladies to bathe their lips in carbolized rosewater before kissing young men, not in a spirit of frivolity but in heavy seriousness. In Detroit a society of young ladies has been formed to oppose kissing. And in Georgia a man has been arrested for kissing his wife in public." Those items led the editor to state; "In short, the world appears to have suddenly opened its eyes to the hitherto unknown bugbear of kissing." He added that; "Pathologically there appears to be no less doubt that the infection of microbes from kissing, increases the mortuary record horribly. Legally the kiss could be readily done away with were it not for the fact that the men who make the laws and the judges who interpret them, are humans and would all walk several blocks themselves to glue their lips to another pair bursting with ruby plumpness."[23]

In Hungary it used to be customary for children to kiss the hands of their teachers when they arrived at school and when they left school for the day. According to a September 1895 report "This practice has, however, recently been forbidden by the board of education, because it is held by the sanitary council that kissing is a dangerous proceeding from a hygienic point of view and should only be resorted to when absolutely necessary." The article said that while most people would likely grant that the kissing of their teachers' hands was indeed unnecessary "but still it is to be feared that whatever terror in the way of infection of disease may lurk in a kiss, where Cupid holds sway the board of education, and even acts of parliament, will be powerless to abolish it."[24]

In a story published in the fall of 1896 it was related that a young man called on his sweetheart at Columbus Indiana when she had diphtheria and a few days later contracted the disease himself, at which point he confessed to the physician that he had kissed her. Following that revelation the press took the matter up all over America. An editor with the *Cleveland Press* said; "The old scare about indiscriminate kissing is about to be revived…Forthwith the doctors are up in arms against the pleasing practice. All the old bogey stories about transmission of disease form mouth to mouth are resurrected and placed in active circulation." The Secretary of Indiana's State Board of Health recommended a disinfectant for the use of lovers and others. The teeth were to be rinsed with it and the lips rubbed well; "Ah, that may do for Hoosiers, but it would never answer in Ohio. What! Quarantine Cupid and put a red card on Hymen! Not much!" The *Baltimore World* newspaper had a talk with the Health Commissioner of that city, regarding the Columbus case. Said Commissioner Dr. McShane; "There's no doubt that bacilli lurk in kisses." When the Columbus story appeared the secretary of the Indiana State Board of Health published a circular condemning kissing. Then a reporter asked the Baltimore Commissioner, McShane, if he could suggest any preventive. Said McShane; "Certainly: warn the people who kiss to stop it at once, or else moisten their lips with some cologne or flower water, 'before and after taking' as it were. When they have to do that they'll stop kissing. It'll take all the sentiment out of it. The only way to stop it is to educate people not to kiss." Then McShane grew reflective and said; "I don't believe they want to be educated, and I don't think it'll ever be stopped entirely. I can't say I believe in stopping it all at once. Such a plan is apt to cause bad feeling. It should cease gradually. When the male part of the kissing syndicate wants to kiss the female part of the firm, the latter ought to say: 'Now, my dear, kissing is dangerous so I won't kiss you, for I have a sore throat.'" McShane concluded by observing; "No, sir; the health department of this city will not prohibit kissing. Our police force state militia, naval reserves and oyster navy combined couldn't quell the riot that would probably result."[25]

An indignant article published on November 10, 1896 claimed that Governor Drake of Iowa owed to the people of Iowa to promptly fire L. F. Andrews, assistant secretary of the Iowa Board of Health. According to this piece Andrews' offense consisted of a declaration he made against kissing. "Andrews must be out of his mind. Quit kissing! Well, not while men and women and lads and lasses know themselves," the newsman fumed. "There are many other serious objections to the Andrews regime. It will never be popular and board or no board, kissing will go on just the same." Andrews said in an interview; "Certainly the state board of Iowa is opposed to all kissing on the lips. The board believes it ought to be abolished." But, he added; "there is no law against committing suicide. Stolen fruit is the sweetest, you know. Sterilized or unsterilized, so long as human nature remains as it is, kissing one's sweetheart will prevail, regardless of consequences or the edicts of legislatures or state boards of hearth. But, seriously, kissing on the lips is subject for thoughtful consideration." He

continued; "Many cases are on record where it has resulted fatally and our state board has especially

declared against it. Nothing is more tempting to kiss than a little babe, yet many a one has been carried

to the grave, the victim of diphtheria communicated by a kiss." He believed all mothers should refuse

all persons who offered to kiss their children, especially on the lips; "Thoughtful people no longer offer

to kiss other people or babies on the lips." When asked if there was any preventive Dr. Andrews

asserted; "There may be, but most preventatives do not prevent. Besides lovers cannot be supposed to

be perpetually sterilized as to the lips." Andrews believed that bathing the lips in certain mixtures

might prove some safeguard, however; "People who want to kiss or be kissed can keep their lips

covered with some sort of colored disinfectant. This could open up a new industry and before long the

drug stores will be advertising kissing disinfecting cosmetics of all colors and tints."[26]

 Also in November 1896 an editorial observed; "Scientists have been trying to discourage the pleasant

practice of sipping the nectar from the lips of loved beauty by intimating that mixed with the honey

were swarms of horrid bacteria that were likely to give the sippers any kind of an old thing in the way

of complaints, from a bad cold to a case of diphtheria." That caused a worry for some but, said the

account, Dr. Hurty of the Indiana State Board of Health had shown how all of those specters could be

driven away. Said Hurty; "all that is necessary to make kissing healthful is to carefully wash the mouth

with a disinfectant before indulgence in the luxury." Facetiously the journalist responded by stating

that when lovers met, if a bottle of disinfectant was handy and if the parties were agreeable; "then

carbolized lips may meet carbolized lips in a dream of bacterialess bliss. Thus romance, with the aid of

science survives, somewhat battered, but alive, the march of progress."[27]

 Another editor commented on the Indiana plan put forward by Hurty that the state of Indiana wanted

to suppress the habit of kissing by an act of the legislature, with the precipitating cause being the case

of the man in Columbus Indiana who purportedly contracted diphtheria after kissing his girlfriend, who

was sick with the disease. This newsman did not see why the board should bother with the issue;

"Nevertheless, it may be said that kissing is wholly unnecessary and is an undoubted promoter of disease, hideous though the thought may be. To the highly practical mind, which argues that it can never be abolished, science points to Japan," because noted the journalist; "the Japanese have either abolished kissing or allowed it to fall into innocuous desuetude."[28]

A report that originated in Chicago noted that, in September 1897; "A noticeable decrease in the public fashion of promenade kissing is due to the popular idea that it is vulgar to smack in public, but now there is a movement on foot to abolish kissing altogether." And, added the report; "Microbes have something to do with this, and a man who lives on the south side and has six daughters, bade them never on any account to kiss or be kissed. And the poor things promised him that they would obey."[29]

Some six weeks later an editorial discussed the dangers of kissing and began by declaring that some time ago a metropolitan newspaper contained a long account of a society, said to have been established somewhere in Indiana, the object of which was the discouragement of the habit of kissing at social parties. Membership in the society was limited strictly to women; "The writer of the article might have employed his imagination more usefully had he described a society of matrons established for the protection of babies against the osculations of every chance acquaintance or visitor in the family, or even passersby in the street." Admitting that babies were very lovable he went on to argue; "but that is no reason they should be subjected to treatment that they would sorely resent were they old enough to appreciate the indignity. And there is not alone the indignity, for the custom, when so promiscuous, is distinctly unaesthetic, and worse than that, dangerous to health." Concluded the editor; "There is no more effectual means of conveying the contagion of disease, apart from actual inoculation, than by kissing. Medical literature is full of instances of the transmission of diphtheria and other dangerous diseases in this way." He continued by stating; "And it is not the baby alone that is in danger through this custom, for it has happened more often than one could believe, that the child has been the one who was ill, and has spread its malady through a wide circle of hysterical osculators. If the anti-kissing society were ever established this is a fact that should be made the subject of its first tract."[30]

Occasionally articles appeared that summarized various illnesses that were sweeping the country at the time. The fear of epidemic-like outbreaks of various diseases such as diphtheria, tuberculosis, influenza, and so forth were real fears. An article published near the end of 1898 detailed the toll that grippe was taking in the northeast section of America. In Passaic, New Jersey, the board of health in that city, as part of its precautionary advice, had placed a ban on kissing, setting forth unequivocally that kissing was the most effective medium for dissemination of the disease. Reportedly, 300 employees of Metropolitan Life Insurance Company were then home from work ill "of the petty plague." That illness was the grippe [sometimes just 'grip'], or the flu, influenza.[31]

According to an editorial published in September 1899, the board of health of Livingston Montana was on record against kissing – at least the members of that board were opposed to "general and promiscuous kissing." It appeared that at the opening of the city schools for the new term that month the teachers were in the habit of kissing the children morning, noon and night for a full week in order, as the teachers said, "to gain their affection and obedience." The board of health believing that was a waste of time and liable to spread contagious disease among the pupils, requested the superintendent of the city schools to notify teachers to take the necessary steps to prevent the "dangerous practice." That request was reportedly being obeyed, though there was talk of a strike on the part of the teachers. With respect to that move a Montana editor said; "We believe it is a false alarm and a restriction of individual liberty. There is no telling where the prohibition will end when once started." He concluded by stating; "Who knows, too, but what the contagion cranks may become so emboldened as to prohibit kissing between man and wife. Of course, in most cast – or in some cases – this would not prove a great hardship or deprivation. Yet it would be a dangerous innovation and interference with domestic affairs"[32]

The fear of microbes and the disease they could transmit was not limited to kissing, but covered many household items and activities. Leon Noel wrote a lengthy column that appeared in December 1900 and which detailed the various ways one could get infections. One paragraph was devoted to kissing.

Noel wrote; "Kissing has been a much-discussed question, and while sentiment defends the practice hygiene is in favor of abolishing it at least as a mark of public affection. Many an infant who has been given a kiss of affection has in reality been given the kiss of death, and in adult life, serious diseases, if not fatal ones, have been transmitted by the kiss of one supposed to be pure, yet saturated with disease. Doubtless the crusade against kissing has been carried to an absurdity, but promiscuous kissing, aside from its indelicacy, is dangerous." Even so simple an action as borrowing a lead pencil could lead to the dissemination of disease in a family. Among children especially, swapping pencils was one method of showing good fellowship and the child who swapped was sometimes the innocent cause of transmitting sore throat, skin disease, diphtheria, or scarlet fever to his best friend. The use of public pencils was also, he wrote, no doubt responsible for the transmission of disease from one to another with the danger being far greater when a person moistened the lead in his mouth. As for penholders they were much more commonly used by many people and the danger of transmission of disease germs by them was therefore greater. At the hotel counter and at the bank desk penholders were handled by thousands in the course of a few days and of that number some probably had skin diseases that might be contagious and were thus transferable to others. Noel also talked about public combs and brushes with the danger from them being too evident and disgusting to need a caution against using, and the same applied to public towels, a public convenience perhaps, but a common source of the itch, or worse diseases. To wipe the hands on public towels was bad enough but to wipe and face and eyes was courting trouble of a serious kind.[33]

Noel remarked that common drinking cups could be a source of infection, including those used in churches; "In fact any article touched by the lips or hands that passes from one person to another may convey contagious virus or infectious germs. Nor is it even necessary to touch such articles." He also argued that library books were, no doubt, often conveyors of disease and although libraries had been urged to adopt some method of disinfecting books few, if any, had done so. He suggested a cheap, harmless and effective way to do so already existed – formaldehyde. [In 2011 the United States

National Toxicology Program described formaldehyde as "known to be a human carcinogen"]. He also worried about postage stamps, and the gummed flaps of envelopes which he believed to be fertile fields for the growth of germs that could be blown or otherwise implanted upon the gummed surface, the danger being increased from the liability that the tongue could be cut by the paper edge in moistening such items. The person who used his tongue to moisten stamps and other such items could be infected or inoculated as effectually as if the person were injected with the disease. "The time will come when the individual will have his individual objects of daily use. Even in the household it is wise to have one's own towel, soap, sponge, and the like, for the toilet…At the table the fad of having individual cups and saucers, and other ware, is a sensible one, though not a necessary one in most cases," predicted Noel. A sick person in the house should always have his own dishes, and so forth. Noel noted that some people even carried the dread of germs so far as to refuse to shake hands with anyone for fear of contamination; a refusal that only created ridicule and contempt although, he thought, that refusal was founded on sound reasons. "The moral of all this is clear. Be clean in your habits and touch not that which is soiled even though it be a bargain offered at a rummage sale, for dread diphtheria and scarlet fever my lurk in the folds of a garment or the crevices of furniture," Noel concluded. "On the other hand do not make yourself ridiculous! In this as in many other questions of health if it is carried to excess it simply makes life miserable, but proper precaution makes life enjoyable and lengthens our days."[34]

An object lesson could be found in Maine. Early in January 1901 Marietta Simmons, a public school teacher in Friendship Maine and sisters Nettie and Fannie Murphy were all ill at their homes in Friendship from a "malignant" form of diphtheria. A week earlier those three young women went to Round Pond, Maine to visit Flora Webber, a friend of all three, who had been ill for several weeks. The visitors stayed for "some time" and at the end of the visit "each kissed the sick girl before they left her." On the following morning Webber died. The Murphy sisters were said to be in serious condition, however, no follow-up report appeared.[35]

Dr. J. Howland Taylor, a medical inspector with the Philadelphia Board of Health discussed kissing before the Woman's Sanitary League in April 1901. He told his audience; "From the standpoint of the sanitarian I object to the practice of kissing. Kissing is most dangerous in cases of tuberculosis. There is just as much risk in touching the lips of one who has kissed a consumptive patient as in inhaling the atmosphere breathed by invalids." Taylor added; "The practice of shaking hands with consumptives is dangerous, too. The germs cling to the cloth and the hand. The mortality in consumption is greater than in almost any other contagious disease. The only exceptions that may be mentioned are bubonic plague and cholera among filthy oriental people."[36]

In an editorial response to kissing that appeared in October 1902 a commentator declared; "And yet the war on kissing appears to be gathering recruits. It was only a year or so ago that the Chicago health department recommended bathing the lips with carbolized rose water previous to indulging in osculatory pleasures. But this kissing antiseptic is never at hand when most needed and it is obviously impossible to anticipate an exchange of microbes in all cases."[37]

Two weeks later a different editor made the brief comment that; "The honorable doctors have opened a crusade against kissing claiming that it is a prolific source of disease. Homeopathy will be a forgotten science long before kissing begins to wane." That was a reference to the recent announcement by the Missouri Valley Homeopathic Medical Association that it was beginning a "war" on kissing, which it declared to be "a nuisance and a breeder of disease."[38]

A day or so later a news story tried to explain the situation and began by saying; "It appears that the homeopath physicians of the Missouri valley have been misunderstood in their attitude toward kissing." According to this report, on November 8, 1902; "Their association did not officially abolish kissing. A few members individually declared that from a hygienic viewpoint kissing must be regarded as a bad practice – a dangerous practice; all the rest of the members professionally nodded assent and there the matter stood." And, the piece added; "That is as far as the crusade against kissing ever gets. The custom is denounced – professionally – the microbes that lurk in the lips are pointed out and their deadly work is pictured, but there it all ends." As far as this newsman was concerned; "It must be assumed that everybody knows by this time that from the hygienic point of view kissing is utterly indefensible…Kissing will continue among us – at least until some convention of doctors officially and positively resolves that it shall cease."[39]

When an Indianapolis editor looked at the issue in December 1902 he began by stating; "Scientists have for some time been waging war against kissing as an unsanitary and objectionable proceeding. Whether they have made any progress in their crusade is uncertain, this form of salute not being a matter open to official record and no statistics therefore being available." However, as a pubic practice he thought; "it is certainly less noticeable than formerly; fewer women are seen to greet each other in this manner when meeting unexpectedly on the street and in the shops, but there is room for belief that the change is not an outgrowth of sanitary intelligence so much as of an increased acquaintance with the well-bred." He also felt the sanitariums had undoubtedly made some impression upon mothers, for there was a "wise disposition on the part of the new mother, at least, to protect her helpless infants from the kisses indiscriminate and indiscreet admirers of dimpled babyhood are so ready to bestow." Not discouraged by the slow progress of reform that was being made, however, he argued that sanitary scientists were then raising a protest against the habit of handshaking. This newsman also made a passing reference to getting germs from doorknobs, streetcar rails, and so forth. In conclusion the journalist mused; "When the pessimist asks sadly, 'Whither are we drifting?' it can be said to him that if the health cranks have their way we are drifting toward a time when human beings will be afraid to associate together or to communicate other than by long distance telephone – with instruments and wires disinfected hourly. How did people manage to save their lives anyway, before the microbe was discovered?"[40]

"Some time ago the doctors placed a scientific ban on kissing but, terrible though it – the announcement, not the kissing – may seem, kissing has gone on just the same," observed an editor in December 1902. "Now comes a doctor with a notion that we ought to quit the friendly, brotherly gasp business. He bases his objections on the ground that diseases are communicated by handshaking more easily than in any other way." That physician was Dr. J. M. Hirsch of Chicago. Hirsch's theory caused the editor to conclude; "It is not likely, however, that the practice of shaking hands will be discontinued any more than the practice of kissing. We must confess that if we had to give up one or the other we would not choose the kissing habit as the one to be cut off."[41]

An article that appeared in a New York City newspaper discussed the practice of throwing kisses, something the piece admitted was not engaged in much in the United States. The journalist brought the subject up because; "there are health considerations to recommend kiss-throwing rather than actual kissing. Cheek kissing went out of style in English society three years ago in consequence of a crusade against it. Numerous physicians, English and American, were interviewed on the question whether kissing was bad. They decided that it was bad for the lips, bad for the mouth and bad for the complexion and worst of all, it was bad for the general health." According to this account; "Kissing went largely out of vogue among society people and is not now nearly so popular as it once was. When girls of fifty years ago met, wherever it might have been, upon the street or in the house, it was their custom to kiss. They even kissed in church, and it is not so very long ago that an English clergyman publicly rebuked two women for kissing while seated in the church pews. Their excuse was that they had not seen each other for several days." At one time, the writer added; "kissing was so common in the street that women and girls, meeting on the pubic thoroughfares, made no bones of saluting each other with a loud smack. It was as frequent in the street as the handshake, and was a commonplace salutation." The article continued on by declaring; "To-day the kiss in public is almost unknown. Women meeting each other in the street, well-bred women, do not kiss, and women meeting in parlors at receptions and in the evening at entertainments, exchange a handshake, but no more." This journalist was convinced that the public discussion on kissing and its evils undoubtedly brought that change in behavior; "And it did another thing in the line of the permanent reduction of the kissing practice. It tended to reduce the amount of kissing bestowed upon children by elderly people." A great many women, some of them old enough to know better; "made a practice of kissing babies. This, the learned authorities will tell you, stops the breath, makes the heart beat irregularly, and in fact, temporarily smothers the child." Said a young mother with respect to people who wanted to kiss her child; "I suppose it offends people, but people who are so foolish really ought to be offended. I put up my hand and say 'please don't'"[42]

A January 1904 news story dealt with the fear of the microbe. "The pernicious microbe is omnipresent and pervasive beyond belief, and acts upon the minds of certain imaginative individuals with the force of a continual nightmare," according to the *New York Medical Record*. Such persons were; "possessed with the idea that hurtful germs are lurking everywhere and are only waiting for the opportunity to pounce upon their unsuspecting victims. To so absurd an extent is this view of the matter carried that in the most simple actions of everyday life deadly danger to health is seen. Kissing had long been interdicted by those advanced thinkers as an especially dangerous custom, and now it is declared that handshaking is the means of spreading a long string of maladies." Handshaking had always been looked upon as an innocent and harmless method of demonstrating friendliness, showing respect, and so on; "It comes, therefore, as a shock to read that handshaking has been denounced in exceedingly strong terms, and that the advice has been given to discontinue the practice on the ground that disease is thereby spread far and wide." The newsman then lashed out at Dr. J. M. Hirsch of Chicago, a leading proponent of the idea that handshaking was a dangerous behavior before concluding; "As to infectious diseases being spread by the hands the event in some instances may be possible, but it is always very improbable. Handshaking will doubtless flourish as vigorously as if there were no possible fear of getting into one's system an obnoxious germ during the process.[43]

"The custom of kissing between children, and more so between adults and children, should be abolished, because it is an injurious practice in more ways than one, and is very likely to spread contagion by direct contact from mouth to mouth," declared Medical Inspector Dr. F. E. Haynes of the Minneapolis City Health Department in a paragraph from his annual report in January 1904. "Parents should be instructed to have their children keep their mouths, noses and teeth clean by frequent washing. At school every pupil should own his own pencils, etc.; should keep them out of his mouth, and should not lend them for others to use in the same manner." Hayes was prescribing methods of preventing the spread of diphtheria in that annual report; "He considers kissing one of the dangerous methods of spreading contagious disease of all kinds, especially diphtheria, and warns the public against it." The medical man stated there were 936 cases of diphtheria in his city in 1903 with 57 of those cases being fatal. It marked a slight decrease from 1902 when there were 960 cases of diphtheria with 72 deaths.[44]

Those comments from Minneapolis by Hayes caused New York City-based columnist Nixola Greeley-Smith to write a sarcastic column. She quoted the statement by Haynes, in the above paragraph, and declared that statement; "outclasses New York's health experts who, in their recently declared war on the microbe contented themselves with a denunciation of the feather duster…Perhaps the Western Health board thinks that with kisses, as with patent medicines, we must accept no substitute and that there is no 'just as good.'" Nixola continued by saying; "But after making the further declaration that 'kissing is the bane of modern civilization and the breeder of diseases' could not Dr. Haynes have suggested a remedial rather than a destructive measure? There is, after all, a universal, even if unreasoning prejudice among human beings in favor of kissing, and so long as it exists would it not be wiser for health boards to consider methods of making the kiss harmless rather than thus waste their energies in vain denunciation and anathema?" She mentioned that when physicians united in declaring that the deadliest disease microbes swarmed in drinking water and in milk they did not suggest abolishing those two items. "Already in Minneapolis the Health board's mandate has divided an enraptured young man from his fiancé who, as a result of Dr. Haynes's report, declined to kiss him, on the ground that 'he had not been boiled.'"[45]

The Board of Health in Neenah, Wisconsin issued an edict in May 1904 against kissing and asked that the custom be discontinued for the general good of the public. In its edict the board claimed that kissing was the direct cause of the spread of contagious disease. It was planned that at the next meeting of the Board of Health in Neenah that a formal resolution would be adopted that denounced the practice of kissing. Members of the board claimed much disease was thus spread, this being particularly the case where school children were permitted to exchange osculatory greetings. The school board would be asked to pass measures instructing teachers to prohibit kissing among the children.[46]

An "eminent," but unnamed, New York neurologist declared in June 1904 that kissing was alright from a sanitary point of view and told New York girls that they could "kiss once in a while without signing their death warrants." The question had been raised in New York when it was claimed that a six-month-old infant had become infected with tetanus by kissing a sister who was suffering from that illness. Said the medical man; "I don't think that kissing between two healthy persons is at all dangerous, excepting where there is a cut or an abrasion of the lips the chances of contagion from kissing are really very slight indeed."[47]

A poem that looked into the future of kissing was published in June 1904. It was attributed to Will S. Adkins, had originally appeared in the American satirical magazine *Puck*, and was titled "In 1954.

With fumigated coat and hat,

And chlorinated cane,

I stand before the portal that

Protects my pretty Jane.

Her worthy father lets me in –

Unlocks the sturdy hasp –

And gives my disinfected fin

A hygienic clasp.

Papa, with wisdom rarely ripe,

Departs with scant delay,

And with his Pasteurized Pipe,

Betakes himself away;

While I to Jane do quickly go -

Upon the sofa snug –

And on that maiden fair bestow

An antiseptic hug.

Before the evening wholly flies,

Upstairs she coyly trips,

And perfumed germicides applies

Unto her dainty lips.

Then cometh gladness – ecstasy –

Just undiluted bliss! –

When lovely Jenny gives to me

A sanitary kiss.[48]

A new peril caused by kissing had, reportedly, been uncovered in the United Kingdom in October 1904. According to the article; "A new danger has been added to the many which, medical men assert, surround the habit of kissing." Dr. Dencer Whittles was a lecturer on dental histology and pathology at Birmingham University in England and he said the "craw-craw" disease common on the west coast of Africa had been introduced into the United Kingdom. Birmingham, he said, had hundreds of cases of the disease while "traces" of the illness had been found in many other places. The disease was due to the presence of what was described as the nematode worm, which had a peculiar penchant for destroying the white corpuscles in the blood. The chief symptom of the illness was an intense itching of the skin. Kissing, Whittles, asserted was one of the means by which the disease was disseminated. There were large numbers of courting couples suffering from craw-craw in Birmingham, he said, and oftener than not "one transmits the disease to the other by kissing." He cited one case wherein an infected boy infected his girlfriend and the disease was incorrectly diagnosed. And the young woman, who slept in the same bed as her sister, transmitted the disease to her, and later on to a younger brother. Today the disease is better known by the name "river blindness" and is caused by a parasitic worm and transmitted to humans by black flies.[49]

When health officials in St. Louis decided to take action on osculation in May 1905 it prompted a Washington state newspaper editor to write an editorial. It began by observing; "Kisses in public have long been a source of annoyance to and cause of protest from non-participants. To the one not in it a kiss in plain sight is the most irritating thing in the world. So legislation has relentlessly pursued the kiss in public and in many states has driven it from the streets and railway stations. Out of consideration for grouchy old bachelors and sore headed old maids, it has been made unlawful in lots of places for a man even to kiss his own wife when he meets her after long separation." He went on to add; "It naturally follows that the kiss flourishes in private with a thousand-fold more business because it is restricted in public…But the world moves. And now in St. Louis, where the primitive innocence of paradise is being restored, war is declared upon kissing in private." Admitting that St. Louis Health Commissioner Simon proposed only to prohibit the kisses of consumptives he added that it was also true that many physicians had asserted the folly and danger of kisses; "but it has remained for Simon to set detectives on the watch and make the calaboose a penalty." Dr. Simon must be a man of great courage, mocked the editor; "He has undertaken a big job. If he succeeds in intercepting all the kissing of St. Louis and holding it up until medical examination has determined the fitness of the kissable parties, he will have accomplished wonders." If Simon succeeded, continued the editor; "it may be expected to become the fashion in St. Louis for the wooing young man to take a physician with him. When the ardent one declares his undying love, wins a confession of love in return, and presses for the seal of affection, he will be told not to 'see papa' but to 'see the doctor.'" Concluded the editor; "There is big business in sight for examining physicians as well as for the detectives. Dr. Simon can hardly be accused of having neglected the interests of his profession. But love is fertile in expedients. If this scheme works, the youth of St. Louis are not up to the average."[50]

A different newspaper looked at the same St. Louis event and declared; "Restrictions on the popular art of kissing have reached St. Louis as a result of the reform idea" and many in Los Angeles "have grave fears that this same fate will befall this community coming in the line of advanced reform." The piece then explained that an order from the Health Department in St. Louis prohibited kissing in public unless it could be clearly shown that the participants "in the osculatory competition are of sound mind and body and free from the contaminating effects of contagion. Dr. J. H. Simon, the health commissioner, has sprang into notoriety through the unusual order to which is affixed his name, and strenuous measures are being adopted to enforce it." And, it was reported; "The detail of detectives furnished the health department has strict orders to arrest everyone concerned in publicly osculating and conveying them to the city bastille, pending an examination into their qualifications and eligibility, according to the code revised by the health department." It was claimed by Health Commissioner Simon that contagion was spread with more alarming frequency through the "deceit" of a kiss than in any other manner and it is his purpose to put an end to it all. It was then mentioned that Dr. Simon was an "ardent admirer" of Governor Folk the reformer and originator of the "Missouri idea" [being a leader in public morality through popular control of law and strict enforcement]. Remarked the journalist; "With prize fights made a felony, pool rooms closed, race tracks shut up, automobiling limited to six miles an hour, thirst parlors, swell restaurants and summer gardens closed on Sundays, saloons closed after midnight and a threat to close all theaters on Sunday, life has not been strewn with roses for the man about town in St. Louis for some time, and now that he is to be deprived of the right and privilege of kissing his best girl or wife, unless he is a perfect man physically, the burden will be altogether too great for the ordinary free and east going natures of St. Louis."[51]

A British doctor writing in the *British Medical Journal* in November 1905 discussed some of the ways by which infection was intentionally spread. One way he mentioned was through paper bags. He referred specifically to the fact that to open them up many people blew against their edges directly into them and that was a common method that was used by most retailers; "The possibilities which might ensue if the breath was infected by the germs of a specific disease can be easily imagined." Then there was the practice of using old newspaper (often bought at rag shops) in poorer districts to wrap food; that was also a practice that deserved attention. Drinking glasses were another problem because even at many high schools the pupils used a common drinking cup for water. The solution he suggested was to provide each pupil with his or her own drinking glass with a wicker cover and which the pupil could take to school. The danger to adults, and particularly children, who bite candies, and other food items, after each other "is obvious and should be explained to them." With respect to kissing the physician stated; "The danger has often been referred to, and the practice of children kissing each other at school should be prohibited"[52]

An editorial appeared in December 1905 that was a complaint about the "heartless scientists who waged war against kissing as dangerous from a sanitary point of view." That aroused the ire of another newspaper the *Louisville Courier-Journal*, which was quoted as declaring; "Will these prosaic and heartless scientists never quit mixing germs with kisses?" He continued by begging the physicians to leave the kiss alone; "It is all right. It is one of the oldest institutions in the world. It would be a shame to put it out of business now."[53]

The Indiana State Board of Health began a campaign against kissing in August 1906 and thereafter every teacher in the public schools in the state was expected to keep his eyes on his pupils and see that they did not indulge in "the harmful propensity." That ban on kissing was included in a set of rules that the board had adopted for the governing of school children and the rules were to be applied to all children in public and private schools; "Do not kiss anyone on the mouth, or allow anyone to kiss you" was one of the rules that was to be posted conspicuously in every school in the state of Indiana. Teachers were expected to enforce the rules and infractions by pupils "will place the delinquent in the same altitude as if other rules were broken." The object of the kissing rule was said to be to prevent the spread of tuberculosis, "which is said to be conveyed from one to another by the practice of kissing." [Today it is said that tuberculosis is spread through the air from one person to another. The tuberculosis bacteria are put into the air when a person with tuberculosis of the lungs or throat, coughs, sneezes, speaks or sings. People nearby may breath in these bacteria and become infected. It cannot be contract from a hug or a kiss nor can it be contracted from saliva shared during kissing].[54]

When an editor responded to the Indiana campaign he began his piece by stating; "A kissless existence is guaranteed to every child attending school in Indiana. The state board of health gives the guarantee. Not a kiss in the long catalogue of kisses will be countenanced in any school in the state when they open after the vacation." He continued; "And, if the state board of health can do it, the war against kissing and kisses will be carried beyond the school. Every kiss in Indiana may be a stolen kiss after a while." In the schools there was to be no kissing at all. The first communication the pupils were going to see on the notice boards of schools when the summer break ended was a sign saying; "Do not kiss anyone on the mouth or allow anyone to do so to you." Reportedly, the Indiana Board of Health had not by then decided whether it would be permissible to accept a kiss on the cheek or bestow one there on somebody else; "The problem is still under consideration and a blanket injunction covering every variety of kiss may be issued." That edict from the board applied to the girls as rigorously as to the boys. Girls kissing other girls was equally frowned upon and taboo. Said the editor; "The board of health has studied the kiss, dissected, analyzed, and examined it under the microscope, and declared against it. Indiana will be better without it was the decision, and the board has started in on a campaign of eradication. Every teacher in the state will be instructed to enforce its abolition from school life and to punish severely the boy or girl who dares to kiss." There were several other prohibitions that had been drawn up and were waiting for the children to return to school, besides the ban on kissing. The other prohibitions included: "do not put your finger in your mouth;" "do not wet your fingers in your mouth when turning leaves of books;" "do not put pencils in your mouth or wet them with your lips;" "do not hold money in your mouth;" "do not put pins in your mouth;" and "do not swap apple cores, chewing gum, or bean blowers."[55]

Another article on the Indiana campaign called it a war against the "white plague." Another health rule adopted for the children was one that said; "Do not spit except in a spittoon or on a piece of cloth or a handkerchief used for that purpose alone…and on your return home have the cloth burned by your mother or the handkerchief put in water until ready for the wash."[56]

Winfield Durban was Indiana Governor from January 1901 until January 1905. When the state Board of Health announced its kissing campaign Durban was spending a year in Switzerland. In August 1906 he wrote a letter to Indiana Attorney General Miller telling him about the reactions Europeans were having towards the campaign in his home state. He said the newspapers of the Old World were inclined to make sport of the board's order and the ex-Governor confessed he was greatly humiliated over the fact that Indiana had taken such a stand against a demonstration so common among the young and heretofore considered harmless.[57]

Near the end of August 1906 a report was published that noted the Indiana campaign to prohibit kissing for sanitary reasons had brought anxious letters from all sections of the state and the state board was, reportedly, "considerably embarrassed" as a result. Dr. John Hurty was Secretary of the Indiana Board of Health and he bewailed the fact that the kissing story was given such wide publicity. He said the board would not be harsh about the matter and that he, personally, thought kissing in moderation would do no particular harm."[58]

An editorial in a New York City newspaper, in September 1906 slammed the Indiana war on kissing by sneering; "The order issued by the Indiana state board of health forbidding kissing in the schools gives a greater impetus to lynch law than anything that has been done by Citizen Dogberry [a pompous, self-important citizen determined to enforce laws] for some time…And a fig for the board of health."[59]

The Indiana Board of Health rules caused some to speculate that such a law might be adopted by the entire country. That caused one newsman to muse, with respect to that speculation; "If the Indiana legislature should enact the proposed anti-kissing law it could never be enforced unless a detective could be concealed beneath the sofa of every home that harbors one or more pretty, kissable girls." He went on to add that; "It is said that Anthony Comstock [notorious puritan reformer] turns the mirrors in his chamber in order that he may not be shocked when he undresses for bed. And he no doubt draws the curtains to keep the stars from peeping in."[60]

The Indiana health rule was still drawing editorial comment late in October 1906 when a Pennsylvania newsman observed; "Scientific discoveries have established the fact that the mouth of a human being is the home of countless bacteria some of which, through infection, lead to disease and possibly to death. Indeed, science has gone so far as to demonstrate the fact the more beautiful the child the more dangerous the kisses. Accepting such demonstration, a great many physicians kiss the children on the cheek only, and the example they have been setting is being followed more and more throughout the country." He said that a recent report on the subject showed that in a community of 1,000 people in which kissing had been tabooed for 10 years the death rate from infectious diseases had decreased a little more than 3.5 percent. That meant in a thousand people three and one-half lives were saved every year. That caused the editor to conclude; "Instead of looking at the order of the Indiana State Board of Health in a humorous way, it will be well for the people of that and other States to take it as seriously as it was intended. If people value human life as they should, they will do so."[61]

In Berkeley California Dr. Edith Brownsill delivered a lecture on hygiene to the women students of the freshman class at the University of California on October 18, 1906. In that lecture she advised against the "pernicious practice of kissing" invalids, particularly those suffering from fevers, smallpox or tuberculosis. She stated that such a practice was likely to generate disease. An impression that her advice included a condemnation of kissing in general was corrected by Brownsill who said she deplored merely the practice of kissing the sick who had infectious diseases.[62]

Alarmed by an epidemic of diphtheria, the board of health at Malden Massachusetts placed a ban on kissing games. "Little Red Riding Hood," was one of those games and was popular among pupils of the local county school. That ban was placed early in November 1906.[63]

The deaths of two children in the area from diseases attributed to children's kissing games was said to have been the catalyst for the ban. Both of those children died from diphtheria within a month of each other and when the Malden Board of Health investigated those deaths it reportedly found the children involved had engaged with other children in games such as "Little Red Riding Hood" and other pastimes of "the osculatory order." After that situation came to light a ban was placed on kissing in all the schools of Malden. When the results of the investigation being conducted by the committee on schools and the Board of Health became known, parents of nearly all the children rose up and demanded the schools be fumigated thoroughly before the children were allowed back in. The school involved was closed twice for a couple of days, immediately after the death of each child, but the indignation of the parents ran high over the revelation that the children had been allowed to play kissing games during the hours of school. A few days earlier school Superintendent Henry D. Hervey, of the Malden schools, while talking to a reporter, claimed neither he nor any of the teachers knew anything about the kissing games. He declared; "Had anything of that nature been brought to my attention I should have investigated at first hand, and you may rest assured that it would have been stopped immediately." And, added Hervey; "Personally I disapprove of any such actions on the part of anybody, and had I the slightest inkling that those tots had the chance to play at kissing games, I would have interfered instantly." Referring to the rumors circulating to the effect that often the same practice prevailed among the older boys and girls of the high school the Superintendent asserted; "I positively do not believe a word of it." Dr. C. D. McCarthy, an officer of the school committee, which took the initiative in the investigation said that in all there were five cases of diphtheria among the children of one class and two cases among the children of another class Two of those children died and the stories came out that some of them had been playing at kissing games. Said McCarthy; "When we became fairly well satisfied that the game had been played, not an hour was lost in giving the superintendent our approval for sending out warnings to all teachers that such practices must be stopped instantly." [Diphtheria is transmitted from person to person, usually through respiratory droplets from coughing or sneezing. It can also be spread by direct contact with infected nasal or throat secretions through sharing food, drink, or kissing someone who has the infection].[64]

Dr. J. E. Drane was a newly appointed health officer for the city of Mesa, Arizona, in January 1907. Reportedly, he was not antagonistic to the kissing habit. A reporter noted that; "He does not believe that every smack means the transfer of ten million germs nor every old fashion exhibition of the osculatory powers sudden death." With respect to the kissing habit Dr. Drane said; "Consumption is a latent disease and may be in the system for a long time. It might have been contracted from a kiss and again it might not. History goes to show that while kissing might have been responsible for contracting the disease yet the patient afflicted in very few instances has been able to trace their infection to a kiss." He continued by stating; "Typhoid fever might be contracted by kissing but there are so many other ways to contract it that the primary cause can hardly be laid at the door of the kissing habit." Concluded Drane; "I would not advise a well person to kiss a person affected with consumption for it is very probable that germs may be transferred, however, it is a well-known fact that man and wife have lived together for years and only one be affected. The kissing habit may or may not be the cause of spreading the disease, yet when it comes to saying that it should be stopped altogether, that is a different matter."[65]

When a newspaper report that originated from a Chicago publication presented a report that peril lurked in kisses it began its lengthy piece be wondering; "Will kissing be indicted? Are laws ready to be passed prohibiting the practice as unsanitary? The suggestion would once have seemed like a joke, but more than one official movement has been made in this ominous direction. Health Officer Somers of Atlantic City is not the only public guardian who has raised a warning hand and science has again sent out a loud note of warning." That latter part of that quote was a reference to remarks made by Dr. Nalpasse of the medical faculty of a university in Paris, France. He charged that the kiss with responsibility for spreading the grip, scarlet fever, measles, mumps, whooping cough, typhoid fever, erysipelas, meningitis, tuberculosis, diphtheria, and the many infectious lesions of the skin such as boils and carbuncles. According to the article those physicians and scientists such as Nalpasse did not so much denounce the lovers' kiss, and so forth, "for they say that adults are generally strong enough to resist successfully the baneful assaults of the myriads of bacteria that lurk in the kiss, but it is the mother's kiss, the caress given to the baby, that comes in for their most bitter denunciations." Health Officer Somers of Atlantic City, New Jersey had convinced himself that kissing and the grip went hand in hand. The grip was said to have been unusually prevalent that year and while most blamed in on the unseasonable weather, Somers blamed it on the prevalence of kissing and has issued a solemn warning the following words; "In view of the rapid spread of grip throughout the city and in view of the known fact that osculation commonly described as kissing, is the most fruitful agent of the propagation of the grip germ, it is advised that temperance and moderation in respect to said practice be more generally observed." Chief Inspector Beck and the Board of Health in Atlantic City were to ask the city council for a special appropriation for printing, and posting that warning in railroad stations, streetcars and in other public places.[66]

Dr. Nalpasse wrote of "the scourge consecrated by the ill-advised acceptance of the ill-advised custom called the kiss, but we can take precautions and do our best to counteract its undeniable dangers." Nalpasse advised mothers not only to refrain from kissing their babies, but to disinfect them whenever they have been out for an airing, washing their mouths with soap and water and their faces and hands with a mixture of equal parts of "tepid water and tincture of quillaya." [Quillaia is a plant, the inner bark of which is used as medicine. People take it for coughs, and bronchitis – it is also used as a foaming agent in fire extinguishers. In South America quillaia bark is used to wash clothes]. Immediately after disinfecting the child with that above noted bath Dr. Nalpasse continued by advising "pass over all the parts so washed a lotion made as follows: one gram of thymol, menthol, and salol, 10 grams of benzoic acid, 12 grams of essence of violets dissolved in 250 grams of alcohol (95 degrees) mixed with a solution composed of 10 grams of bicarbonate of soda and 15 grams of boric acid dissolved in 1,750 grams of distilled water. A simple filtering will make this lotion clear and limpid."[67]

When the American Medical Convention held its annual national convention in Atlantic City in June 1907 a spokesman for the physicians told a reporter that the group was "too busy and life is too short to tackle the kissing bug." When it came to a vote at that convention whether or not to put osculation under some type of ban the medical men voted neither yes nor no but unanimously voted to simply drop the whole subject. Discussion at the convention began when Dr. C. W. Drake of the Hollins Institute of Virginia addressed the delegates and declared; "This kissing habit is terrible enough when confined to lovers but let the kissing fad get started among college girls and you have a source of danger that is appalling." Drake continued by saying; "Why college girls kiss when they greet each other good morning, they kiss when they say good-night and they kiss all day between. The kissing devotion of the average college girl exceeds that of any lovers of fact or fiction. Pretty students have kissed the most alarming grippe epidemics through many of the largest female seminaries and universities. It is high time the doctors of the country should speak out, to save the educated fair sex from kissing their lives away by transmitting tuberculosis and fever bacilli." Dr. Drake's resolution, that state legislatures place "unnecessary" kissing under a legal ban, was lost in the confusion of an attempt of the by the delegates to define "unnecessary." Dr. C. W. Irion of Detroit stated' there are too many other reforms needed in this great health war before we can tackle the kissing bug. As long as the little god goes around with his bow and quiver there will be kissing. I move we leave it up to the kissed and the kissers." That resolution was adopted unanimously.[68]

During that same week that the doctors convened in Atlantic City in June 1907, several hundred members of women's clubs from all over the nation met in the same city at the same time. They were an auxiliary to the Anti-Tuberculosis League and one of the slogans they adopted was; "Don't Kiss the Babies." One speaker before that group was Franklin Dye, secretary of the New Jersey State Board of Agriculture. He demanded that the sign "don't kiss the baby" be hung in every household. That, he said, would block aunts, cousins, and other callers from kissing the infants. He was applauded for his ideas but when Dr. J. S. Perth, a western delegate offered a resolution that the society commit itself to a movement to suppress kissing at all ages he was received with silence. Perth declared; "Kissing is dangerous at all times, and I know a whole family that has been wiped out by disease first communicated by osculation." After the defeat of his proposal, Dr. Perth offered the proposal that sweethearts carry a special brand of perfumed germicide for use when kissing. But that proposal, noted a journalist; "was also received very coldly."[69]

An editor with a Pennsylvania paper thought that in his area, in June 1907, kissing was not going to go out of fashion; "It is true that stern-faced scientists have been telling us for many years that infection lurks in the kiss. They exhort mothers and lovers and others to resort to some less dangerous method of manifesting their affection. They are becoming increasingly urgent with the flight of the years and with the discovery of new forms of bacilli that delight to lay in wait for the human race." He added; "They tell us that tuberculosis and various other deadly diseases are communicated by the kiss and they are at the present moment earnestly engaged in the effort to organize anti-kissing leagues in all sections of the world. They are in deadly earnest." While the editor admitted that there was a "large measure of truth" in the declarations of the scientists he went on to state his newspaper; "holds with them that danger lurks in the kiss…It hold that those who are troubled by dangerous or infectious diseases should be compelled to forego the osculatory salute." While willing to concede that much it went on to state that it was unwilling to join the league that would ostracize that salute. Concluded the editor; "The scientists are right. There is danger in the average kiss. But it is likely that human nature is going to be too strong for the scientists and that a fashion which probably came into the world when Adam looked upon the first woman and pronounced her good to look upon will not vanish."[70]

An announcement came out of Philadelphia in July 1907 that kissing games were to be banned in public school playgrounds and that; "Stringent regulations against the old-fashioned plays in which the penalty is a kiss will be suppressed by the board of education and the medical inspectors." According to the story the Philadelphia authorities "are simply shooing away the dread microbe and discouraging the visitations of infectious germs." Kissing by children which had for generations been the accompaniment of such games as "spin the plate," "going to Jerusalem," "clap in and clap out," "drop the handkerchief," and a host of other games "is now looked upon as unhygienic and a transmitter of germs." Said William A. Stechler, director of physical instruction in Philadelphia; "There are so many more educational forms of recreation now than there used to be that it is not necessary to permit the old kissing games." Stechler added; "Games that require muscular activity and skill and bring into play the development of brain and body have been substituted on our recreation schedule and we do not anticipate any trouble in doing away with the unhealthy practice of promiscuous kissing." Dr. Thomas J. Beatty was an assistant to the chief of the Bureau of Health in that city and sentiment did not enter into his mind when he issued his mandate prohibiting kissing on the playground; "The practice is disease-spreading and will not be tolerated," he said, with scientific finality.[71]

When Philadelphia school Superintendent Martin G. Brumbaugh was asked about the Philadelphia move he said the orders to prohibit those games have been issued as a sanitary and hygienic precaution. He declared; "Under no conditions will the children be permitted to play 'spin the plate,' 'drop the handkerchief,' 'post office' or any other similar games and any boy caught stealing a kiss from a girl on the sly will be ejected from the playgrounds for the rest of the season."[72]

Another lengthy newspaper piece about the dangers of kissing appeared in a Boston publication in July 1907. It started by stating: "Science has pronounced another anathema. After attacking many ancient institutions and customs; after discovering the sources and cures of mysterious diseases; after revealing to us the ravages of the armies of germs that infect the places we live in, it has made the most sweeping attack of all. Science had directed its shaft against love. It has uttered its judgment on the kiss." The piece went on to declare; "That kissing is productive of more diseases than the flesh would ordinarily be heir to is the statement of world-renowned scientists, such as Pasteur, Roux, Netter and others. At the convention of the American Medical Society in Atlantic City a short time ago a physician advised the placing of a sign on every cradle in the land, 'Don't Kiss the Baby.'" Dr. Franklin Gifford of New Jersey declared before a convention of the dentists of Ohio; "Germs and microbes lurk in every kiss. I would advise that every kiss be sterilized and that if this were found to be impossible, to take a sanitary gargle after every kiss." Declared Dr. G. W. Drake, house physician at the Hollins Institute in Virginia, at that Atlantic City gathering; "The kissing habit is terrible enough when confined to lovers but when the fad gets started among college girls you have a source of danger and disease contagion that is appalling." An unnamed physician was quoted as saying; "When you bend over to kiss the lips of a charming girl you are possibly giving her death warrant. Unconsciously you are about to murder her. Or she may impart to you disease which may blast your life…The mouth is the most unclean part of the body, and at the same time the channel most admissible to the armies of disease microbes." This account listed the usual disease whose germs could be found on the lips; pneumonia, tuberculosis, diphtheria, whooping cough, typhoid, grippe, influenza, and skin infections of "innumerable varieties." That unidentified medical practitioner went on to say; "Before you kiss the sweet little one who lives in the sunlight of your smile, pause. Think of the danger to which you are heedlessly rushing. Tuberculosis, pneumonia, diphtheria – the possibilities of disease are appalling." The journalist concluded by saying; "Ought we not, then, hail the sanitary kiss with rejoicing. A prominent physician has advised the gargling of the mouth after every mean and every kiss with water into which a few drops of the following mixture has been dripped 'tincture of eucalyptus, 15 grams; alcohol, 100 grains; and peppermint, 10 centigrams.'"[73]

Mrs. Avis Boyce was said to be on a mission, in July 1907. She was traveling through the United States on the mission of making mothers stop kissing their babies. She intended to establish anti-kissing missions throughout America, branches of the United Sisterhood for the suppression of baby kissing, noted a reporter. He did admit, though, that she did not call it that; she referred to it as the Woman's Auxiliary of the Anti-Tuberculosis League but she said it was the same thing. According to Boyce; "If you kiss the baby it'll get tuberculosis. Only babies that never have been kissed escaped tuberculosis. It is wrong to kiss the baby. In fact, it is wrong to kiss at all, unless you want to have tuberculosis." The reporter once again acknowledged that the above quote was not her exact words but insisted that was the lesson she was spreading. She did not say that if you kiss a baby it would get sick and die. But she did say it was dangerous. The reporter said; "and she's in deadly earnest about it. She is so earnest that she has accepted the post of vice-president of the Anti-Tuberculosis League and is carrying the anti-kissing war right into the house." So earnest was Boyce that she went before the American Medical Association at its Atlantic City gathering earlier that same year and tried to get them to endorse her anti-kissing campaign. Some of the doctors reportedly sided with her and some of them even "urged the abolition of kissing entirely." But most of the younger doctors were against her ideas and the physicians declined to take any action with respect to kissing.[74]

It was at that point that Boyce decided to start out on her mission, but, noted the journalist; "She has given up the grownups as hopeless cases and despairs every of making them quit kissing, even if it is legislated against." Said Boyce; "An adult can care for himself or herself and refuse or accept tuberculosis kisses. I have in mind the helpless, defenseless babies, who are victims of dangerous and pernicious kissing and who should be protected by their parents. The helpless babe is kissed by the mother, the father, all the family, the nurse, the servants, the friends, the neighbors, by all the other nurse girls in the neighborhood, and by their friends and relatives." She continued by stating; "A pretty baby is kissed perhaps fifty times a day. Probably one person in 50 has tuberculosis in some form, so you can see what a large chance there is for a child to get a tuberculosis kiss. I am sure that if the mothers can be brought to realize what the peril is they would be horrified into some kind of drastic action." As far as Boyce was concerned there was also an ethical side to the question; "The sacredness of the kiss is destroyed by this promiscuous osculation and the child that grows up on a diet of miscellaneous kisses, if he or she is not killed in the process, will have a perverted or blunted idea of the most delicate and uplifting act of the affection."[75]

Later in July 1907 it was reported that Avis Boyce "whose mission in life is to form anti-kissing clubs" was in Denver and reportedly heading toward Salt Lake City. "Mrs. Boyce, for some reason best known to herself, has the anti-kissing mania in its most acute form, although according to her photograph she isn't a bad-looking woman," wrote a journalist. "Her chief object tis to form anti-kissing societies among mothers, and get them to agree not to kiss their babies. She imagines that all kinds of diseases are transmitted by kissing."[76]

Another editor who railed against the scientists had his say in print in January 1908. He declared; "The doctors have been having their innings just now over the kiss. All the sins that can't be bundled away on some one's shoulders are laid at the door of that delicious little morsel – the kiss." And, he added; "The doctors may talk as they will of the sanitary kiss – of the unromantic purification of microbes of contagion which are liable to lose you your best beloved. I'm not saying anything about that."[77]

A report published in May 1908 remarked that schools in London England were making an effort to stop kissing games. The children were in the habit of playing those games at school "and to the practice is traced much disease." In issuing instructions to have the games stopped, the medical adviser of the board of health of that city said: "Promiscuous kissing among children might easily lead to a most serious epidemic of diphtheria, scarlet fever, measles or any other infectious disease. Organized games are now played in the council's schools and no rational teacher would allow kissing to form any part of them. That is a sanitary practice all teachers ought to be acquainted with…" A reporter felt that the notice was probably intended merely as a reminder to a few teachers who had overlooked "the grave danger to health involved." According to this account a single child suffering from an infectious disease might easily cause a whole school to fall victim to it. The medical adviser continued by warning; "I remember the case of a little Irish girl who died from diphtheria. Her parents held a wake and 27 children in her class kissed her. They all contracted the disease and three or four of them died." The advice went on to include the following; "Kissing any adult is just as dangerous as among children and this fact cannot be too widely known. Personally, I could never understand why two girlfriends who meet or part in the street kiss each other. Surely they can show their affection one for another in a more sensible and less risky manner than kissing." In conclusion the medical advisor told the London

England board of health; "If I had my way I should abolish kissing altogether. Besides being a positive danger to the public health generally, it is a stupid, insipid custom, unworthy of twentieth century enlightenment."[78]

The feature of one day's session in June 1908 of the national convention of the American Anti-Tuberculosis League was an anti-kissing campaign started by Dr. Walter M. Tyzzer of St. Louis. According to the doctor it was dangerous to be in love unless you had a clean bill of health from a physician and unless the object of your affection also insured against certain dread germs. At the least lovers should ever kiss until they were certain that they were not affected with tuberculosis, he asserted, in a paper he read to the convention. Dr. Tyzzer estimated that there were 200,000 deaths in the United States each year due to tuberculosis a disease, he thought, that was easily transmitted.[79]

A story that appeared in the newspapers on November 9, 1908 stated that; "Boston is the source if the latest crusade against unhygienic kissing. The same old story about microbes reveling in the osculatory contact, and spreading disease, is being told – with the same lack of result." The article continued by noting; "Maiden ladies of advanced years easily become convinced that kissing is dangerous business...Yet all that the anti-kiss crusaders say is true. It is a scientific fact that the lips should be carefully sponged with carbolic acid before kissing and after." In conclusion the journalist remarked; "But the world must first be convinced of its error, and until that happy consummation is reached, the great majority of humanity will kiss when the inspiration strikes it, in the same old way, and with the most reckless disregard of the damage which vital statistics may receive from their thoughtlessness."[80]

Later in November 1908 an editor reported that an unnamed female physician in Philadelphia had declared; "The number of diseases which kissing causes in unbelievable. I firmly believe the day will come within a generation when a formidable anti-kissing movement will be established, and when kissing practically will be confined to the lower classes, the educated people having been brought to see the evils of the habit." She continued; "Next to the evil of kissing babies comes the sweetheart's kiss. This is one of the most dangerous of all. A husband's kiss generally soon loses if fervency, but the kiss of the two sweethearts is the paradise of the tuberculosis germ and the diphtheria germ and other germs too numerous to mention."[81]

It was reported in May 1909 that if you followed the instructions of Professor Kepford of the Iowa State Board of Health a person would refrain from kissing every baby he met on the street. Kepford thought that the kissing habit should be abolished in all walks of life and stated emphatically; "Don't kiss the baby." Cards containing that message were to be printed by the anti-tuberculosis department of the state board of health. They were to be distributed to the fathers and others of Iowa. When mothers took their babies out for walks they were to be urged to have one of those cards fastened conspicuously to the baby buggy. Lip kissing had to go, declared A. E. Kepford, the state lecturer against tuberculosis for the state board of control. While kissing babies on the lips was the first "menace" to be choked off "if possible Mr. Kepford proposes to direct his energies against kissing in all its types from that of the giggly school girl who will greet all of her girlfriends with an osculatory caress to the lovers who spoon in the twilight. Even the bridal kiss must skidoo." Said Kepford, as he explained that the new cards warning against baby kissing had already been put into effect in the east; "It is difficult to make people see the danger in lip kissing. If the people could see the bacteria that develop from lip kissing they would be astounded. It is the most dangerous practice imaginable. In making our fight against tuberculosis we have found that tuberculosis has been communicated by the kiss in thousands of cases and deaths without number may be traced directly to the lip kiss. It must go in time but, of course, it will take some time to work up the proper sentiment along that line."[82]

In Seattle, Eugene Robert Kelley the "prominent" anti-tuberculosis worker in that west coast city was asked what he thought about the fight being made against kissing in the state of Iowa. "Yes, I believe in eliminating kissing to a certain extent" he replied. "I do not believe in indiscriminate kissing when there are so many cases of tuberculosis, because kissing is a means of spreading the disease. I wouldn't stop kissing altogether. A law against kissing would be nonsensical, as it would be a lot harder to enforce than the cigarette law." The catalyst that started that discussion was a story from Iowa saying that the state government had appropriated $1,500 a year to maintain a campaign against kissing, led by

Kepford. He had been appointed Iowa state government lecturer on health, but his real title, joked a

reporter "is state kiss exterminator. The kiss exterminator has started in on the schools and has the

pledges of 10,000 pretty (and otherwise) teachers to give their earnest support in stamping out kissing

in the public schools." The reporter mentioned the "don't kiss me" signs and said they "are being

printed to be hung around the necks of the babies." Added the journalist; "If it becomes known that a

young man has been going to see a certain girl an extraordinary number of times he receives a card

from the exterminator saying, 'hold her hand if you must, but don't kiss her,' or maybe it is a note from

his former teacher saying, 'do not expose the one you love to the germs that lurk in kisses '"[83]

 A few months later a reporter noted that a government-backed campaign against kissing was

"actually" taking place in Iowa and that a dozen state governments were watching the experiment with

interest. Then a poem was added to the brief article. The poem was credited to Lue F. Vernon.

The doctors – oh, those prophylactic,

Antiseptic microbe fiends –

Cry out in many a sacred didactic,

Kisses are the deadly means

Of pathogenic bug transmission,

Dread bacilli far and wide,

Strange to Cupid whose ambition

'Tis to stem race suicide.

But where's the girl who'll most gladly

Risk ten thousand weird diseases

For a kiss when fondly, madly,

Both her hands a fellow squeezes?

And where's the man who'll not defy

The ills of other worlds and this

If there's the slightest chance thereby

Of winning one sweet maiden kiss?[84]

That Iowa campaign was slow in getting underway and nothing more was heard about it until Lue Vernon (the man who penned the above poem) wrote an article about the Iowa effort, in August 1910. Vernon declared; "The oft-threatened and long-dreaded scientific crusade against kissing is actually advancing in Iowa," and that a dozen other states were watching its progress – part of Iowa's fight against the "white plague" [tuberculosis]. "If Iowa really proves that her crusade against kissing stamps out the white plague, other States may follow suit, the lipless kiss may be proscribed by law, and marriage bureaus will become as deadly dull as a graveyard," said Vernon. According to this account Iowa had appropriate $3,000 per year as a salary for its "professional crusader against the time-honored habit of kissing." That crusader was Aretar Edward Kepford and his official title was "State Government Lecturer on Health." Kepford took the advice of Benjamin Franklin who once said; "What you want in your nation introduce in your public schools." Some 2,000 school teachers were said to have pledged Kepford their earnest support in stamping out the kissing habit. Said Kepford; "Kissing, my dear supporters, belongs in the stone ages of courtesy along with rubbing foreheads, noses, and chins. There is no reason why rubbing lips should be more reasonable or logical. About 10,000 of the cards being the slogan "Don't Kiss Me" had been printed for use in decking out babies with that warning. "There are 100,000 babies in Iowa to-day and five times as many growing children, whom we are educating to forswear kisses, commented Kepford. Before an audience in Des Moines he asserted; "In one generation I can stamp out kissing. It's merely custom, and holds no real joy." As well, Kepford was reportedly making efforts to have a number of Iowa philanthropists offer a prize of $100 to each unkissed girl of 15, with an added prize of $5 annually for every year she remained unkissed until she was married. As yet those philanthropists had not materialized, noted Vernon, "but Crusader Kepford has hopes."[85]

Another anti-kissing effort got underway in Washington, D.C., in November 1909. The legend "Don't Kiss Me" printed in gold on brightly colored ribbons "is being sold to many of Washington's best families," according to a journalist. That slogan was being worn by babies and "It is the well-dressed gently nurtured child playing in the charmed neighborhood of Du Pont Circle that most frequently is seen with the 'Don't Kiss Me' mandate fastened from shoulder to waist." That effort against kissing was said to have grown out of the "anti-germ craze" and the mothers of Washington, and also Boston, were joining in a concerted effort to prevent "the promiscuous kissing" of their little ones by adoring friends. "The movement has taken the most practical direction and leagues have been formed in all the establishments for trained nurses and in the schools where girls are prepared for service as governesses or nurses, the members of which pledge themselves to stand against the kissing of their little charges," reported the journalist. Those ribbons had been designed "to save the nurses or governesses the embarrassment of actively interfering with those unduly affectionate individuals who shower their caresses upon defenceless children."[86]

The advertising industry was in its infancy back in 1909 but one company tried to benefit from the hype that surrounded the idea of not kissing the baby. Ad advertisement for Dr. Lyon's Tooth Powder told the reader not to kiss the baby unless the mouths of those involved had been "cleansed and purified" by the daily use of the product.[87]

In November 1909 the Tennessee State Board of Health sent the following rule to be pasted in all the school books used by pupils in that state; "Do not kiss anyone on the mouth or allow anyone to do so to you." That rule was said to be one of several that the state board had put in force to prevent the spread of consumption.[88]

In Columbia, South Carolina in May 1910 Dr. C. Fred Williams, state health officer, was shown a copy of a New York newspaper that contained a story about the "kiss not" campaign and asked if South Carolina was ready then to do something similar. "No, we are not ready yet to tackle that subject," said Williams. According to the article some of the health organizations throughout the West were strenuously advocating non-kissing. And that the circulars sent out by the non-kissing societies contained the following; "Why not stop kissing? It is a time-honored custom, and one person can not stop it. It is only in unity that sufficient strength can be gained to convince the world that kissing is pernicious and unhealthful."[89]

An editorial in a Boston newspaper in July 1910 outlined that Dr. M. P. Ravenel, head of the Wisconsin Anti-Germ Society, said he was going to do everything in his power to abolish kissing in that state. Remarked the editor; "Why waste your time, Doc? The kiss is too old an institution for any one man or combinations of men to make war against…If you insist on backing the kissing bug, Doc, you'll never make any headway and the world will never hear of you. The kiss is here to stay – whether it's antiseptic or not!"[90]

Robert J. Newton was secretary of the Municipal Commission on Tuberculosis in St. Louis. In October 1910 a matinee crowd of women was attending the board's exhibit and Newton advised the women in that crowd to insist that when their husbands refused to part with their beards that "the germ-ridden beards be subjected to fumigation before every kiss." Further advice he offered that day was a directive to friends; "Don't swap germs. If a kiss is aimed at you dodge." He told fathers not to kiss the baby, except on top of the head and he advised sweethearts; "Don't kiss the bare hand until you are satisfied it is thoroughly devoid of bacilli."[91]

An article appeared in print in April 1911 that was split into two brief parts, on each side of the kissing issue. Dr. Anna G. Freedman of New York City said; "It is wrong for any person under any circumstances to kiss a child on the mouth. This applies just as well to the baby's mother and father. Many diseases may be conveyed to infants by a kiss on the mouth and no mother who loves her baby will ever expose her innocent child to possible contagion by kissing its mouth." She added; "I do not think kissing between healthy adults is attended by the same danger. I think kissing between women who are utterly indifferent to each other should be abolished." The other side of the issue was given by Mrs. Calvin N. Gabriel, described as a "prominent suffragist from Baltimore." Note that both these women were against kissing as it then existed. Freedman was somewhat opposed to it while Gabriel was extremely opposed to the practice. Said Gabriel; "Kissing should be abolished. The utter meaninglessness of the performance, to say nothing of the unsanitary element of it, should have killed the kiss long ago." And, she added; "The menaces to health that are difficult to get rid of, such as open sewers and such things, are bewailed and bemoaned, but one of the most dangerous practices, one that constantly endangers health and spreads disease, is allowed to flourish on account of the mere maudlin sentiment that surrounds this form of caress."[92]

The Indiana State Board of Health came up with a poster in May 1911 that contained some two dozen small photos of babies with a header that stated "Indiana State Board of Health" and a text in all capitals that said "Please do not kiss me, I do not want your germs, they are harmful. You should protect me from possible disease and death." The poster was the idea of Dr. William King assistant secretary of the State Board of Health – it was a unique idea as an illustration for the board's crusade against kissing the baby. They were what Dr. King called "baby charts." One of the posters was to be sent to Los Angeles as part of the Indiana exhibit at the annual convention of the American Medical Association that was to take place in the California city in June that year.[93]

Dr. Charles J. White of Boston who was described as an "authority" on disease of the skin, gave a lecture at the Harvard Medical School on the afternoon of March 1912. In that talk he condemned Boston barbers and their brethren as "the worst disease spreaders," due to the poor sanitary condition of the barber's implements such as brushes, combs, razors, and so forth. As well, he favored the abolition of the cigar cutter from store counters saying that it constituted a health menace. While the bulk of his lecture consisted of slamming barbers he also declared that women friends should not exchange kisses.[94]

A health-related article that appeared in July 1912 had as its focus ways of keeping the baby cool in the summer. It branched out a bit to speak to the subject of kissing. "Never kiss your baby on the mouth…Keep your microbes for older people if you feel that you must kiss someone. Transmit your million or so of germs to someone your own size," declared the article. "Baby's mouth should be washed out daily with a weak solution of boracic acid, This will, perhaps, counteract the trouble made by someone who kisses the baby when you are not looking." The journalist who wrote this article concluded by declaring; "No baby has ever said it likes to be kissed. Indeed, one sees more babies cry than smile at the salutation. Most of us kiss a baby from the surely selfish desire to feel its soft, sweet-smelling flesh against our lips…kiss it any place but on the mouth."[95]

The message of the Wheeling West Virginia Board of Health to those who osculated, in November 1912, was, according to a reporter; "Lovers and others who are inclined toward osculation are advised to cleanse their lips regularly, as disease may be transmitted through the common habit of kissing." It was said that was a substitute recommendation for one which was brought up by a Board of Health member prohibiting kissing entirely in Wheeling. That resolution had been strongly urged owing to the large number of infectious diseases that had prevailed in that area during the past few years. Noted the journalist; "Rather than be made the butt of jokes, cartoonists and humorists the world over, a majority of the members of the board of health agreed to appease the righteous wrath of the opponents of kissing and issue a warning to all who inclined to enjoy the sweets of osculation, advising them to use extreme care in cleansing their lips and cheeks before indulging the pastime.[96]

The presses running off the weekly bulletin of the Chicago Health Department were stopped in August 1913 while Chicago Health Commissioner Dr. G. B. Young eliminated from the edition being printed an article warning the public against kissing. The warning had been prepared by one of the assistant commissioners. Said Young; "Kissing is not dangerous if kept within due bounds. Kissing has been going on since the world began and I shall not raise my voice against it."[97]

An epidemic of influenza [grip] reached serious proportions in the northeast part of America in December of 1915. It reached such proportions in Camden, New Jersey that the Board of Health in that city placed a ban on kissing issuing the following bulletin; "Don't even kiss your wife. Put the duty or pleasure off for a time till the epidemic has passed. Let the sweethearts wait; they can stand it. See that little children and aged persons are not kissed. Kissing spreads the germs of the disease and the epidemic may become severe." In Philadelphia the epidemic had "seriously inconvenienced business" and had caused the death rate to climb with 122 grip victims dying in that city in the previous one week.[98]

The danger of kissing as a means of spreading disease was pointed out during that epidemic to residents of Petworth [a suburb of Washington, D.C.] by Raymond E. Adams, chairman of the committee on public health of the Petworth Citizens' Association at a public meeting on the evening of December 21, 1915. He noted that persons carrying contagious disease easily transmitted it through the habit of kissing.[99]

Later in December it was reported that the epidemic of influenza had spread throughout the Middle West. As a result people were advised to sleep out-of-doors in possible, avoid the common towel and common drinking cup, avoid the careless cough and sneeze and; "Don't kiss infected persons – or anyone if you yourself are infected." In Milwaukee some 20,000 people were said to be ill in the epidemic. During the previous two weeks nearly 40 percent of all school children had missed classes at some point during that period. Several million sufferers were located in Illinois and Minnesota. Chicago health authorities followed the example of Milwaukee officials in banning kissing. Commissioner Rusland of Milwaukee warned against "kissing of any sort." As well, serious flue epidemics were reported in Camden, New Jersey, Jackson, Mississippi, and a number of other cities. Said Dr. W. C. Rucker, assistant surgeon general of the United States Public Health Service; "Children's kissing games spread the grip. Kissing between infected and non-infected persons should be avoided. Guard against being sneezed or coughed upon. Infected persons should be avoided, and avoidance of towels and other articles they may touch with their hands, mouths, noses, should be observed."[100]

In Canton, Ohio, during that epidemic, Health Officer Lamont advises that Christmas mistletoe be thrown away. Why did he want it thrown out? Because, he explained, it served as an excuse for osculation and kissing, he declared; "is one of the worst means of spreading disease, particularly colds and grip."[101]

On December 30, 1915 an editorial cartoon was published that mocked Camden, New Jersey's response to the flu epidemic; "America's only and original kissless city threatens to jail all kissers committing the osculatory act within its bounds, and has become the hotbed of propagation for an anti-smacking movement that may inundate the nation."[102]

On that same day in Camden it was estimated the city had 3,500 people who were then the victims of influenza. To that date there had been close to 100 deaths. Dr. John F. Leavitt, health officer in Camden said; "Grip is sweeping through whole families here. Germs were the cause. They are everywhere in the air, but they are most likely to be communicated by contact. Promiscuous contact of lips is especially dangerous. The human lip contains 40,000 microbes per square centimeter. For these reasons I have forbidden kissing in Camden for the duration of the epidemic. Of course I can't enforce my decree – but the people are with me." Reportedly, Camden jewellers were selling both kissing screens and kissing fans. Drugstores were selling "Osculation Lotion aux Violettes," a sterilizing agent, in accordance with a formula given out by the "famous" Dr. Nalpasse of the University of Paris.[103]

In the first week if 1916 Mayor Tom Lea in El Paso, Texas declared he would not emulate the action of the mayor of Camden, New Jersey who had issued a proclamation forbidding kissing. Lea said that no ban on kissing of any kind would be issued by him; "Besides, kissing s a time-honored constitution." Lea added; "Far be it from me to issue a proclamation prohibiting a love-lorn swain from kissing the maid of his choice. It is no part of my affairs as mayor to say that a husband shall not salute his wife with the usual morning and evening kiss." Concluded Lea; "No such proclamation ever will emanate from my office. The kiss shall ever be held sacred. People may kiss unrestrained, without reserve and in full confidence that at the worst, they may catch nothing worse than a cold – if they confine their kissing to bounds that do no trespass upon the right of other kissers."[104]

Later in January 1916 Camden and its ban on kissing was mentioned in connection with Phoenix Arizona. That city had no flu epidemic but it was said there were some cases of the disease there. The fear that there might be a spread of the malady caused some "public-spirited" citizens to suggest to Mayor George U. Young that he issue a proclamation similar to that of put out by Camden. Said Young; "This mayor (the Camden executive) has given us westerners some new information – that is that Camden is not a live but an academic community. Too much schooling, too much of the wrong kind of parental authority – the young people not allowed to grasp just how small the world is, what life was intended to be – a place that must be overflowing with old maids, made so by fear – a place Roosevelt would scorn to live in because the men of Camden have no idea what a kiss is, and thus have proven their absolute unfitness to assume the responsibility of the ballot." Young was not finished attacking Camden and went on to say; "If the mayor is married his wife is to be pitied. If he is not married then the most vicious suffragette should pass him up, for if we analyze him, he is not in the nominative case, where he should be, and the subject of some good woman's loving, but he has proven himself strictly in the passive case, not fit to be left for a moment with the care of any good woman's children." Would Mayor Young ever consider imposing on Phoenix a no-kiss rule as had been put in place in Camden, wondered the reporter. "No, it would require a more selfish man than the resent mayor of Phoenix to be guilty of such ignorance, for with all the Phoenix feminine loveliness and masculine manliness, if there be two who cannot impart sufficient vitality to their kiss to kill the germ of any influenza the mayor's worst wish is those two die the death of rag babies and be removed from this community."[105]

In Boston in May 1916, Dr. Charles E. Page, head of the Health School and a practicing physician in Boston for 30 years commented that; "There isn't half enough kissing going on – that is what I think about it." When Page heard that Dr. C. V. Chapin, a Providence health official had stood up before an audience of the Harvard Medical School and "put the ban on kissing" Page felt he just had to speak up on the subject. "Why, it is nothing short of foolish to even suggest that one can catch germs. In the first place germs, or bacilli, are the product, not the cause of disease…One does not catch a cold from any little bug." [Maybe his medical knowledge was not among the best].[106]

"Cease kissing" was one of the suggestions made in July 1916 by the Connecticut State Board of Health for preventing the spread of infantile paralysis [poliomyelitis, polio]. In the bulletin the Health Board issued was a how to prevent the spread of that disease section, which included; "stay away from theatres and public gatherings, forbid kissing and the use of common cups and towels…[107]

It was reported in March 1917 that almost 3,000 Aurora, Illinois residents were suffering from an epidemic of "septic sore throat." City Health Commissioner Dr. Schwachtgen declared that as one measure of checking the epidemic he suggested a ban on kissing.[108]

A week of events for a Better Baby Campaign that took place in Tacoma Washington in the spring of 1917 featured tips on the proper care of infants, nutritional advice, and so forth. An illustration that appeared for the event showed the drawing of a resolute, grim-faced child staring ahead and saying "Don't Kiss Me; You Carry Germs."[109]

People who wanted to avoid the Spanish influenza, or the common garden variety of the same disease were warned by the New York City Department of Health in September 1918 not to kiss "except through a handkerchief."[110]

A ban on kissing and on "political" handshakes was suggested, in January 1920, by Dr. George W. Finley County Commissioner of Health in Brazil Indiana as a preventive against the spread of influence. Six cases of the disease had been reported in the county but they were all, said a report, "of a mild nature." Dr. Finley suggested that the military salute take the place of the handshake for a greeting, and that kissing be abolished entirely until the danger of an epidemic was removed.[111]

Practically all people, especially those living in cities, were infected with the tuberculosis germs before they reached middle age, according to Dr. T. C. Hempelmann of St. Louis, who addressed the American Child Hygiene Association at the concluding session of that group's annual convention, in St. Louis on October 14, 1920. To protect against infection the doctor told mothers they should guard the milk supply "and prevent promiscuous handling and kissing of the baby," and he emphasized; "Don't kiss the baby on the mouth."[112]

A kiss hygiene warning was issued in Cincinnati in June 1921, from Leo B. Forst, the retiring head of the United States Pure Food and Drug Laboratory. He said; "It has been the custom among some girls to scent their lips with violet, lilac or rose toilet waters. This custom gives rise to the perfumed kiss. The Government now is warning women not to anoint their lips with these perfumes, because anyone kissing them might receive a violent chemical reaction."[113]

Kissing was blamed by physicians of Uniontown Pennsylvania, in September 1921, for the spread of an epidemic of blisters that had then grown to such proportions that the board of health might be called upon to place a ban on osculation until such time as the disease had abated or disappeared entirely. It was a skin disease and while not all the sufferers were in their teens and early twenties a "great majority" of them were in that age group, what was known as the "kissing age." However, the hint dropped that the board of health might be asked to declare kissing taboo until the epidemic was over, had subsided after, said a journalist; "it aroused a strong protest from all over the city."[114]

St. Louis Health Commissioner Dr. John Simon was one of many city officials who took action against kissing , or threatened to do so, most of that activity occurring in the first decade of the 20th century.

This 1907 photo shows Mrs. Avis Boyce, whose mission in life was to get people to stop kissing babies.

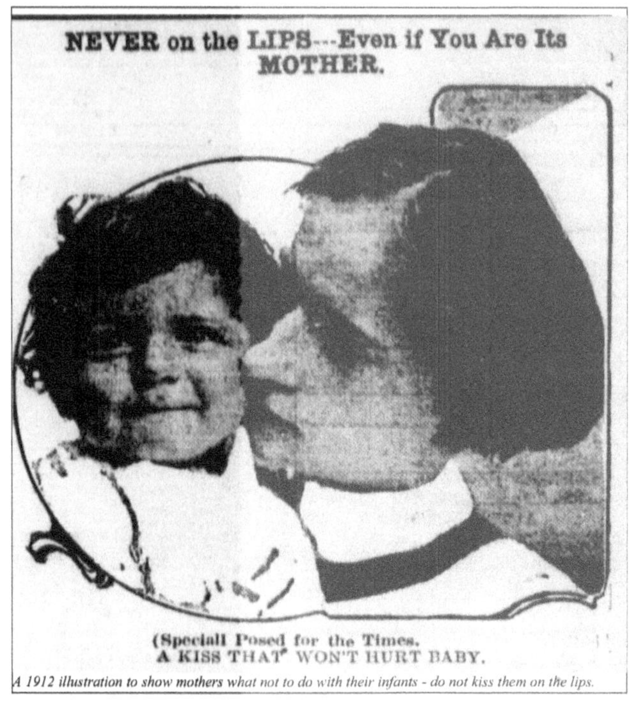

A 1912 illustration to show mothers what not to do with their infants - do not kiss them on the lips.

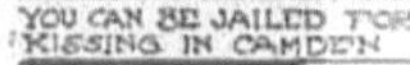

This series of sketches in 1915 spoofed the efforts the city of Camden New Jersey was then taking in its efforts to eradicate kissing.

Ch. 3. The Sanitary Kiss.

The growing fear in America over microbes and germs in general, and from the kiss in particular, fueled many movements against the practice and was the catalyst for many attempts to regulate kissing in some fashion. Since science had been responsible for setting off the controversy and the fear it was only proper that science should step in with the remedy. And so it did, or pretended to do so. And thus was born the sanitary kiss.

The earliest appearance in print of that concept was headlined; "The kiss hygienic: guaranteed innocuous." That article appeared in a New York City newspaper in September 1909 and gave a brief account of a German inventor by the name of Herman Sommer and his sanitary kiss apparatus, along with a picture of the item.[1]

Not much more was heard about the device until the middle of December of that year at which time a fuller account was presented. That story began with the declaration; "And now we have the kiss hygienic – an answer to those who have started a crusade against the kiss on the ground that it spreads contagion." It was explained that the kiss hygienic was made possible through the medium of a very simple little contrivance designed by a German "genius" named Herman Sommer. It consisted of a small ivory or metal frame, made to look somewhat like a small tennis racket, across which was stretched a bit of silk gauze. That gauze was soaked in disinfectant and then, in the words of the reporter; "interposed between the kisser and the kissee at the psychological moment and then – well, then follows the kiss robbed of all its terrors and but few of its delights, so the inventor says." According to the account; "There can be no exchange of disease germs in the kissing when this device is used. The disinfected gauze prevents that absolutely." A journalist observed that; "Of course this kiss hygienic isn't quite the old time kiss. For instance the disinfectant isn't particularly agreeable to the taste even when its flavor has been concealed by perfumes as the inventor advises. Then, too, the interposition of the device may seem something like the presence of a third party." The reporter also noted that the device raised a question that was highly embarrassing to the modest young woman; "shall she presume to provide herself with the contrivance in anticipation of the visit of the young man who is attentive to her, but who as yet is nothing more? Then, too, something of the spontaneity of the old fashioned kiss is likely to be lost, and also something of that thrill which poets have sung of the meeting of lip with lip."[2]

Another report about the device was published in April of 1910 when it was noted that the gauze was soaked in disinfectant and to that was added the scent of roses, cloves or peppermint, to cover the unpleasant taste of the disinfectant. However, it was also noted herein that the device "is more of a joke than a serious invention, so also are the stories being published in many European newspapers concerning American children who are wearing hat bands with the words 'don't kiss me' upon them, the idea being to prevent the infection that may come from promiscuous osculation."[3]

If ridicule about the sanitary kiss was starting to emerge it did not put an end to the contrivance invented by Sommer. It was announced on April 30 that the New York branch of the National Pharmaceutical Society had given its approval to an "osculatory screen." It was described in the same way as had been Sommer's invention, although the German was mentioned.[4]

A couple of weeks later a lengthy article appeared about Professor Harry Butler, described as the inventor of the "kissinette." That story contained a picture of Butler and of his "little sanitary implement." It looked remarkably like the device invented by Sommer but the story contained no mention of the German. Enthusiastically, the article began with the words; "At last, the antiseptic kiss!" Professor Harry Butler was described in the story as a student of germs and an experimenter in germicides who said he had found the antiseptic kiss. He declared, stated the journalist, that in the future those "who acquire the kissing habit will be able through his newest invention to kiss in security hunted by no fears that that wicked little osculatory germ, the bugaboo of certain distinguished medical men, will render their kisses less soulful or less thrilling than nature originally designed them to be.

The germless kiss, the kiss hygienic, is to be the kiss of the future." Those words of the reporter were, obviously, somewhat sarcastic, written with tongue in cheek. Butler exhibited his invention, designed to bring about the antiseptic kiss, in public for the first time one evening in May 1910 at the exposition and bazaar held by the National Pharmaceutical Society of Registered Drug Clerks and, it was reported, the device "won instantaneous favor, and the available supply was exhausted in exactly fifteen minutes." The device to protect kissers and "kissees against the grave dangers of kissing germs" was called the kissinette and while it looked like a simple enough contrivance there was said to be a secret in its preparation that was known only to Professor Butler and he guarded that secret carefully.[5]

Upon examination by the journalist the kissinette appeared to be merely a piece of fine white silk gauze stretched over a loop of white silk wire. It was about four inches in diameter with the ends of the wire being fastened into a wooden handle about three inches in length. Kissers kissed with the device placed between them and their lips. In the gauze lay the secret, according to Butler because before being attached to the loop the gauze was steeped in an antiseptic, and then perfumed. "For three years he has experimented to find the right combination of chemicals, but not until recently did success crown his efforts," declared the reporter. Butler would reveal nothing about those chemicals used in his formulation except for one fact – that the mixture contained "positively no acetanilide." That meant there was nothing in it to depress heart action. The professor was a member of the National Pharmaceutical Society. At that exhibition a kissing booth was set up to demonstrate the device and all 300 kissinettes on hand at the fair were quickly sold at a price of 25 cents each. Those who had the honor of testing the device that night did so at a cost of ten cents a kiss or three kisses for 25 cents.[6]

At that exhibition, according to the journalist; "A few careless persons, evidently without a proper respect for germs, were inclined to treat the new invention with levity, but after listening to the exposition of its merits they were gathered into the fold of converts." One sceptical youth remarked that he saw no reason why the germs could not crawl through the interstices in the gauze. Professor Butler explained that the antiseptic preparation lured the bacteria to the strands of the netting, "just as

Circe of old lured sailors to their death on the sunken reefs. Besides, he declared, the ways of germs, like those of all evil things, are crooked, and they would never go straight through on principle. He also explained that an immersion in water after any kiss rendered the kissinette again germ proof." Butler engaged in some of the test kissing himself. When a reporter asked the professor if he found it a pleasant experience Butler replied; "The pathogenic interest I had in the demonstration precluded my giving attention to what would otherwise have been a pleasurable experience." He continued by saying; "When men and women realize that osculation can become perfectly harmless it will be more generally practiced. There is a certain modesty about the kiss given through the kissinette that does not pertain to ordinary kissing, and the most prudish girl will feel that she can allow herself to be kissed with the hygienic kiss." A journalist then asked Butler if the charm of the kiss would not be lost when the lips no longer met. To that the professor replied; "On the contrary…I am convinced that there will be an added charm when the new device is used. The threads of the gauze create a vibration which will add to the thrill of the kiss and will I am sure be something intense between true lovers. In farewells this vibration will express sympathy, sometimes pathos, since the net responds to the osculations. There is one other advantage. The vibrations cause a musical note in the kiss waves which fill a room when two persons kiss each other."[7]

 According to the story Butler had given all the rights to his invention to the Pharmaceutical Society. He also pointed out that a smaller sized kissinette was soon to be made which a man could hang from his buttonhole after the manner of an eyeglass. The reporter stated that the kissinette was really the result of experiments made several years ago by Butler to find an antiseptic gauze that could be used on the drinking cups passed around in church communion services. It was difficult, explained the professor, to find a germicide that was not poisonous to man. "I recognize that kissing is a custom as ancient as it seems to be agreeable and so general that we can scarcely abolish it if we would…it seems to me to be the duty of science to rob it of its dangers," he stated. "That, I think, I have succeeded in doing. Unfortunately, while there is danger in the kiss there is no terror attached thereto, and the hilariously inclined are prone to make merry over the kissinette. But it is not a matter for merriment."

Reportedly, the demand for the device was so great that the manufacturer was working overtime to

meet that demand. In conclusion Butler declared; "I am inclined to think that the custom of osculating

by means of the kissinette will become general. I am satisfied that it will be hailed as reverently by the

serious minded as it appears to have been hilariously by the light hearted."[8]

Almost two years passed before the kissinette was heard from again. In February 1912 it was reported

that the National Pharmaceutical Society planned to give away samples of the device at their annual

ball to be held in New York City on February 28. It had apparently been redesigned and then had a

sterling silver handle.[9]

In May of 1912 the senior class at Northwestern University in Evanston Illinois took a secret vote to

determine if they were for or against the sanitary kiss. The vote was reported to have been "almost

unanimous" against it. That class numbered 170 men and 113 women. Secretary Drugee of the class

said; "This means that we consider the anti-germ kiss and sanitary kiss advocated by physicians to be

'bunk.' The class believes in kissing in the old-fashioned way. Why, the doctors would cut all the

flavor out of osculation and leave a kiss as dry and mechanical as a clinic." As well the female

students took a vote on "fussing," the college girl term for "spooning" and the ayes had it by a "big

majority."[10]

Dr. W. F. Snow, secretary of the American Social Hygiene Association, suggested in October 1914

that if people must kiss they should kiss through a square of tissue paper that had been prepared in an

antiseptic bath.[11]

That suggestion from Snow provoked at least one editorial that sarcastically addressed the issue in a

tongue in cheek fashion. The editor began; "As indicating that science and invention are still busy in

the service of humankind, the discovery of the sterilized kiss has just been announced by hygienic

experts." And, he continued; "The ordinary old-fashioned kiss was barred from active practice some

years ago, when investigations made it known that dangerous diseases lurked in the affectionate greeting. The mortality arising from these practices had never been particularly remarked, but investigators told us that the kiss was just a clearing house for disease, and the habit has since been discouraged. Whether or not the general death rate has been diminished thereby has never been satisfactorily demonstrated." With respect to the sanitary kiss the newsman declared; "But the new kiss is not an adventure to be attempted in haste. On the contrary, the sanitary kiss is to be deliberate act, consummated only after effective preparation." All that was required to prepare for the "sterilized osculation is to step into the corner drug store and purchase a supply of sterilized tissue paper, especially treated for the purpose. The rest is simple. The kisser holds a small portion of the paper over his or her lips, as the case may be, the meanwhile pressing a like piece of paper over the mouth of the kissee. Contact between the pieces of paper is then made, and the act of osculation is completed. Could anything be more conservative, or more effectively sanitary?"[12]

During the summer of 1915 the latest version of the antiseptic kiss was introduced. An article published in July included a photo in which a man was seemingly going to slap a girl's face. But no, he was merely going to administer the "pat-pat" which was described in the story thusly; "It is the very latest in salutations – the sanitary kiss." The pat-pat was being advocated by Dr. E. F. Otis, a delegate from Dominica to the Pan-American Medical Congress, which had recently concluded its session in San Francisco. Otis was very much against the lip kiss stating; "It is the most common way of spreading tuberculosis…The spread of the disease has been traced in many cases to the kiss and for this reason we have waged war on osculation in Dominica." He continued by declaring; "The 'pat-pat' is the accepted form of greeting in our country and I advocate that in the interest of humanity, the health authorities of the United States launch a campaign to establish the 'pat-pat' as the standard method of saluting in this county." In a pat-pat exchange each partner patted the other lightly on the cheek.[13]

Several weeks later another article mentioned the pat-pat and announced that it had a champion in America by the name of Dr. E. W. Grover who was described as "vigorously opposed to the osculatory mode of greeting friends and expressing affection. Grover was president of the local health board in

Huntington, West Virginia and said that kissing was a "sure manner" of spreading tuberculosis and other diseases. He told a reporter that the latest substitute for kissing was the pat-pat and then proceeded to explain to the journalist how it was done. Grover declared there was too much kissing in Huntington and that the health authorities ought to start a campaign against what he termed "the habit."[14]

According to another report Grover's campaign to do away with kissing and substitute the pat-pat had gained nation-wide publicity. He was president of the Huntington Board of Health. In the wake of that publicity his three nieces, who all lived in Los Angeles, wrote back to Huntington to declare; "When it comes to osculatory pursuits our uncle was a humdinger in by-gone days. The other boys didn't have a chance with him. He was some kisser." Doctor Grover had reportedly received hundreds of letters protesting against his pat-pat system. A Cleveland man termed him "a superannuated old stick."[15]

Late it December 1919 it was reported that Dr. Grover, by then the former city health officer in Huntington and who had "originated" the sanitary kiss several years earlier had by then retreated from his position. At that time Grover announced the following policy; "All men are born free and equal, endowed with certain inalienable rights – among those being life, liberty and the right of unrestricted osculation." He said he had reached that conclusion after over a year of careful consideration of the general subject of kissing. Grover formerly believed there might be a considerable exchange of disease germs from osculation but, by 1919, had completely reversed himself. Apparently he had given up on the pat-pat idea not too long after having introduced it. Then, a year or so after that he introduced his wire frame covered with medicated gauze for the sanitary kiss, perhaps the kissinette itself, or a copy thereof. When he introduced that, said a reporter; "He was both commended and condemned on all sides."[16]

Earlier in 1919 it was observed that the town of New Castle Pennsylvania was not taking very kindly to the sanitary kiss. This version was performed with a piece of cheese cloth being used as a shield. "New Castle people seem to prefer their kissing unfiltered. They may have premonitions of dangers lurking in city water, but when it comes to kissing they take a chance. They are willing to defy the germs of bacilli," observed a newsman.[17]

Nothing more was heard about the sanitary kiss, at least with respect to the using of some type of device or material placed between the lips of the kissing couple. And thus died the sanitary kiss.

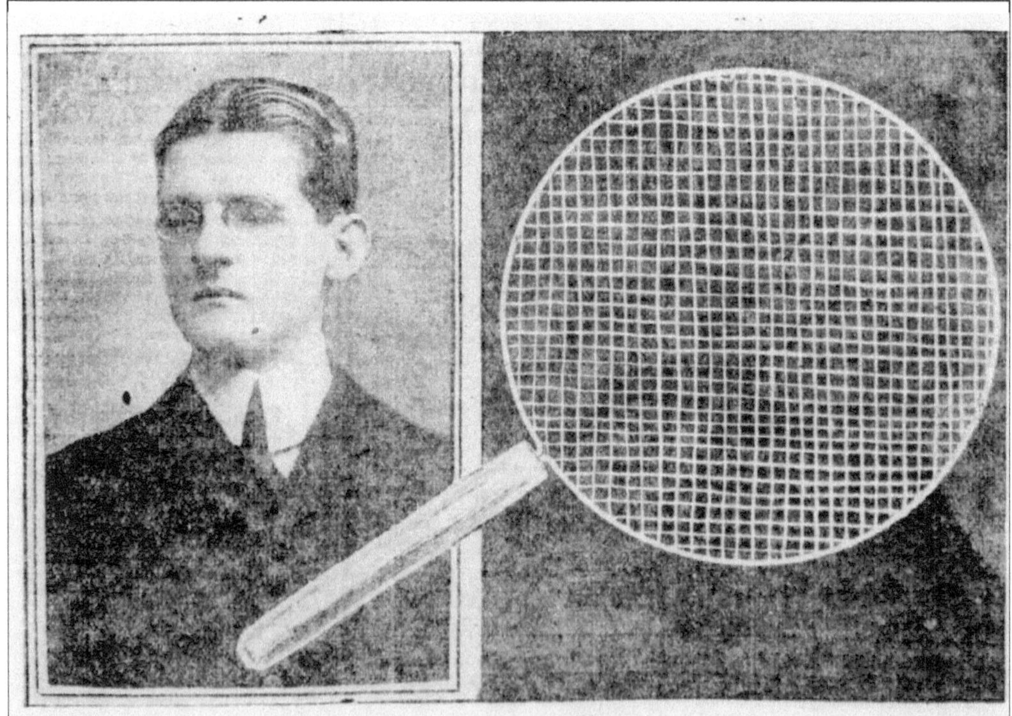

Professor Harry Butler is shown here in 1910 with the contrivance that he called a "kissinette." It looked very much like the invention of the German inventor Sommer, but that man was no longer mentioned.

The sanitary kiss apparatus invented by a German named Herbert Sommer made its first appearance in the fall of 1909; it was guaranteed to make kissing a risk-free activity.

NOW YOU CAN KISS YOUR LADY FRIEND AND YOU NEEDEN'T WORRY ABOUT GERMS

This sketch shows the kissinette and a drawing of a couple putting the item to use.

This man looks like he is about to slap a woman but it is not what it seems. The time is 1915 and he is about to give the woman a pat-pat, a substitute for a kiss. It was the latest, and last, version of the sanitary kiss. And what could be more sanitary than to abandon the kiss altogether?

Ch. 4. Morals and Crusades.

Some of those opposed to the practice of osculation were driven exclusively, or almost exclusively, by health concerns, be they legitimate or not. Some were in positions where they could impose rules, regulations, or laws, or attempt to do so. Some of those people were concerned with health to some extent, but many contained morality concerns underlying their official efforts, such as railroad officials, city councilmen, or state legislators. In between were those driven mostly by morality; they were crusaders for "purity." Sometimes they masked their crusade under the guise of health concerns but mostly they were zealous agitators, determined to impose their value systems on others.

One of the earlier issues that revolved around kissing was that of females kissing each other. It raised much ire from time to time but the underlying motives for such animosity were never articulated. For reasons never explained at the time the act of one woman kissing another was very much unacceptable. An article that appeared in print on May 26, 1881, told of a "very animated" parlor discussion on kissing that had supposedly taken place during which a young woman expressed herself opposed "to the practice of ladies kissing each other when they met, as many do, on the street cars, in the street, at their offices, and at all times and places, in season and out of season." The young lady said that, for her, she had kisses enough before she was 12 from people such as relatives, friends of her parents, and so forth. The reporter declared; "It is a foolish and injurious practice; and besides being distasteful to most children to kiss tobacco consumers and beer drinkers, the little innocents take diseases in this way and are the victims of 'cruelty to children.'" The journalist then stated that he was in agreement with the woman in being against women kissing each other; "Many ladies actually submit to as much torment as though they were children, for if a partial acquaintance, someone who apes familiarity, kiss them, they take it as meekly as a lamb." In conclusion the reporter asserted; "It actually amounts to rudeness some time, and I doubt if a genuine lady will presume on the patience of a friend with whom she is not most thoroughly acquainted. Old and very dear friends find kissing a pleasant pleasure; but even there need not forget that there are times and places where the salutation should be omitted."[1]

An editor on a Wheeling West Virginia newspaper related a story to his readers in June 1885. He wrote that on a public thoroughfare in Wheeling four young women met three young women and then there were seven; "They stopped, after the manner of women, kissed." He then determined how many kisses were involved. Each one kissed the six others so six times seven equalled 42 kisses. They got through all their kissing and were chatting when four more acquaintances came along and then there were eleven. The four newcomers fell to kissing the seven original ones. How many did that make, the editor wondered. Four times seven equalled 28 so that the total number of kisses bestowed was 42 plus 28, or a total of 70. But, if each mouth constituted a kiss then there were really 140 kisses in total; "For if it be not in good taste – however sweet the osculation – to exchange seventy kisses in a public place, how much less so to give and take a hundred and forty kisses." He then pointed out that the old "Blue Laws" made kissing in public punishable by a fine; "The immutable law of propriety lay at the bottom of this public kissing interdict. If the kiss be a sacred thing, as it ought to be, then it ought not to be aired in public places." He believed that in the United States women kissed as a matter of course; "It is not confined chiefly to kinfolk or to dear friends, but embraces as well casual acquaintances. After two women have kissed and one has turned away it is inspiring to hear the other remark, 'I hate this horrid thing, but I must keep up the acquaintance.' The kiss hypocritical is poison."[2]

At the beginning of 1886 an editorial that originated in a Philadelphia newspaper began by stating; "Some recent observers have remarked that the kiss as a salutation, except among near kindred and friends, is passing out of use. We should be glad to believe that this is so, but in many portions of the country it is certain that the kissing habit is still almost universal among women. Those between whom an actual dislike is known to exist touch each other's lips in their calling rounds, and even on the street and at railroad stations." According to this editor a few years earlier; "when the kissing furor was prevalent" at a certain girl's school, a sort of social was formed, which was dubbed the A.K.L. (Anti-Kissing League). It was said at one time that society embraced most of the 'solid' girls at that school; "We understand that it is no longer in existence but its influence was most salutary and is felt even to the present time." Concluded the editor; "If the teachers in girls' schools and colleges would only take the matter of kissing in hand and create a public sentiment against the indiscriminate indulgence in the practice there would be much less of the absurd 'mash' epidemic among the callow maidens in our education institutions."[3]

A month later an editor with a Boston paper replied to the above editorial by observing; "The Philadelphia Press wants to abolish kissing. Tut, tut, bother! Let the young folks enjoy themselves. Because one's kissing days are over, he shouldn't wish to deprive others of sweetmeats."[4]

According to a report published in September 1889 the "Wideawake and Christian Union" was conducting a crusade against the kissing habit; "As the remarks of these periodicals have reference to the kissing of women by one another, there is not a man in the country who will object."[5]

A female writer on a London England publication asserted, in November 1889; "And why must we kiss each other every time we meet? Kisses are really not agreeable greetings to exchange…Of all my girl friends who kiss me when we meet there is only one from whose osculatory greeting I do not involuntarily shrink." She wondered if it would be possible for women to forge a non-kissing compact; "The rules would not forbid a kiss after a long absence, nor would it interfere with lovers' kisses or anything of that sort, but only combat the custom of daily greeting by osculation." In conclusion, she declared; "I feel quite sure that woman's friendship would be firm and more durable if they would abandon all such heavy demands upon it."[6]

Later in November 1889 an editorial was reprinted in various newspapers that had originally appeared in a periodical called *The Housekeeper*. The subject of the editorial was "the foolish habit of kissing which prevails among women." It continued; "It is hard to see why it is done. If you ask women about it, one in four will tell you that she does not like it and would like to drop it but that 'they expect it, you know.'" And, declared the editor; "Indeed, so far has the objection to indiscriminate kissing among women gone that there are anti-kissing societies in many places, the women who belong pledging themselves not to kiss any woman in public, and only those whom they really care for in private."[7]

A journalist by the name of John Armoy Knox wrote in October 1891 that; "The kiss that one woman gives another may be called the instantaneous, and may be considered the most unsatisfactory known to the human race. It is a shadow, a base counterfeit, a wretched substitute. There is no enjoyment in it, no lingering pleasure in it." Knox went on; "It is as perfunctory as the peck of a hen in a gravel bed; compared to a genuine mutual male and female kiss it is in flavor and value as the canned fruit of commerce is to the juicy peach fresh plucked from the tree." He even included a short poem on the topic;

Men scorn to kiss among themselves,

And scarce will kiss a brother.

Women oft want to kiss so bad

They smack and kiss each other.[8]

Writing in March 1893 a New York City newspaper editor thought the crusade against kissing seemed to have abated somewhat but the practice had not; "It must be apparent, however, to everybody that the custom ladies have of kissing each other is a very absurd one, and should the crusade accomplish an abatement of it the movement will not have lived in vain. The number of ladies who kiss and dislike each other would be startling if made known."[9]

An editorial from *The Demorest Magazine* was reprinted in newspapers in May 1895. The founder of that periodical was William Jennings Demorest a man who, among other things, was a well-known prohibitionist, ran for Mayor of New York City on the Prohibition ticket, and organized the Anti-Nuisance League. "A vulgar display of mawkish affected," he declared in his piece, used to be the unkind comment that came so often from kindly folk at the sight of women kissing in public; "but since her Majesty, Queen Fashion has announced that she not only approves, but recommends, kissing in public, no one hears on any hand the old sneer at the affectional demonstration." Demorest added; "Tis the fashion now to kiss one's hostess when calling, to kiss one's guests – women guests, of course – who arrive for an informal cup of the best Oriental brew or for a stately dinner party." Readers of the piece were advised to; "Give the salute lightly, like the touch of a butterfly's wing, just in the center of

the cheek; give it the soft sound of swaying silk draperies or falling rose petals, holding one hand of the

woman you kiss." He concluded; "On the street it is perfectly proper to kiss a woman through your

veil; or very prettily the kiss is given by lighting the gauze a bit and pressing a little kiss on your

companion's chin, just below her lip."[10]

Kisses delivered on the stage came under scrutiny as early as December of 1882. It was noted by a

journalist at that time that those stage kisses were regarded as a "necessary evil," or an advantage of

stage life, depending of the perspective. He remarked; "But this is an age of progress, and there is an

intimation that even stage kisses must be reformed." Some people then argued those stage kisses "must

have their limits, that, as it were, they must be delivered decently, in order, and without undue

lingering." It was all said to be part of a movement to abolish from the stage the "more passionate

kisses.[11]

A brief item that appeared originally in the *Christian Union* publication and was reprinted in

newspapers in April 1889 declared; "it is really a nuisance and in these days of societies and crusades

against evils, presents a good object. We mean this kissing habit. Girls are the guilty ones in this bad

practice."[12]

The above item may have inspired the Reverend P. S. Twitty of Cuthbert Georgia who was, in June

1889, said to be trying to organize an anti-kissing society in that community. Up to press time, sneered

an editor; "the society consisted of the Rev. P. S. Twitty." A few weeks later a different editor scoffed

at Twitty by writing; "The Georgia fanatic who is attempting to abolish kissing is on a cold trail. It

can't be did. This is a matter in which every man must be his own abolitionist."[13]

According to a January 1890 news story a bitter church war was then in progress at Dighton,

Massachusetts because the pastor of the Brick Church had put a stop to public kissing. "The church

sociables were veritable kissing bees, and the sport was not indulged in exclusively by the younger

people, either. Old spinsters were just as enthusiastic over it as were the young ones," noted a journalist. When the Reverend Asa Dyer accepted the pastorate he immediately declared that there should be no more kissing at church sociables; "The result was pandemonium and persecution without end. About the only collection which was even taken up for some time was one of empty rum bottles which reckless young men left in their pews. The voice of the faithful pastor was often drowned by the kissing sound made by slow kisses on the back of the hand." Various tricks were said to have been played on the pastor such as powder burned slowly at the door of the church, with smoke blown inside. Finally, a deputy sheriff drove one young man out of town for insulting the pastor, "and the overt acts have been stopped, for the time being at least."[14]

As he boarded a train to leave Pittsburgh in February 1890 United States President Benjamin Harrison "kissed Baby McKee goodbye at exactly 12 o'clock." The baby was his grandchild and there was nothing special about the event. But less than four months later, early in June, wrote a journalist; "President Harrison's refusal to kiss a baby of this city [Pittsburgh] is attracting the attention of many of our contemporaries." It was said that some applauded Harrison's "self-denial and some do not." The reason for the refusal to kiss the baby was said to be unknown. The reporter remarked; "However he was actuated, we think Mr. Harrison did right. The practice of kissing babies promiscuously is not wholesome or beautiful…Circumstantial evidence indicates, however, that kissing, if maternal kisses be excepted, is not relished by most babies." In conclusion the journalist stated' "As an act of mercy to the baby Mr. Harrison's refusal merits our approval. It should be an unspeakable relief to the infants of this broad land if their osculation for political purposes sunk into desuetude. And candidates for office would not be sorry either."[15]

A poem entitled "Enough of Kissing" appeared in a Washington, D.C. newspaper on September 13, 1890.

Aid me, ye muses mine, and eke ye graces!

While Pegasus I mount and try his paces;

My theme a kiss – or say a thousand kisses.

Yet, not to praise, but to denounce them this is.

Loves my kiss, at least in moderation;

Now kissing husbands wake my indignation;

To kissing babies I do much incline,

Especially if the darling cherub's mine

Their laughing lips exhale the only nectar

But from promiscuous kissing heaven protect or

Give us rest. Worthless the gift that's shared with all…

But kiss when we come and kiss when we go,

Kiss at the church and kiss at the show;

In joy or sorrow, trouble or bliss,

We begin with a buss, and we end with a kiss!

I'll still object to this contact of noses.

It makes one feel so like a hypocrite

Saluting those we'd rather not have met.

For nearest kindred let's reserve our lips,

Shake hands with friends (nor give our finger tips).

Sisters, I pray, let's make this new beginning,

And once again each kiss shall have a meaning.[16]

In June 1891 a newsman launched into "a consideration of the latter-day state of kissing in this country." He believed that kisses could be divided into several classes such as mother's kiss, sister's kiss, the conjugal kiss, the lover's kiss, the young woman novelist kiss, and so forth. None had ever been prohibited by a civilized people, he claimed; that is, until the last two or three weeks and then only in Boston and Philadelphia. Two weeks earlier, related the newsman, a young man of Boston who was from a "good family" and "of excellent position in society" was standing late at night with his wife in a doorway waiting for an East Boston streetcar. While waiting he kissed her two or three times. But these proceedings were observed by police officer Maguire who was in a doorway across the street and who promptly arrested them and took them to the station house on a charge of disorderly conduct. The next morning the Boston judge "reluctantly" discharged them on account of their previous good character. However, he gave the pair a warning not to do it again. Concluded the newsman, with regard to that case; "It is the understanding in Boston now that there must be no more kissing in public, and the pleasant pastime has been abandoned throughout the city." Something similar had reportedly happened in Philadelphia just two or three days earlier. Isaac Purnell and Sallie Senseman, young people who hoped to get married were walking along a quiet street in Philadelphia at about 9:00 PM. They stopped in the shadows of a tree and kissed. Policeman Stanton was nearby, saw them and arrested them. Then he took them to the police station. There the magistrate held them for the grand jury. On the following day that body indicted each for assault and battery upon the other. No outcome of the case was reported.[17]

Kissing at Bucks County Pennsylvania Sunday school picnic during the summer of 1891 was to be banned. The ground upon which kissing was to be banned was that while kissing itself was not immoral; "the promiscuous indulgence fostered by [the kissing game called] Copenhagen tends toward immorality." It was also reported that; "Just how the movement originated to abolish the game is not known. It is certain that the young people themselves did not start it, and the clergymen deny any knowledge of it." But the movement did exist and speculation was that; "the numerous old maids who infest Bucks County, and particularly the vicinity of Bristol, where the movement is said to have started, have risen up in arms against the favoritism shown toward the young girls in the matter of kisses."[18]

The subhead of a December 1, 1894 article stated; "Society woman's meeting against the anti-kissing crusade." It was said that for some time the society woman had been bowing before the shrine of Hygeia; that she had sacrificed her corset and even demonstrated a willingness to wear shoes that greatly magnified the size of her feet; "but there is one hygienic measure upon which she determinedly draws the line. The anti-kissing crusade will never become a popular fad, and though scientists prate of bacilli until doomsday, kissing has come to stay." The reporter then cited a writer in a Kansas City newspaper who said; "Of course kissing, like quail-eating and over indulgences in other luxuries may be overdone. The indiscriminate kissing of a baby, the meaningless osculation of two women." The newsman then argued; "Because the Princess Alice caught a fatal disease from the lips of the dying child, it does not follow that no mother shall kiss her baby." And, he concluded; "Ordinary common sense will regulate kissing as it governs other pleasures in life. The octogenarian grandmother who passes quietly away full of years and kisses, might have died sixty years before had she happened to kiss the wrong party…she took her reasonable chances and was no more the worse for them."[19]

According to a message from Burlington, New Jersey, in June 1897, there was woe among the Presbyterians of that town, because the management of the church said there would be no more kissing games engaged in at Sunday school picnics. The officers of the Sunday school stated they had determined to stop the kissing because dangerous microbes were in that way passed around among the people. Said the journalist; "The movement against kissing seems more on account of health than for other reasons. There are, however, others who desire to prohibit kissing at Sunday school picnics on account of the immoral aspect of the case."[20]

"I hope to see the day when kissing is entirely unknown. I wish it could be made illegal. It is not a clean thing to do. It should be discontinued by every clean, thinking woman," said Miss E. Marguerite Lindley, in an anti-kissing lecture before the Household Economic Association, in New York City in March 1899. After she had delivered her lecture some of the girls in the audience crowded around her and asked if she had not been carried a little too far by her ideas. "Nothing I said was too strong," she reiterated. "Kissing spreads disease. It is especially mean to kiss babies and children who are too small to object and who cannot escape. I never let anyone kiss me. It is a very undesirable expression of regard. I hope no one will ever try to kiss me, as I should not let them. I take care that no one ever gets a chance." One girl asked Lindley what about the situation in which the girl was engaged to a man, at which point Lindley looked in astonishment at the girl who became flustered and hastily added "and his mother wants to kiss you when she's welcoming you as her daughter." Lindley relaxed and stated; "Even in that case kissing is wrong. There are no exceptions to the rule. Why, even among some savages kissing does not exist." Another girl in the audience asked Lindley; "Do you really think that kissers should be put in jail?" She replied; "No, I don't say that, but kissing is unhygienic, unpleasant and very disagreeable. It should be dropped because it's not nice."[21]

With respect to Lindley's crusade, a newspaper editor declared; "Judging from her picture there is no need for her to do so on her own account. She will never be the victim of the osculation habit."[22]

In May 1899 Lindley appeared in Cleveland where she attended the convention of the International Woman's Health Protective League. At that gathering she declared that she had been misquoted concerning her theory that kissing was extremely dangerous to public health. "The papers say that I am in favor of the passage of a law to prohibit kissing, which is perfectly absurd, of course," she declared, "and they also say that I said in my address to the Household Economic Association in New York that I had never been kissed. They quoted me as saying that I never let any one kiss me and that I should not let any one if he tried. It's true that I believe kissing is dangerous." Lindley continued; "I had been delivering an address and some of the ladies said they were going to kiss me. Then I said I should not allow them to do it. I spoke of the unhygienic and insincere kissing between women and said it was unwholesome. A friendly grasp of the hand is enough for me. I did not say I had never been kissed as there was no occasion for such a remark."[23]

President Rogers of Northwestern University in Evanston, Illinois, announced in November 1899 that he was prohibiting kissing in the stage plays given by the students at his institution. While witnessing a play rehearsal a few days prior to his announcement the university head found himself "startled" at the "profusion and vigor" of the kissing between the young men and the women during that rehearsal.

Rogers declared that he left the hall in a "state of indignation" and then issued an order against kissing in all plays; "The students will hereafter not be allowed to embrace so ardently."[24]

A lengthy editorial appeared in print in November 1900 wherein the editor began by writing; "And now even kissing is being reduced to science! Once upon a time when people wanted to kiss they just kissed and that was all the fuss there was about it. Now all this is charged. The woman who want to be absolutely 'correct' in kissing, as she is in the selection of her hats or gowns, stockings or petticoats, must kiss according to rule." He then quoted one of the new authorities [unnamed] on polite osculation; "It is no longer good form to kiss even your best friend on the lips. That kiss is sacred to lovers and to husbands and wives. In polite society the kiss upon each cheek is now the accepted form of greeting between friends and relatives. When women are about the same age either one may offer the caress, but between a young woman and an older woman the younger must always proffer her lips and the older will gracefully turn her cheek to receive the kiss. Then, if the older woman desires to be exceedingly gracious she may in turn kiss the younger but there is no discourtesy if she turns the other cheek and becomes the recipient of the second kiss." The newsman continued by remarking that the well-bred woman was always cordial but never effusive in her caresses; "She is also chary of them. Promiscuous kissing is in bad taste. Of course, to kiss even one's nearest relative in the street is not permissible. A woman who is the possessor of self-respect and dignity will take care that her kisses are not meaningless" He thought there were several reasons why the kiss upon the lips had become obsolete with the principal one being that it was unhygienic; "Especially is it bad for children to be kissed upon the lips by elders. Mothers who study health never kiss their own children in this way, and are careful that the nurse does not thus show her love for her little charge. Kisses may be pressed upon a child's cheek, brow, eyes, chin or neck, but never on the mouth." In his conclusion the editor noted that a hurried kiss was almost an insult and that; "Some women put off the good-bye kiss until the last moment, and then give it in a peck on the cheek. The proper way to give a kiss is to press your lips lightly, but firmly, against the cheek and let them rest there for an instant. There must not be anything suggestive of a smack."[25]

The young people of St. Joseph's Roman Catholic Church in Jersey City, New Jersey, were reported to be much concerned, in December 1900, over remarks made by the Right Reverend Monsignor Seton made at several masses on a Sunday in that month. He said; "I am strongly opposed to certain Christmas entertainments. I am particularly opposed to what are known as kissing parties held by the younger element. They do not understand the importance of their religion or they would stay at home or go to church and read their prayer-books." Seton continued by asserting; "Mothers and fathers are not doing their duty when they allow their children out at night. I am much opposed to those gatherings and warn the young folk against that curse – parties." Seton declared, in conclusion; "I am particularly opposed to kissing parties on New Year's Day, when young men and women kiss each other under the mistletoe. The vigil of Christmas is a fast day and must be observed in such a manner. I hope you will take heed of what I say and will not go to theatres or parties or read novels."[26]

The Demorest branch of the Woman's Christian Temperance Union (WCTU) in New York City declared itself against the kissing habit, in December 1900. It did not advise temperance but urged prohibition as in the case of the saloon issues. At the regular meeting of the group in New York on December 27 Dr. Anna Hatfield said she thought kissing to be the worst thing a young woman could do. She said; "The amount of hugging and kissing that some girls – of our best families, too – submit to is literally a menace to our morality. I know a young man well who declares that he rarely leaves a girl without kissing her good night. He says that they not only eagerly accede to his request, but that several have insisted on being kissed." Hatfield added; "I have carefully inquired into the matter and I find many young women imagine this is the way to get husband. It is reprehensible. These are the supposedly well brought up daughters of rich parents. The girls must be taught that it is wrong, not only to kiss a stranger, but to kiss the men they are engaged to. Too great care cannot be taken." At that meeting it was suggested that an excellent way to stop the habit "would be to instruct young men as to the evils of kissing."[27]

An account of the WCTU meeting in another newspaper commented; "The kiss, like the saloon, must go." That decision was reached at the regular meeting of the group, which was held at the home of Mrs. Shirley, on West 23rd Street in New York City. The matter came up during a discussion on the group's vice crusade when Dr. Hatfield interrupted that discussion to unleash, according to a reporter; "a torrent of eloquence apropos of the saloon as the source of all evil to prove that the nectar quaffed from red lips was more fruitful of consequences than any alcoholic beverage ever distilled." Journalist Lavinia Hart covered the WCTU meeting and the start of its anti-kissing campaign. Hart wrote that Hatfield "has studied the kiss from both the medical and human standpoint, and knows whereof she speaks." According to Hatfield; "It is a vicious habit and if vice crusaders really want to purify society they should commence by tutoring children from their earliest infancy that kissing is an evil." But what of the kisses of a mother for her child, wondered Hart. "They should be fewer. Mothers have kissed their children to death," fumed the crusader. As far as Hatfield was concerned, who was married, the only exception to the no-kiss rule was for married couples. That caused journalist Hart to wonder if then, there were no bacteria in married couples' lips. "There are, at least, no moral bacteria lurking there, but from a medical standpoint no person should kiss another unless an antiseptic wash is used on the mouth daily. If you take a microscope and examine the teeth you will realize how limitless are the dangers of kissing," replied the practicing physician. That caused Hart to wonder about the moral bacteria. "You won't require a microscope for that. Kissing has come to be a greater plague than drink. It is more insidious. It is more deadly. Girls are not taught to view a kiss with awe, as they were in the days when I was young. Girls then considered a kiss a betrothal," asserted the crusader. Could engaged people kiss, asked Hart. "No, engaged people should not kiss. A betrothal kiss is a different thing. It is simply a token of respect – the sealing of a pledge." Hatfield continued; "Now, to most people these ideas may seem very extreme, but they are not. Almost all of my dealings have been with women. A large part of my practice consists of young girls, because for some reason I win the love and confidence of young people." Those young girls confided in her and nine out of 10 of them confessed they kissed the men they knew; "When I warn them against such a course they say, 'Why, what's the harm in it?' To think that mothers should neglect to answer this question. Mothers who rear their daughters with a view to perfect culture and endeavor to provide them with an ethical education."[28]

Hatfield went on to explain the situation by exclaiming; "The mothers of to-day are to blame for nine-tenths of the evil that exists. They don't know how to train children. When their sons and daughters are babies they are kissed incessantly. Everyone who comes in is allowed to torment the infant in the same fashion. By the time the infant becomes a child of several years it has become used to the kissing, and you will find that most children before they are five have cultivated the kissing habit. It is like any other vice, which…we first endure, then pity, then embrace." Reporter Hart observed; "Of course the crusaders know the habit is a very deep-seated one and will be hard to break up." To which the physician replied; "Certainly, but they must begin with the mothers. Girls are left alone too much. When a young girl and a young man are left night after night down in the parlor their conversation becomes exhausted, and they resort to billing and cooing. The trouble is with modern mothers, that they are too liberal, and their daughters do not receive the protection that is their due. If some of the hours spent in solitary association with young men were given up to teaching them how to become good wives and mothers girls would realize that the way to win a husband is not through the medium of spooning." The crusader thought that kissing between women "is quite as unwholesome a practice as could possibly exist. I have seen women kiss each other – not once or twice, but hundreds of times – who hate each other, who talk behind each other's backs, who would kill each other through the medium of their kisses if it were possible. Yet it is expected of them, and so they are hypocrites." In the conclusion of her interview with journalist Hart, Hatfield declared; "The kiss has gone too far. It usually does, and that's one of its great setbacks. It's time somebody made war upon the kiss. I'm willing to go down in firing the first gun." Hart believed it to be doubtful if Hatfield would raise a large army in her battle against the kiss.[29]

An editorial cartoon about the anti-kissing crusade was published on January 1, 1901. It depicted Father Time and Mother Earth embracing and noting that they had been at it for so long that they could not reform.[30]

An editorial published on the same day but in a different newspaper sneered at the Hatfield campaign by declaring; "Girls, thou shalt not kiss one another, and thou shalt not kiss a man!" Added the Montana editor; "There is talk among some of the old maid circles in Butte of abolishing the kissing habit. The idea of a girl kissing a man an affection 'good night' is preposterous; it's horrid in the first degree, and both participants ought to be shot on the spot. And the idea of women kissing each other under any circumstances, conditions or previous conditions of servitude, is horrifying. The wonder is the clock in the court house doesn't stop again."[31]

Still another editorial appeared around the same time. It also mocked the WCTU effort and declared; "The W.C.T.U. of New York will prohibit kissing, claiming the practice is intoxicating. Hereafter the ban will be placed on kissing as well as drinking. We are getting too good to live in this old world."[32]

In the wake of the WCTU crusade came the announcement of a little town in Massachusetts wherein, said a journalist; "a churlish and surly selectman has announced that he will prohibit kissing at church entertainments. It seems that there is some law authorizing him to do this and all the kissable girls of the town are on the war path."[33]

"The kissing girl has now an active and declared foe in the Demorest branch of the W.C.T.U.," declared the editor of an Atlanta Georgia newspaper, on January 9, 1901. "By formal vote, after an exhaustive discussion pro and con, the ladies of that society adopted a radical anti-kissing policy, pledging themselves to put a stop to promiscuous osculation among young women and young men, calling in a policeman if necessary. Not even an engaged couple are to be exempt. 'No kissing (except of babies or kin folks) for the unmarried' is the hard and fast law laid down by those foes of osculation," the newsman explained. With respect to the end of that WCTU meeting the editor noted

that; "No specific method was agreed on but it was decided that all should do their utmost to break up

the kissing habit wherever found. They went away from the meeting feeling a profound sense of their

duty toward misguided osculators and resolved to be stern and inexorable in their warfare."[34]

A little more than two weeks after the New York branch of the WCTU made the headlines with their

stance on kissing, Mrs. Clinton Smith, president of the WCTU in the District of Columbia announced

that her organization would not take part in the crusade against kissing. Smith exclaimed; "We have no

time for such nonsense…"[35]

With respect to the WCTU's announced campaign against kissing, Ida Husted Harper, a reporter with

a New York City newspaper, suggested; "It will be wholly useless for the W.C.T.U. to labor for a

favorable vote in the House of Representatives on its resolution that kissing between men and women

must be discouraged as it will be sure to be hung up in the senate committee on privileges."

Commented an editor; "Verily Miss Harper sees well into the future – and sees through the lens of

human nature in its finest evolution – when she predict the dismal failure of the W.C.T.U.'s latest

propaganda…No, no, this generation will not be sacrificed to the dire demands of arid hearts and

vengeful disappointment."[36]

An editor with a Tennessee newspaper commented on the WCTU campaign against kissing by

writing; "A crusade against kissing has been started in the East. Will it result in abolishing the kissing

habit? Not much! Neither deadly germs nor the majesty of the law will prevent osculation." He

added; "It may be true that kissing breeds disorder from germ transmission, but death will be defied.

The kiss habit is implanted as deeply as the tobacco and whisky habits. The grave is the only absolute

cure for any of them."[37]

The crusade by Hatfield prompted a lengthy article on the general subject of morbid fears. "Even

among people of the greatest intelligence and apparently sound mind there are many who are victims of

emotion obsessions which control their actions and thoughts beyond the power of reason or resistance."

Mentioned in the article were such "obvious and well-known" ones as agoraphobia (fear of open spaces), claustrophobia (closed spaces), hematophobia (blood), and many others. However, the journalist wrote; "The most common of the modern phobias is beyond question bacillophobia, a fear of germs, thousands of people being possessed by this fear of the little things about which they know so little and have heard so much that is dreadful and fear inspiring and they take extraordinary precautions to escape infection and avoid contagion, dreading to touch anything publicly used, even the handrail of a [street]car, and sometimes going so far as to refuse to shake hands with their dearest friends. This phobia has been brought to especial prominence by the crusade against kissing."[38]

Professor Algie R. Crook, a bachelor member of the faculty of Northwestern University in Evanston, Illinois, surprised his students during a "heart to heart" talk he had with them in the laboratory, on April 25, 1901, by saying the "frivolities of the world had not tempted him." Crook declared; "I have never uttered a profane word, never have smoked, chewed tobacco, drank intoxicants, nor hugged or kissed a woman." Crook was a graduate of Ohio Wesleyan University, a coed institution, and he also studied for two years in Munich He was 37 years old, had been teaching at Northwestern since 1893, and, said a journalist; "is known as one of the most athletic and erudite men at the Evanston institution, and he is a favorite at Woman's Hall."[39]

That declaration by Crook set off a large amount of attention and media coverage. Reportedly, within a few days with every mail delivery to the university came letters from all over the United States offering proposals of marriage to Professor Crook. The professor did not answer the letters and was tired of all the notoriety. He said he was not angry at the women who were writing to him but he was angry at the undergraduates who tattled and gave the story to the newspapers. "He is abashed and humiliated over the gossip the affair has provoked," it was reported. As a sort of spoof one reporter interviewed a number of New York City chorus girls to get their reaction to the pure and chaste Crook. Said Madge Relyea; "What an idiot he must be. Case of sour grapes, I reckon. He probably never got the chance to kiss a girl anyway." Margaret Hobart remarked; "I don't believe a word of it. He's posing for the goody-goody. I don't believe any man ever lived thirty-seven years without every casting sheep's eyes at a girl. He is a humbug." Ruby Reid commented; "Now wouldn't that jar the preserves in the cellar. What a crank. He'd kiss a girl quick enough if she'd let him. I'd hate to offer him the opportunity. I don't believe any man is so everlastingly straight-laced as all that." Said Catherine Bartlett; "Why, the man is a freak…Lucky he never married…Such goodness is wearisome." Jessie Gordon offered the comment; "There is only one of him, I guess, and one will be plenty, thanks. This world would be too good if there were many men like that."[40]

An editor on a Boston newspaper stated that; "The unkissed Chicago scientist, Prof. Crook, is making lots of copy for the newspapers. Thus far no man has come forward to dispute the non-kissing professor's claim to the distinction."[41]

Near the end of April 1901 a letter to the editor from Professor Crook was published in Chicago. It stated; "You and other newspaper men of Chicago are getting unnecessarily excited over my statement that I have never hugged or kissed a woman or girl. I should think it would have occurred, even to a newspaper reporter, that women and girls might have hugged and kissed me. Some men have more tact than others."[42]

One month after that Crook was still speaking out, still trying to distance himself from his original utterances. He declared; "The idea that I never kissed a woman is preposterous. Saying nothing of the members of my family, my relatives are numerous, and the idea that I would refrain from saluting them on occasion is not to be thought of for a minute." Crook reiterated that he was greatly annoyed by the immense quantities of mail he had received daily, and was still receiving. Around the same time as the professor's latest outburst of denial a satirical poem about Crook was publishing, as the university man continued to be mocked far and wide. That poem was credited to Josh Wink and titled, "Crook, the Unkissed."

Professor, Oh, Professor,

Did you never shyly slip

Your arm around a damsel with a red and pouting lip?

Did you never feel a quiver

From your fingers to your toes

When you sought to kiss her rightly, but caromed upon her nose?

Professor, Oh, Professor,

Did you never take a drive

When the moonlight and the maiden made you glad you were alive?

Never guide the horse one-handed,

Or, through one part of the trip,

Let him amble slowly homeward with the lines wrapped round the whip?

Professor, Oh, Professor,

Did you never feel a tug

At your heartstring, when the moment was approaching for a hug?

Did you never get the tingle,

Like a strong magnetic breeze,

Which is the peculiar symptom of a frank and honest squeeze?

Professor, Oh, Professor,

In you tan-and-freckles days

Did you never try "postoffice" and such osculating plays?

Did the girlie of your fancy

Never kiss you on the cheek

And you, to prove devotion, wouldn't wash it for a week?

Professor, Oh, Professor,

Of your failings I take note,

And it's hard to think that really you have got the right to vote!

And my only hope, Professor,

If it's true you've not been kissed

Is that Fate has fixed it some way that you don't know what you've missed.[43]

One commentator on the kissing habit observed, in August 1901, that kissing among relatives went by families and it was quite true that certain households were known to all their friends as "great kissers." The members of such families, men, women and children, kissed each other the first thing in the morning and the last thing at night, and on any other occasion that they consider sufficiently emotional. Still, the commentator thought, it was possible to go too far the other way. He wondered what type of problems would occur if a woman who came from a kissing family married a man who came from non-kissing stock.[44]

It was reported in December 1902 that; "An association of physicians out in Iowa has declared against kissing. In other words the embers have joined forces with the railroad magnates who are seeking to suppress osculation in depots. It is now the allied forces of the doctors and the railroaders against the world. Sentiment is fast crystallizing and you must soon line up for or against an ecstasy as old as Adam and Eve…doctors say we must desist or shorten our lives."[45]

Women teachers in Scranton Pennsylvania were said to be "highly indignant" in September 1904 during a week when they were attending the sessions of the teachers' institute. They were upset over the publication in local newspapers of statements to the effect that the women teachers of Scranton were fond of kissing. They particularly took exception to a caption in one morning paper that read; "Are fond of kissing. By unanimous vote the city teachers decide in favor of the osculatory pastime." That story had its origins with Dr. Bigelow, one of the instructors of the women at the institute. In one of his lectures he offered the thought that all teachers liked to be kissed. "I will prove it to you," he said. "All who are opposed to kissing stand up." No one arose.[46]

A lengthy article that appeared in October 1906 discussed the morality and cultural fashion of the habit of kissing. The piece began by stating' "The twentieth century woman who would be thought to be familiar with the most approved social customs must curb her emotions in public. For the time being fashion has forbidden manifestations of affection except in private." And; "There must be no parade of the affections in the public eye, the example of European royalty to the contrary notwithstanding, says the *Washington Post*." The writer continued by declaring; "The bursts of tears, ladylike hysterics, fainting spells gracefully done, and affectionate greetings, countenanced by the highest society of long ago, are no longer considered good form. The woman brave enough to embrace her own husband in a public place proclaims her ignorance of the cannons of smart society." If the reporter was accurate then, at that time, the curriculum of "nearly every finishing school includes a course on how not to show what one feels in public. It has come to pass that when the big steamships leave this port the farewells between the fashionable who sail on them and their friends who see them off are of the mildest description…Tears are no longer in evidence. Some hugging may be indulged in in staterooms but might little is seen on deck. In other avenues of travel it is the same." Such exceptional outbursts of emotion on the part of a female – or a female allowing such outbursts from a man – were considered to be low-class. An unnamed society dowager told a reporter that she had watched a man who just got off a bus kiss a girl, an event the dowager found "shocking." She then saw two school girls joyously embracing a third girl (also from the bus) and declared it was obvious that none of those young females had ever attended a "high class school." This elderly dowager watched another group from the bus. It involved a wife and husband who greeted each other with a hand clasp and the ceremonious lifting of the hat by the man. Then the wife turned to greet her brother and sister-in-law, with handshakes in both cases and to offer her cheek to be kissed by their son, aged 10. That dowager declared; "That woman and her friends are the only ones in that crowd whose manners will pass muster" She went on to add; "And yet when I was a girl a woman wasn't considered hopelessly vulgar if she kissed her relatives and friends in a public thoroughfare. I for one always kissed my women friends if I felt like it, no matter where I met them and when my husband came to us from the city, when I and the children were spending the summer out of town, I never stopped to consider who was watching us when I met him at the station…I didn't need to, for every other woman was saluting her husband just as I did mine. And in those days I went in just as good society as I do now."[47]

 At that point another woman joined the conversation with the dowager and the reporter. The newcomer commented; "The teachers are right. Of all senseless customs, in my opinion, indiscriminate kissing is the most senseless, and the sooner children are taught this the better." She added; "Few women, I believe really care to kiss each other. Frequently they do it simply because they imagine the salute is expected…As for a man and wife kissing before two or three strangers, the custom is shockingly bad form to say the least. I never allow my husband to kiss me in the presence of anyone." Then the dowager remarked; "There can be no doubt but that kissing is fast going out of fashion. A good nurse will never allow the baby in her charge to be kissed, and small children are now taught to refuse to kiss persons they don't know well…Thus brought up, naturally as they grow older, the children will not be inclined to osculation under any circumstances in public."[48]

 Picking up on the same topic around the same time a reporter named Susan Ball noted; "Kissing has become almost entirely tabooed in the higher circles of society in this country since the persistent outcry against it…for fear the kissed may be an adherent of these germs communicating theories." Ball continued; "To confidently approach a friend or relative, not seen for a long period, ready to add a kiss to the greeting and then be held off, at arms' length, by a handshake, is apt to make one feel rather cheap to say the least. Some of the most ardent kissers, those who have been in the habit of so saluting friends upon arrival or at the departure of a call have joined the ranks of the non-kissers, which complicates the situation." After a few such rebukes Ball thought the kisser tended to become timid, and so forth. She declared that change in attitude toward kissing was because; "the papers had been so full of startling head lined articles decrying the kissing custom as barbarous, a disease spreader rather than a form of greeting in polite society." In conclusion Ball said; "It might be well for people to wear a little badge denoting what cults they belong to so that in meeting those not frequently seen, one may know the situation…Especially might it be advantageous to get out kissing and anti-kissing badges."[49]

A brief poem titled "The Spice" appeared in April 1907 and it captured the sentiments of many.

The wise may expurgate their bliss,

But who with friend or stranger

Would want a sanitary kiss?

The fun is in the danger.[50]

In July 1907 a reporter spoke to a female physician about the Reverend Dr. Bass' anti-kiss courtship theory. Bass argued that young lovers should hold each other's hands in token of their "pure" affection and in parting the lover should bring his sweetheart's hand to his lips "for a fleeting, gentle, respectful pressure and nothing more." Dr. Ellen M. Miles disagreed emphatically with Bass and favored the kiss; "It strikes me that this kiss denunciation is simply another instance of evil to him who evil thinks. Certainly a pure woman would only too quickly recognize and resent an impure kiss, and a true lover would never give her an occasion to do so." She added; "I very much doubt whether this Anti-Kiss Courtship crusade will gain much in popular favor." Asked what she thought about the idea of holding hands as a substitute show of affection Miles asserted; "All nonsense. Affection is not centered in the hands. It is centered in the heart and truly a moment when the heart is in the mouth us when the lips of two true lovers meet." She thought that; "The wooer who would court without kissing would never win the lady. Possibly that is the reason the Rev. Dr. Bass is still a bachelor. I certainly wouldn't want him for a sweetheart." Mrs. H. Herbert Knowles, a prominent member of the New Century Study Circle, the Woman's Health Protective Association, and a charter member of the New Yorkers also was a staunch opponent of the kissless courtship. She said; "A kiss evil and impure, indeed! Why, what could be more pure than a little child, and the tiny tot raising up its rosy lips to be kissed is its first most natural way of showing affection. A kiss is the first impulse of childhood." Knowles added; "Of course I do not approve of two young people who are merely acquaintances indulging in promiscuous osculation. A kiss is a sacred symbol, to be exchanged between true overs or those of near family tree." She concluded; "But to bar kisses from a courtship is to take away half the pure joy of love's young dream. In fact, I would even go so far as to say that kissing is absolutely essential in a courtship."[51]

 The Reverend D. L. Bass had originally been a preacher in South Carolina but by July 1907 he was preaching at Cairo, Illinois where his recent sermons on the evils of kissing created a stir in Cairo and spread to other places. He continued his attacks on the "kiss devil" that month when he said; "The kiss devil is doing more to fill Hades than the whiskey devil, the drug devil, and all the other devils all told." He added; "Sweethearts should never kiss until they are married. In the days of our grandparents in the Southern states at least, any attempt to kiss a girl was rightly declared as great a wrong as could be committed against her. Such an attempt was a gross insult, and the man who offered it and the young woman's father or brothers met with pistols at the next sunrise.' Reiterating his idea that sweethearts should limit themselves to holding hands and to a fleeting touch of his lips to her hand upon parting he fumed; "But that's all. God will deliver us from the kissing devil."[52]

 "Because young women will allow men to kiss them before becoming engaged a lax condition of morals has arisen which threatens the downfall of our country," declared Bass, in July 1907, in defense of his recent sermon on "The Kiss Devil." He believed the precipice leading to moral collapse was near. Second only to the kiss as a factor in what he saw as a frightful condition of immorality, Bass placed "prosperity." He asserted; "Too much money is adding to the downfall to which we seem bound. For when wealth comes in at the door, virtue goes out of the window." Bass continued by stating; "For I believe that the highest and purest form of civilization is impossible in any age or country if the men believe that the young woman they have led to the marriage altar have been guilty of kissing half a dozen other men before her marriage." Those "liberties" before marriage often led to infidelity and quickly destroyed the marriage bonds, claimed the preacher. The journalist who wrote the piece noted that the anti-kiss crusade of Bass, who was pastor of the Calvary Baptist Church in Cairo "is attracting much attention in various parts of the country. The start of his campaign was made in a sermon in which he declared that the kiss devil did more to fill hell than all the whisky devils, drug devils and all other devils put together."[53]

In another newspaper article Reverend Bass was quoted as saying the following about the kiss; "There is something wonderfully magnetic and thrilling in the kiss…A kiss goes straight, like the shock of a galvanic battery, to the heart, and the weaker party is always paralyzed under the blow, whether for good or ill or for weal or woe." He continued by observing; "Nothing has more of heaven's fire or the fire of hell in it than the kiss of a lover or of a villain, and the first step of the fiend incarnate in order to destroy the innocent but deluded victim in his clutches is to get his lips to hers. The lips are often the gate to the citadel of virtue in the young and loving heart, and thousands have surrendered the fortress of character to the thrilling kiss of the licentious libertine, who well knows its psychologic and dynamic power when affections and confidence have won in a woman's heart. Great God deliver us from the Kissing Devil." Bass was described herein as a Southerner but had Puritan blood in his veins. He claimed to be a descendant of Samuel Bass, who settled in Massachusetts in 1630.[54]

The Reverend John L. Scudder delivered an address on January 31, 1909 in the Congregational Church at Jersey City, New Jersey. That talk was in the interest of the Anti-Spitting League and he stated; "The twentieth century commandment is, 'Thou shalt not spit.'" He said his church was interested in the "annihilation" of disease and to be in the forefront of the crusade against tuberculosis. Scudder enthused that the; "villainous, unhygienic custom of kissing the lips" should be abolished. As well, he declared that many people had been "kissed to death."[55]

The Reverend Dr. John L. Scudder preached at the First Congregational Church of Jersey City, New Jersey and added; "I am thinking of starting an anti-kissing society. I may import Dowie junior, whom his father described as 'the great unkissed' as a distinguished figurehead for my new cult." Then the "progressive clergyman," as he was described, amplified his views on the "pernicious habit" of kissing by saying; "Kissing is a pretty custom, but there is such a thing as kissing a person to death. If the kisser has tuberculosis or diphtheria there is great danger that the disease will be communicated to the kissee." And, he continued; "In this way diphtheria has carried off its thousands and tuberculosis its tens of thousands. Many a little one has been sent to the grave by the loving kiss of a consumptive mother. Many people have caught tuberculosis by kissing consumptive dogs and cats, canary birds, parrots and other household pets. It is time to start anti-kissing leagues throughout America, and if I could be the agency for this new departure I should consider myself a public benefactor. The whole land should ring with the cry, 'quit your kissing.'" Scudder concluded; "Any mother must be demented who permits a stranger to kiss her child for, mark you, a man may have consumption in an early stage and not know it. Yet it is communicable. Even kissing the Bible in the courts should be abolished, for court bibles are nests and breeding places of bacilli."[56]

Said the Reverend Dr. Henry W. Ireland of the Disciples Church at Mt. Gilead, Ohio, in February 1909; "The kiss is an intoxicant and, like the saloon, must go." He also declared; "And, I have carefully inquired into the matter, and I find that many young girls imagine that to kiss is the only way to get a husband. It may help some, but kissing is not all that is necessary." The journalist who wrote this article mostly mocked Ireland and his views. Also quoted in the piece was Mrs. J. B. Marion, described as a prominent lawyer and suffragette, who said; "Of course it is absurd to speak of passing a law against kissing. You could not more stop it than I could stop Niagara Falls with my hand. I cannot believe that Dr. Ireland has been quoted entirely. There are probably modifying portions of his sermon that have not been repeated."[57]

Miss Ellen M. La Motte of Baltimore was the name of a young woman who was said to have started a new crusade against kissing, early in 1910. La Motte pointed out that the contact of lip and lip gave an ideal passageway for the marauding germs and the act of kissing should be discouraged, to say the least. A reporter thought that; "Babies that have never been kissed may grow into men and women who will not tolerate osculation, but this generation is not likely to be influenced by such crusades."[58]

A couple of months later, in March 1910, it was reported that Syracuse, New York mothers who did not believe in the indiscriminate kissing of children had been aroused by the formation of leagues and societies for its prevention in other cities and the general sentiment seemed to be that such a movement

if started in Syracuse would meet with general approval. The journalist noted that the habit of friends

and even strangers of kissing babies all the time became such a nuisance in the cities of Washington

and Boston that mothers in those cities were banding together to prevent it. Mrs. Caleb Candee Brown

believed such an organization would be a good thing for her native city of Syracuse; "I never could

understand persons offering to kiss children. I have seen the most pained expressions of resignation on

the faces of my children when they were little when even dear friends would inflict them with caresses.

It is just as annoying to children as to their parents; and why persons, who should know better, do it is

beyond my comprehension." Mrs. Paul M. Paine of Syracuse said; "My children have never been, to

my knowledge, subjected to such practices and even our own family do not kiss them on the mouth. I

should be very indignant should persons take such liberties with my little ones."[59]

Nixola Greely-Smith was a well-known columnist in the early 1900s; her grandfather was the famous

newspaperman Horace Greeley. Her column of November 10, 1911 included a collage of illustrations

that spoofed the anti-kiss crusaders. In the text of her column that day she created a fictional situation

in which a woman declined to promote in any way the project that had been outlined before a

federation of women's clubs – that of forming all the young girls of the United States into an

organization opposed to kissing, holding hands, spooning, or taking solitary walks with young men.[60]

Dr. Harvey W. Wiley, a pure food expert and former chief of the Bureau of Chemistry in the United

States Department of Agriculture declared himself, in August 1912, to be utterly opposed to the

movement for the abolition of kissing on the ground that it was a menace to public health. Said Wiley;

"Prohibit kissing? Oh, no! I'm not in favor of that procedure by any means. I don't want osculation

prohibited…I think it is rather a danger to one's health to refrain from kissing. Many a young man or

young woman is likely to be made ill by being kept from experiencing the joys of osculation."[61]

During a Bible conference held at Winona Lake, Indiana, in September 1912 Dr. Elizabeth Muncie

gave a series of lectures on eugenics to a large gathering of girls. Muncie was a practicing physician in

Brooklyn. Several hundred young women attended her lecture wherein, among other things, she urged all girls to pray God to send them husbands. She also told the girls; "Never let any man kiss you, that is, unless you are engaged or married, then kiss to your heart's content." Muncie also told the women in her audience to have nothing to do with traveling salesmen, stating that many a girl was "ruined by one kiss from a drummer."[62]

In Europe, in Madrid Spain in March 1914 Queen Ena had reportedly inaugurated an anti-kissing campaign crusade in her nation. Rebelling against the time immemorial custom that required the queen to kiss every youngster presented to her King Alfonso's British consort announced that hereafter she would refrain from kissing those presented to her, unless she felt so inclined.[63]

A report published in August 1915 noted that Dr. Anna T. Quensel, a "noted zoologist of the Swedish University at Uppsala, does not believe in kissing." She lectured on the subject and hoped her talks would have a beneficial effect upon the younger generation. She said; "My husband has never kissed me and I have never kissed him. Neither of us has ever kissed anyone. We are both very active members of the Continental Anti-Kissing League. We believe kissing is unsanitary and a menace to good health." Quensel added; "In Europe agents of the league are assigned to public parks, railroad stations and steamship piers. It is their duty to separate persons who are about to kiss and deliver a lecture on the perils of osculation. Every kiss leaves thousands of bacilli." Those remarks caused an American newspaper editor to comment; "If the lady has never been kissed, she is hardly a competent authority on a subject of which she is ignorant. See here, Anna, why don't you and your hubby insure your lives and try just one smack and let his microbes and your microbes fight it out in the lip trenches."[64]

An editor with a different newspaper also summarized the remarks of Quensel and added his own by observing; "Kissing may be unsanitary, but there is a lot of romance in it, and the average American is strong for anything that savors of romance. The American people have stood for sanitary drinking cups, sanitary towels, telephone screens and about a thousand kids of microbe catchers, but they will insist upon kissing once in a while, just to keep the doldrums away."[65]

On the afternoon of March 19, 1916, a group of Columbia University seniors canvassed 40 of the "most prominent students" in Barnard College and Columbia. By a vote of 39 to one they declared their scorn of the 43 un-kissed seniors at Princeton University. The students canvassed included athletes, social leaders, and editors of college publications. According to a reporter; "The result is considered a direct answer to allegations of Princeton's un-kissed that osculation is neither hygienic nor moral."[66]

That poll was in response to a canvassing that found 43 out of 300 members of the senior class at Princeton University had gone on record as never having been kissed. Columnist Nixola Greeley-Smith went to Princeton in March 1916 to meet those 43 and to deduce the kind of young man who was still un-kissed at the age of 21.7 years, the average age of a Princeton senior that year. In that anonymous survey 160 men answered that it was not morally wrong to kiss a girl, while 40 said that it was. Nixola, with tongue-in-cheek, admitted she had some difficulty in locating the un-kissed on the institute's campus. The rest of the piece was a spoof on her hunt to find the un-kissed men.[67]

Betty Brown was an actress who wrote an opinion piece that appeared in newspapers in June 1919 in which she addressed the question as to whether or not it was immoral to kiss in the park. Brown declared; "Already this season six embarrassed couples have been hailed before the magistrates if New York on charges of 'disorderly conduct' preferred by unsympathetic policemen who found them billing and cooing in Central Park after sunset." Two of the culprits were soldiers who indignantly protested that in Paris the police never interrupted such activity. "But this isn't Paris" was the court's rejoinder. Declared Brown; "it is no more immoral to kiss on a park bench than it is to kiss on a parlor sofa…It seems to me kissing should be an intimate and sacred rite never performed before third parties. Kissing in public profanes kissing." She concluded; "Of course, there is no self-respecting girl who would permit her beau to kiss her in a public place…"[68]

A journalist rounded up some "expert" opinions of the subject of kissing in April of 1920. At a tuberculosis convention Dr. Brown of Saranac Lake, New York told her; "If you would be sanitary, kiss your girl in the evening or afternoon. Disease germs lurk in the morning kisses, because the sun and fresh air have not had a chance to sterilize her sweet lips." According to tuberculosis expert Dr. John G. Frey of Ohio; "Afternoon and evening kissing is as dangerous as morning kissing." Much of the article was given over to the opinions of Olive Thomas, a well-known actress and model of the time. Because of her film work she claimed the record as "most kissed woman." In answer to the reporter's query as to whether or not kissing was dangerous to health Thomas replied; "With all due respect to the doctors, I don't believe that kissing is unhealthy at all. I suppose I have been kissed as often as any woman alive…And my experience has been that kissing, whether by moonlight, sunlight or flashlight is equally innocent of danger to health." Thomas added; "The propagation of the germ theory will have no more effect upon kissing than the discovery of the law of gravitation had upon the growing of apples…It is part of the fundamental make-up of the race. Doctors might as well try to banish love itself as to place a ban on kissing."[69]

A November 1920 article about law enforcement began with a comment about Lucy Page Gaston [a famous anti-cigarette crusader of the era] and that her campaign for enforcement of an anti-cigarette law directed public attention to the fact that the law was being violated by local merchants and; "It also may serve to call to mind the fact that there is continuous violation of many other statutes and to arouse an inquiry as to why so many laws are ignored by the public and the officers entrusted with their enforcement." The piece then went on to mention a book on American police systems by Raymond B. Fosdick, formerly undersecretary general of the League of Nations. In commenting on unenforceable laws in the United States Fosdick said; "Another disadvantage under which American police departments are laboring is to be found in the presence on our statute books of laws which, because they interfere with customs widely practiced and widely regarded as innocent, are fundamentally unenforceable. The willingness with which we undertake to regulate by law the personal habits of private citizens is a source of perpetual astonishment to Europeans." He went on to state; "Often the laws are such as to defy enforcement even if they had behind them a substantial body of public opinion. Thus there are laws against kissing, laws against ear-rings, laws regulating the length of women's skirts, laws fixing the size of hatpins. In Massachusetts one may not play cards for stakes even with friends in the privacy of one's home. In Texas cardplaying on trains is illegal." Fosdick concluded; "Nowhere in the world is there as great an anxiety to place the moral regulation of social affairs in the hands of the police and nowhere are the police so incapable of carrying out such regulation."[70]

Frederick Haskin was a well-known American journalist and author. He wrote a lengthy article in March 1921 about the reform movement in the United States and all that it encompassed such as length of skirts, motion picture censorship, and so forth. Said Haskin; "This leads naturally to the matter of kissing, which has come in for much thought and denunciation the part of reformers recently. It has been asserted by many of them that the practice of promiscuous kissing is steadily on the increase and that great moral danger is bound up in this fact unless something can be done to stop it." And, he added; "Disease as well as immorality is among the results of the nefarious practice, the reformers point out. Tonsillitis, measles, hiccups, encephalitis, hay fever, acute palpitation of the diaphragm and chronic conjugal discord are all caused or aggravated by promiscuous and unregulated osculation." Haskin's article was, of course, a spoof piece. "It is felt that with a strong department of public morals having branch offices in all parts of the country, the regulation of this form of immorality will be comparatively simple. A new law will be passed making it a felony for a man to kiss a girl unless she had made and she has accepted a proposal of marriage," Haskin continued in the same vein for the remainder of his article.[71]

The tide was clearly turning away from the idea that kissing should somehow be regulated, in some way. Mockery was wearing away the enemies of osculation. Still, a few remained, gamely soldiering on. Mrs. B. C. Howell was a lecturer on morals and a delegate to the International Purity Conference that was in session in Chicago at the beginning of 1922. At that gathering she urged the American girls to turn over a new leaf and get back to the moral code of 1914. Howell said; "Spooning never has been

indiscriminate – never has had such disastrous results to the morals of the girls in the 'teen' ages." She

continued by asserting; "I know. For fifteen years I have been making talks to grammar and high

school girls, hearing their stories – stories they wouldn't tell their own mothers. The girls say the men

expect to be kissed; most girls think it is all right; they say, 'Every girl does it.' Is it any wonder that

the average age of girls admitted to the Florence Crittenton Missions [homes for unwed mothers] has

dropped in ten years from the age of 26, to 16, with some as young as 10?"[72]

An article that featured comments on the question as to whether or not mates should kiss in public

appeared in print in February 1922. Those commenting were all "society" women. Mrs. Jacques H.

Goodby Mills Jr. of New York City felt so strongly that a husband should never kiss his wife in public

that she had begun a suit for divorce basing her action on the ground that her husband Jacques kissed

her right on the lips in front of hundreds of people who were "mere strangers, at a New York City

dock." It was all deemed to be "impolite and vulgar." That case drew comment from some Milwaukee

women. Mrs. Benjamin Fuelleman, a "prominent club woman" agreed, stating; "I think caresses

between husband and wife should be given in private with no outsider to desecrate the moment."

However, she thought that suing for divorce carried the matter too far. Mrs. John B. Brisbane of

Milwaukee's West Side Mother's Club declared; "Kisses are too sacred to be given in public." Two

other women named and cited in the article thought the public kiss between husband and wife was

okay.[73]

Marguerite Lindley delivered an 1899 lecture against kissing in which she called the practice "unhygienic, unpleasant and very disagreeable."

PREACHER ATTACKS THE KISS DEMON.

The Reverend D. L. Bass went after the "kiss devil" in 1907. He believed the kiss devil was worse than the whiskey devil and the drug devil and all the other devils combined.

Columnist Nixola Greeley-Smith went after the anti-kissing movement in one of her columns in November 1911.

Ch. 5. Organizations.

One of the other outcomes of the fear of microbes in general, and of kissing in particular, was the formation of a large number of organizations dedicated to the proposition of fighting the evil. These were all single issue groups that arose just for the purpose of doing battle with the kiss. Most seem to have been very short lived with no media coverage other than a brief report as to their formation and/or existence. Some lasted longer and some got a fair amount of media coverage.

A few of these organizations emerged before microbes became an issue, illustrating that for many of these groups there was a morality element involved in the subject. That was also true, of course, for many of the groups that emerged after the arrival of the fear of microbes. A very brief report was published in March 1871 that announced that an anti-kissing society had been formed by the girls of Galena, Illinois. "No kissing before marriage" was said to be their motto. Later in that same year, in September, it was revealed that Saratoga girls were organizing an anti-kissing society. The rules of the society imposed a $1 fine for each kiss bestowed on anybody from "the masculine gender." Reportedly, at the end of the first week some of the girls were actually indebted to the society in sums ranging from $5 to $25. The journalist writing the story declared; "The association will disband." A second reporter wrote about the anti-kissing society favored by the "fascinating damsels at Saratoga" and that it did not seem to have worked out very well as 15 of the 23 members were fined the very first week. The location of Saratoga was not given in either report; likely it was the one in New York State.[1]

A few more such groups appeared in the 1880s. Another brief report remarked that an anti-kissing society was organized in January 1880 in Pascagoula Mississippi, by "a few ladies." Commented the reporter; "We imagine there will not be any great number of young men who will join this club."[2]

A report that originally appeared in a St. Louis newspaper in December 1884 declared that young ladies in that city were contemplating the formation of an anti-osculatory society "for the purpose of putting down the barbarous practice of kissing brides immediately after the marriage ceremony. The usual rule was for every male relative and connection to the most distant degree and every woman present at the wedding to form in line and mouth the poor bride until the last one has claimed the privilege and has been satisfied." Declaring that the whole procedure must have been a horrible experience for the bride to have to kiss all those people the reporter concluded, with respect to the group that might be formed; "The society will shut down on all kissing at public receptions and will countenance only private salutations from the members of the two families.[3]

In April 1889 27 girls in Atchison Kansas had reportedly formed an anti-kissing society. One of those 27 was a young woman 17 years old who was interviewed by a reporter from the local paper. According to his account; "she frankly stated that the girls were becoming tired of kissing the boys, and then hearing afterwards that the boys had told about it." She added that a girl never told such things "but the boys rejoice in it, indeed, they keep a list of the girls that kiss, and show it to every new fellow that comes along." Anti-kissing organizations that formed in the 1870s and 1880s were few in number with only sketchy details provided. However, those societies became much more numerous with the vast majority of them appearing in the 22-year-period from 1890 to 1911. After 1911 they had mostly disappeared.[4]

An editorial that appeared originally in a Philadelphia newspaper in April 1890 mocked an organization that had recently been established by declaring; "What a miserable lot they must be, that handful of cold-blooded creatures who have formed a society in New York to protest against kissing, on that ground that it is a powerful medium for communicating disease." That editor concluded; "There are some forms of caprice so fantastical that the human race – patient as it is – openly revolts against them. The kiss is inviolable. No vandal need hope to profane it by hurling medical sophistries at it." A different publication editorialized about the same organization by declaring; "A set of unsentimental callous cranks in New York have organized an anti-kissing society. The objection which they urge against the osculatory exercise is that it communicates disease."[5]

It was reported in December 1894 that prominent society people in Detroit, including several physicians, proposed to organize an anti-kissing club. The idea was said to have originated at a gathering of friends a few evenings earlier when one of the visitors refused to kiss a child of the household because it had a sore throat. A long argument over the matter ensued, the upshot being that an anti-kissing crusade was begun on the spot. It was arranged that each member of the proposed group should wear a small piece of red ribbon or a red button on the coat lapel or on the dress. As soon as sufficient interest was manifested in the movement it was planned to hold a public meeting and to establish a permanent organization. The whole purpose of the movement, said the promoters, was to prevent the spread of contagious throat and lung diseases.[6]

A few days later an editor observed; "If the idea of the people of Detroit in organizing an anti-kissing society was to promote a smile, they are to be commended. If it is really the purpose to place a ban on kissing, they have proved themselves to be a squad of simpletons." He went on to say; "Kissing will endure. The edicts of either Fashion or Fashion's place – man – can no more control kissing than a blind cow could run a chromatic scale on a piano. The man or woman who cannot kiss and draw from its velvety, electrical thrill an ecstatic, fevered, pulsating throb of intensified bliss is fit for treason, stratagem and mouldy pie." In conclusion this newsman asserted; Kissing does more for pure optimism than all your high-sky philosophy, or hogsheads of gold…People can crusade against it all they want to. It will not hurt kissing or destroy it. It is the currency of the heart, the coin of the realm of emotions, and it is not measured by a gold standard, either."[7]

Two months later a different editor wrote about "a peculiar society in Detroit called the 'Anti-Kissing League.'" He noted that; "Its sole purpose is to discourage those emotional persons who find relief from high pressure feelings only in osculation. The platform of the league is 'kissing must go.'" Mentioned also was the bright red bade adopted by the members; "This flaming red challenge is not intended to invite to contest, but to warn all would-be trespassers to 'keep off the grass,' figuratively speaking." Concluding his piece this editor said; "In view of the fact that thus far the membership includes only unmarried women over 40 years old, perhaps it is just as well to label them plainly in order to prevent waste of time and emotional energy." [Those "details" about the Detroit membership were likely false as no other account reported those details.][8]

In May 1895 a journalist observed that, upon further inquiry into the report of the anti-kissing club in Detroit, it was revealed that none of the active promoters were willing to have their identity disclosed until the time for permanent and public organization arrived. According to this account the movement really had its inception in the refusal of one lady at a small social gathering to kiss little baby Bessie of the host's family because the child had an ulcerated throat. The mother of Bessie was offended at her guest's action and pointedly said so. A "spirited" discussion then took place. "I never heard of such nonsense," said the mother. "People have been kissing each other since the world began and I cannot see how a young woman like you can hope to reform the world" To which the non-kissing guest replied; "I have simply reformed myself. I kiss my own children very little, and I never kiss my husband on the lips. Outside my home I never kiss any one, nor allow even my relatives to kiss me, if I can help it. I can see nothing whatever in kissing; no advantages, while there are scores of disadvantages." At the suggestion of a young man present at that gathering, the anti-kissing club idea was finally decided upon. It was also arranged that every person favoring the movement should wear a small disk of red ribbon or a red button on the coat lapel or dress, as the case might be. Said the journalist; "Any one may adopt the badge, and if it appears to the promoters after a time that the movement is likely to be successful, a meeting will be arranged and preliminaries gone into for active missionary work."[9]

That Detroit movement was said to have received "very hearty support" from many of the leading physicians of Detroit and; "Almost to a man they pronounce against the kissing habit." Dr. E. L. Shurley, one of the best known throat and lung specialist stated; "The sooner people are educated against kissing the better for the community at large. Frequently in my practice I have been called to attend patients suffering from the most revolting skin and blood disease resulting from kissing."

Shurley added; "Eczema and other chronic skin troubles, cold sores, as they are commonly called, diphtheria, thrush, diseases of the tonsils and even tuberculosis have frequently produced corresponding disease in some one the sick person has kissed." Dr. John E. Clark declared that Americans could learn a valuable lesson from the Japanese because that country, by law, prohibits kissing. Clark said; "Most people are ignorant of the fact that the lips are peculiarly sensitive. They are covered with a mucous membrane peculiarly susceptible to the active germs of disease. It will be a step in the progress of the nation when people stop kissing." Dr. E. W. Jenks, of the local board of health, suggested a law be made forbidding kissing during the current epidemic of diphtheria. Dr. E. Younghusband called attention to the "ridiculous habit" some women had of kissing dogs, cats and other animals. He said the tongues, mouths and noses of such pets were frequently covered with the eggs of the tapeworm and through the lips of the kisser were carried into their systems.[10]

Near the end of 1894 a brief news story noted that a "lot of people" in Chicago had organized an anti-kissing club and the organization was said to be in the process of growing. Its object was the prevention of the spread of throat and lung diseases. An editor remarked; "We do not believe the benefit to be derived is commensurate with the price to be paid." Just a week later a brief account declared; Tombstone Arizona has formed an anti-kissing society, as a safeguard against diphtheria, love and other plagues."[11]

Two more very brief reports were published in 1895 about newly-formed societies against kissing. In one case it was stated that the anti-kissing club that was organized by some Clearfield Pennsylvania young women "is now reduced to two members, and they are of the opposite sex." In the other account it was noted that the hygienic crusade against kissing had taken practical shape in Philadelphia where an "Anti-Kissing Society" had sprang up.[12]

Weston, West Virginia women, said to have been impressed with the danger of the transmission of disease bacilli, had organized, in October 1897, an anti-kissing club. At around the same time, a different report observed that some Boston women had also organized an anti-kissing crusade.

According to the story; "That's right. The spectacle of a couple of women kissing each other when there is plenty of better material in sight makes the average man very tired." Just one week after that it was reported, with respect to the Boston group, that; "The anti-kissing crusade in Boston has ended in fiasco. The girls of that town call kissing osculation, but they like it just as well by one name as another."[13]

Reportedly, in February 1898, the young men of Atlanta Georgia were determined to redeem the reputation of their city on the osculation front and to that end they had formed an anti-kissing club that imposed a penalty of $10 for every case of kissing in public. Another by-law of the new society prohibited members from talking for more than 10 minutes with any particular girl and if it was established that any man had serious intentions toward a girl he was "tried and heavily fined."[14]

A few days later another account was published that was somewhat different from the confusing report above. In this version the Atlanta anti-kissing group was led by Mrs. Joseph Kingsberry who published a statement in which she defended her position against kissing. She cited an op-ed piece she wrote that appeared in a northern newspaper on "The abuse of osculation in the south." Kingsberry stated; "The South takes kissing like other fashions, periodically, and some young people yield to its fascination. But the bulk of our Southern girls and boys are carefully taught at home all the good, old-fashioned virtues. Therefore, there can be only a little abuse of what under right conditions is a sweet and dear privilege." She added; "A funny side to my dilemma has been the approval of my views by the women principles of boarding schools and seminaries, and their desire for my influence in behalf of their schools."[15]

Mrs. Kingsberry was said to be "well-known" in society circles in Atlanta. She had written her newspaper piece against kissing from Florida where she was spending the winter. In that piece, which created a furor, she cited several instances in which well-known young society people in Atlanta had been caught kissing when it was known that "there was not the slightest tie between them." Discussing another case she told of a young lady visitor to Atlanta; "charming, beautiful and modest in speech and manner, who was kissed in full view of the drawing-room windows while she sat in the full glare of the

electric lights on the enclosed piazza." And, she continued; "At another recent event one young man

spoke of the indiscretions of Miss _____ in allowing herself to be kissed, not under the mistletoe, but

under the palms at a recent social function in the West end." The real indiscretion, she seemed to

think; "was in allowing herself to be seen."[16]

A story that was published in August 1899 remarked that an anti-kissing league was the latest fad in

Columbus, Ohio, among a number of "east side society girls." Its membership "which was at first

limited to but a select few, is rapidly growing and now takes in the majority of the ultra-fashionable

girls in that section of the city." The league was of a secret character and neither the names of the

regular members nor the names of the officers was disclosed. One of the members explained to a

journalist that the attitude of the group toward kissing was "of a restrictive and protective nature rather

than totally prohibitive." Membership was limited to girls between the ages of 17 and 25 "and each

applicant is carefully examined before being voted in. It is necessary that she must have been kissed a

few times in order that the nature of the sacrifice made may be clearly appreciated." The reporter

concluded his story by writing; "The young men in that section of the city are considering means by

which to prevent further additions to the league, if they cannot induce the withdrawal of those now

in."[17]

Most of the anti-kissing groups were American but on rare occasions a foreign organization emerged.

In March 1901 it was announced that a new anti-kissing league had just been formed in France and that

its motto was; "If you would enjoy good health you must strictly refrain from kissing anyone." The

object of that society was to secure legislation that would in the future make the art of kissing a

misdemeanor except under specially defined conditions. "Not on the ground of morality do the

founders of the league ask that kissing be prohibited, but on the ground that osculation, as not

habitually indulged in, is a constant menace to the public health," declared the account. A French

newsman by the name of Maurice Spronch wrote, of the league; "These persons want to prevent parents from kissing their children and children from kissing their parents, and if they have their way all those who were wont to distribute a few kisses daily among their friends and relatives will be in future debarred from testifying to their love and affection in this old-fashioned and delightful manner." In the future, after legislation had been achieved, the group hoped to see that betrothed couples would be permitted to kiss each other only once before marriage, "as it is feared that if they kiss more often one of them may transmit to the other germs of an infection disease." Said the reporter; "How often they will be permitted to kiss after marriage the founders of the league do not inform us; neither do they say how they propose to find out whether married couples, who are really in love with each other, strictly obey the anti-kissing law." Discussing the motives of the league founders the journalist stated; "Of course it is the dread of the ubiquitous microbe which caused this singular league to start on its novel crusade, and from the indefatigable manner in which its founders are going to work there is reason to hope that the microbe of kissing, which would doubtless be styled by scientists 'bacillus osculatorious' will be discovered at any early date. If so, young persons may be so inoculated that kissing will do them no harm." Meanwhile, the general opinion of unscientific people throughout France, concluded the journalist; "is that the league, no matter what it does, will be utterly powerless to prevent parents, children and sweethearts from kissing each other whenever and wherever they please, microbes or no microbes."[18]

Thirteen men of Mount Hope, Kansas, a small town near Wichita were adherents to the belief that men should not kiss women. All 13 were married and had just formed, in June 1901, a new club known as the Mount Hope Married Men's Anti-Kissing Club. All of those members were said to be "quite prominent in the business circles" of Mount Hope and the organization of the club had been kept secret for some three weeks, but the secret had finally leaked out. In a statement to reporters club president Wilson said; "All this talk about our wives going to sue for divorce because we have pledged not to kiss them is rot of the worst kind,. We went into this with the understanding that it was to be carried out as an experiment, and we will stick to it if the women uphold us in it. Of course, every member has taken a pledge not to kiss his wife for one year, but there is a proviso that if we all get tired

of the proposition we can disorganize the club and no one will have broken a pledge." Wilson added;

"I have been in it now for about three weeks, and am perfectly satisfied with the arrangement, as is my

wife. I find that kissing is a filthy habit and that without it a man can love a great deal more strongly.

If Wilson was to be believed; "All of the boys have kept their promises, so far, and the prospects are

that we will make this club a thing of permanence. The 13 members were; B. R. Wilson (president), T.

J. Cox (secretary), A. L. Rite, F. N. Johns, L. R. Densmore, J. B. Smith, S. W. Karnes, G. A. Snow, F.

N. Jones, P. T. Burris, A. L. Koren, B. Q. Chains, and T. V. Quincy."[19]

In an editorial about the club that appeared about 10 days after the announcement of its existence, the

newsman said it was not surprising that some of the wives of some of the members were reportedly

applying for divorces; "Who is to administer the chaste Kansas salute if not the men who were legally

entitled to perform that office? Let the witnesses in the divorce courts answer." Then the editor

printed an extract from the by-laws adopted by the group; "We, the following undersigned members of

the Married Men's Anti-Kissing League of Mount Hope, do agree between ourselves that in the future

we will not kiss either our wives, daughters or any other women whatsoever. We believe that kissing is

an unnecessary thing by which one may express their affection and further that it is a filthy and

unhealthy habit. We agree to stick to this constitution, no matter how much trouble it may cause in our

families, but will use every means in converting the members of our household that kissing is not the

proper manner for sensible people." With respect to the club constitution the editor concluded; "The

grammar is unhealthy if the idea be wise. The wives have not decided what they will do about it.

Some have suggested that they allow the benighted husband to go his way as one riding for a fall."[20]

At the same time a different newspaper editor mentioned the organization and its founder and went on

to comment; "The latest Kansas freak is a man named Wilson." He went on to add; "This freak claims

it is unmanly for a man to kiss his wife. A society to keep men from kissing other men's wives might have some excuse for existence, but this one has no other than the craving for notoriety or a form of idiocy."[21]

Later that same summer yet another editor weighed in with his opinion on the Mount Hope group. He started by observing that his local board of health had issued an anti-kissing circular and that he had looked at it with some misgivings but was glad to see "that hopeless idiots" were not confined to the local health board. That brought him to the Kansas group. He then printed what he called a declaration from that group; "That henceforth we will not kiss our own wives or any other women, but that we will still hold the same deep affection for our wives and retain admiration for the feminine beautiful. We do not believe that kissing is right, and therefore we agree not to practice it. Any member of this organization who is found guilty of disobeying the order will be dismissed at once." According to this version of the group's formation the 13 wives of the 13 members at once held a meeting and decided that they would leave their husbands within one month if they did not break up the club. But after two weeks had passed and the club still retained all of its original members the women agreed not to leave their husbands, but to await developments. Said president B. R. Wilson; "I do not see anything so extraordinary about our club. We are only following the lines laid out long ago. We have believed this for a long time, but some of the members did not like to form an organization to carry it out. But some of us who believed thus were continually violating the principles of our belief, and we agreed that the best way to keep from falling by the wayside was to form a club and then one member could support another." He added; "I will use all my influence to get other young men, and old men, too, for that matter, to join us, for I think our principles are right. I am now fifty-one years old, and I have never kissed my wife or any other woman more than a dozen times in all my life." Wilson then explained to a reporter why he was opposed to kissing; "I think it a dirty and filthy habit – one that is apt to spread disease and against the true principles of love. One does not need to kiss to show his affection. The grasp of a hand is sufficient to do that, and as for loving, I think one's actions speak for that and not the number of times you kiss your wife. I have not kissed my wife for five years, and I do not intend to, but I love her just as strongly as I ever did." As a final comment the editor added; "What will the next freak movement be?"[22]

The last article about the Mount Hope group appeared at the end of August 1901 when it was reported that the wife of club secretary T. J. Cox, had revolted and was suing for divorce, after three weeks without any kissing, but Cox boasted he had not kissed his wife in many years, maintaining that it was unmanly. President Wilson said; "Kissing is for women only – the weaker sex. Kissing is a weak manner of showing affection. We love our wives more than those men who are all the time kissing them every time they leave the house. Some wives may object, but that will not induce us to desert the cause. My wife is in favor of the plan and looks at it in the same manner as I do,"[23]

A society known as the Anti-Kissing Club was formed around January 1, 1902 by several of the unmarried females employed by the Davis Medical Company in Fort Wayne Indiana. By-laws of that new club stipulated that any girl who was "so rash or forgetful as to permit herself to be saluted with a kiss by any one not of her family shall buy a pound box of candy for the enjoyment of the rest of the society." According to the reporter the pledge was for a year and "kissing is really, rigidly prohibited.[24]

In July 1902 a journalist wrote of a group of eight young men and six young women who were attending Northwestern University in Evanston, Illinois and who had established an organization called "The Kiss Shunners." As its name implied the society was going to discontinue "the labial method of expressing affection." In this account the journalist said he did not know why the group were shunning kissing. At the previous meeting of the group the followed resolution was offered and referred to committee; "Realizing that kissing is demoralizing and detrimental we, the undersigned students of Northwestern university, solemnly swear that we will refrain from all kissing and that we will try to persuade others to likewise refrain." The members of the organization proposed to wear a badge indicating their attitude on the issue. It would therefore be understood that when one met a girl with a badge on her right arm that she did not desire to be kissed. In conclusion the newsman declared; "When all is said and done, the old way will be most popular and will therefore probably stand the test of time. If a young woman is willing to be kissed, and there is nobody looking, she will continue to be kissed in spite of all the anti-osculation societies formed now or hereafter."[25]

Reportedly, this new group had decided to follow the "teachings" of Professor Crook of Northwestern who had publicly declared himself to be "the man who was never kissed," even though he was then middle-aged. In this account those students, herein 16 in number and not 14, were said to describe the practice as "vulgar, demoralizing and entirely unnecessary in respectably courtships". They were determined to work, through their new society, for the purpose of discountenancing "the evil." According to this story the following was the pledge taken by the club members; "Realizing that kissing is very demoralizing and detrimental, but still delicious, and that it is exclusive and contagious we, the undersigned students of Northwest university, following the example of our beloved professor Algie R. Crook, solemnly swear that we will refrain from all kissing." Professor Crook, noted the journalist, "who inspired the idea has been elected an honorary member of the organization and chosen sponsor for his disciples."[26]

About one week later another article was published about the society. It claimed that; "The Kiss Shunners is prospering." Since its organization only several days earlier the membership was said to have double, "although the strictest attention is paid to the standing of the new members admitted." The campaign against kissing was to be conducted exclusively in the club "but the increase in membership, it is believed, will make its influence extensive in the town." No student of Garrett Biblical Institute [located on the Northwestern campus] had to that date been able to gain admittance to the society. All members were required to sign a pledge to refrain from kissing as long as they were identified with the group, and if anyone was found guilty of an infraction of the rule that member was summarily dismissed from the organization.[27]

Another account of this group looked at the influence Professor Crook had upon it. Said a reporter; "The words he let fall in his unusual claim to virtue have had subtle influence on the students at the university, and are responsible for the present sudden opposition to kissing. Strange to say, a group of co-eds are at the bottom of the conspiracy to discourage the osculatory endeavors of the young men."

The men, in this account, were said to be less enthusiastic about the project, but from the force of circumstance were brought into the movement. To assist the anti-kissing members in keeping their pledges fasting was absolutely prohibited and a hearty diet was recommended, "on the theory that love cannot flourish except on bread and water. Hugging and goo-goo eyes are not tabooed by the society, although the members are not permitted to hold conversations over five minutes in length in couples." Boating was allowed to the society members provided four people were in the boat. Herein the membership rules were said to be as follows; "To be eligible for membership in the Anti-Kissing League, persons must be between the age of 16 and 30, good looking, with past experience in the art of osculation, and students of the Northwestern university."[28]

Before the end of July arrived it was declared in an article that; "Kissing can't be stopped. Even its regulation is impossible. The more one tried to discourage the time-honored custom the more popular its indulgence becomes." Those were reported to be the conclusions which a dozen young men and women had reached; "Their unanimity became public today when the announcement was made that the United Order of Kiss Shunners was no more." A schism among the faithful apparently had surfaced almost at the outset when one of the officers of the group was caught in the act of kissing a new recruit and, observed a journalist; "From that time it may be said that the society had a precarious existence." Wrote the newsman; "The Kiss Shunners started out with a heroic task before them. They were chiefly from among the students of the Northwestern University who aspired to achieve great things during the summer vacation months. Vacation was at hand and the co-eds didn't know what to do to keep their minds of their studies, so they proposed the kiss shunner crusade to their admirers and the united order came into being." And, the newsman concluded; "They were bent on seeing the passage of an anti-kissing ordinance in the Evanston city council before the resumption of classes."[29]

However, the report of the demise of the club was, it seemed, premature. Because in late September 1902 Ethel Merrill, one of the founders of the group, spoke on behalf of the club, and said; "Kissing is a habit which grows on one, and I believe it is a good thing to kill it off." A newsman sneered in response; "Of course, only some real mean man would insinuate that Ethel's sole chance of ever being kissed would be by mistake on the part of someone, due to darkness."[30]

In June 1903, almost a year after the group had formed, it was observed that anti-kissing pledges taken back then from John W. McClinton and Miss Frances C. Lemery, when the pair joined the anti-kissing society, proved to be an unsuccessful restraint upon matrimony because the couple announced their engagement and made it public on June 15. A journalist remarked that those two "leaders in the formation of the club were the first to be found guilty of a love affair engendered within the ranks of the society itself." McClinton was herein called the president of the group "and other members of the club assert that he was the originator of the anti-kissing regulation. Miss Lemery was one of the enthusiastic champions of the banishment of the kiss." According to this reporter; "With the desertion of two of the members, the anti-kissing society speedily broke up, and its cherished ideals rudely dashed to the ground. The pair were expected to be married in the fall.[31]

Frances Lemery [perhaps Lewery] joined a church choir in January 1903. McClinton attended the same church always sitting near the choir loft at each service. The society held its last meeting in June just before the engagement was made public. At that meeting McClintock got up and said; "It's all off. I tender my resignation from this society. Its tenets are not suitable for a co-educational institution." He then announced his engagement to Lemery and a notion to disband the organization carried unanimously.[32]

A newspaper editor, writing on January 15, 1903, stated that some American men and women "have conceived so strong a distaste for kissing that they have banded themselves into an association with the pleasing title of the Anti-Osculation Society." The members pledged to not kiss anybody and the female members, and most members were women, pledged not to kiss each other, or even their nearest relatives. People who were or had been much given to kissing were preferred as members "so that they can be 'reformed.'" One of the members, a middle-aged man, claimed that he had never in all his life given or received a kiss; "He is naturally the pride and glory of the strange society." The editor declared; "It is worthy of note that the lady members are not taking precautions against non-existent dangers; that is to say, some of them are both young and charming. It is indeed a question whether the fact of their being pledged against kissing would not offer any new and irresistible temptation to unscrupulous young men." No specific identification of this group was given by the article. In conclusion the editor wrote; "Certainly a cynic might suggest that some idea of this sort is at the root of the anti-kissing movement so far as the girls are concerned."[33]

"No more kissing is the watchword now in Oakland," or at least that was what a journalist wrote in April 1903 about a new anti-osculation society that had been formed in that California city. And in the ranks of that group, continued the reporter, were some of the city's "choicest bits of masculinity. Doctors, lawyers, bankers, writers and politicians have joined in the crusade against kissing, declaring that not only is it an aid to microbes, but a trap by which innocent young bachelors are lured to matrimony." Reportedly, the society had grown rapidly in strength and numbers since it was organization a few months earlier by Dr. Frank Huis, a young physician and Lunt Fritsch, the treasurer of the Unity Club, and the membership list then included a number of married men. "For the sake of peace and quiet the latter are given 'osculatory permits' but their oath of membership binds them to oppose in theory and practice the art of kissing as a promiscuous pastime," explained the account. Dr. Huis, president of the organization, said to be opposed to kissing only upon medical and sanitary grounds, was then hard at work perfecting a "microbe killer" that could be rubbed on the lips and would render immune from disease those who engaged in osculation. A list of names was published in the article and amounted to 30 names, all men, with at least half a dozen being physicians, several listed as professors, and Oakland City Attorney J. E. McElroy. An elaborate membership card was provided by the "Oakland Anti-Osculation Society." The card declared; "This is to certify, That [name] being a duly qualified member of the Anti-Osculation Society of Oakland, and having unimpaired possession of his mental faculties with full courage of heart and a desire for the health and happiness of mankind, hereby solemnly swears to renounce and abstain from all worldly pleasures derived by the Art and Practice of Osculation, usually known as kissing." The card was dated and signed by club secretary Fritsch.[34]

At the end of 1903 it was reported that the Oakland organization, then apparently renamed as the National Anti-Kissing Society of America, already had 100 members who declared themselves "of sound sense" and who were pledged "to abjure all forms of the kiss, from the amatory to the perfunctory, for the rest of their natural lives." They renounced kissing from a "heroic desire to promote and preserve the health and freedom of the human family generally." At this time the club president was K. I. Sweet and the secretary was M. Early. The organization declared that it would soon have branches. A. S. Rutherford of Oakland was also an officer of the society and explained the mission of the group as a "cause and that they took themselves seriously. Declared Rutherford; "The practice of kissing is a menace not only to the morals but to the health of the community. Through promiscuous contact of lips disease is spread, and the evil effects of such marks of affection cannot be estimated. Then just think what a shield against temptation an antiosculation pledge must be. With such an ironclad resolution as that in his pocket a man is proof against the wiles of a Cleopatra."[35]

A reporter then canvassed some prominent New York City residents as to the possibility of a New York branch of that Oakland society. Said Mrs. Cornelia Stewart Robinson, a well-known social economist; "Kissing is one of our oldest social amenities. It did not come into being without reason. It could not be killed without disaster…Abolish it and you disintegrate the universe." She added; "To treat the subject economically, if it be true that the microbe is fostered by the practice of kissing its cessation would put many physicians out of business, and the pauperizing of the medical profession would be a serious consideration." Emma Fields, actress, stated; "The kiss, more than all the cosmetics in the shop is a rejuvenator…The child and the woman were made to be kissed." Fields continued by saying' "If we could abolish the society kiss, which means nothing, I should favor an antisociety at once. But as for its bad effect upon health, I do not think the microbes transmitted in a kiss weigh against the pessimism and premature old age of those who languish for kisses that they never receive."

Belle De Rivera of the New York Equal Suffrage League asserted; "Kissing is a relic of barbarism. We

shook our enemy's hand originally to discover that he had no weapons concealed. The promiscuous

kiss is the thing to go, but the abolition of the entire practice might have a political significance."

Harriet Ostrom of the West End Republican Club said; "It is the habit of kissing in public and the

kissing between women on every occasion of a social sort that call for an antisociety. In my opinion

the French habit of kissing on the cheek should be adopted." Remarked Mrs. George Studwell of the

Professional Woman's League; "In the matter of kissing the 'antis' have more to contend with than

they reckon for. There are, for instance, the people born in the month of May, who are supposed to be

constitutionally inclined to this expression of their affections. I believe that those who are not included

to kiss the people they are fond of have something radically wrong with them." And, she continued;

"Everything when carried to extremes is bad, but as kissing goes by favor it seems to me that should be

sufficient protection for the evils of promiscuity at least, and all other evils are a matter of individuality

and not of the kiss per se."[36]

 Mr. A. S. Rutherford, of the National Anti-Osculation Society of America, believed that it was more

important to enlist the kisser than the kissee, and so frankly stated that he would rather bring under his

anti-kissing banner the men than the women. Rutherford had attached to his anti-kissing pledge the

rider; "to abstain from the use for purposes of attraction, allurement or fascination of all such facial

expressions and contortions as are known and designated by the names of cat's eyes, sheep's eyes, goo-

goo eyes, winks, blushes or other designing alterations of countenance." The members of the club also

bound themselves "not to make use of any terms of endearment, such as lovely, sweetness, birdie,

littlest, onliest, tootsy wootsy, etc., to any one, whether a member of this organization or not."[37]

 The Oakland California Anti-Osculation Society made the news again in February 1904 when it was

reported that its membership rolls contained "scores of business and professional men and not a few

women." Emil Fritsch, 30, was described as secretary of the society and its founder. Members of the group were pledged to "forego, renounce and abjure forever all pleasure, gratification or enjoyment to be derived from the use and practice of osculation, commonly known as 'kissing.'" According to this article; "The society is based upon the theory that kissing is a relic of paganism and a menace to the health and ultimate happiness of the country at large." It was also stated that the scope of the society was quite radical in that radicalism could be inferred from a rider in the pledge statement by which members were pledged to refrain from using the various terms of endearment that were mentioned above.[38]

A month later a wit was moved to produce a poem about the anti-osculation groups. It was a general poem and not specifically about the Oakland group.

She's joined an anti-kissing club,

She fears the microbes, she declares;

Her nose is what is known as snub;

She's joined an anti-kissing club –

But why did she need to? There's the rub!

She's plain and thirty, so who cares?

She's joined an anti-kissing club,

She fears the microbes, she declares.[39]

As of the middle of September 1904 it was reported that half a dozen "pretty" Georgia girls discussed kissing from various standpoints and decided that it was a silly and unsavory practice. Accordingly they organized as the Anti-Kissing Club and adopted a constitution that provided, among other things: "Each member shall sign the following pledge with her own blood secured from her lips – I pledge myself to never kiss anyone except father, mother, brothers, sisters, husband and children. I pledge myself furthermore to never kiss my betrothed until I become his wife." Commented a newspaper editor; "These girls, unwittingly, have organized an old maid's club."[40]

A different account noted that the Georgia women were from the town of Lexington and that they had organized their society because they decided that kissing was a "silly" custom. Other clauses in the group's constitution declared; "The object of this club is to promote hygiene, candor, saneness and finance among members." The constitution also provided that is any member failed to keep the pledge she "will pay a fine of $25 and ask the club to erase my name from the roll." Upon the marriage of any member of the group, each member was to pay $5 to the treasurer, who would then present the amount raised as a bridal gift to the woman who was to be married. The amount of money paid in as fines by those members who fail to keep the pledge was to be held by the treasurer as a fund to be divided among "those who prefer spinsterhood." Any member who applied for a divorce was to pay $50 to the treasurer and have her name removed from the roll.[41]

Pottstown Pennsylvania girls had reportedly formed an anti-kissing club in October 1904 under the name of the Four Leaf Clover Club. While the club was said to be of a social nature, the principle obligation each member took was to refrain from kissing anyone, either male or female, except relatives.[42]

A little red button worn by some 300 women, old and young, married and unmarried, who were among the leading social sets in Mexico City, said a reporter in December 1904; "marks a new departure, or rather a new step, in progress." That little round red button signified membership in what was known as the Anti-Kissing League. Members of the society took a solemn pledge not to kiss each other, in public or private, and to spread the idea that kissing was contagious, or rather, the means of conveying contagious diseases from one set of lips to another. According to the journalist; "There is nothing visible to the naked eye in the constitution of this league against kissing other than members of the female persuasion and, in fact, the practice aside from the supposed danger of infection, is decidedly, to the male sense, not only deplorable but unnecessary. How far this new league will conduct its offensive and defensive campaign remains to be seen."[43]

Five young ladies in a high school in Urbana Ohio formed what they termed the "Anti-Kissing and Hugging club" in February 1906. One of the rules adopted by the group was that when young men called on them they had to sit on the opposite side of the room "and not to talk about love." Reportedly, "the young men have already entered a vigorous protest."[44]

A different account some ten days later called the organization the "Urbana Anti-Kissing Club" and declared the origin was a lecture given by the principal of that high school to the girls of the sophomore class, in which he criticised the girls who allowed young men to kiss them. Said a journalist; "Whether the girls took this talk seriously cannot be said, yet three of them met at the home of a fourth member of the class and started the anti-kissing club." The reporter added that; "No young man will be allowed to kiss any of the members. If the girls violate the rules they will have to pay a heavy penalty. The girls are reticent about the club's affairs, and especially as to how offenders may be detected. Meetings are held every Wednesday night."[45]

A few days later more details about the Urbana group were made public. If a member of the club violated the rules she had to pay a fine of $5 or be suspended from the group for 15 days. Meetings were held every Wednesday night after prayer meeting and; "A large number of society girls have applied for admission." Helen Leonard was president of the club with the other officers being Belle Best, Edith Turner, and Clara McCreary, with all of those women being described as "members of the best families in Urbana."[46]

Early in February 1908 Professor Anders of the Medico-Chirurgical College in Philadelphia delivered a lecture on the subject of tuberculosis in Schuylkill County. One unexpected result from the lecture was that a movement was started by young women in the town of Schuylkill Haven to form an anti-kissing society. In his lecture Anders spoke strongly about the danger of the transmission of the tuberculosis germ by kissing. Somebody followed that up by sending to "prominent" young men of the county a magazine article, then current, that contained a statement that a celebrated doctor found germs of half a dozen different diseases on the lips of a young lady upon examining her with a microscope after she had been kissed by a young man with a moustache. That discovery and the emphasis placed by Anders on the dangers of the transmission of the tuberculosis germs decided the young women to request all the young men with whom they had influence to have their mustaches cut off. One man who attended the Anders' talk had already been notified by his wife that he would not be allowed to kiss her until he removed his mustache.[47]

Actor Zelda Sears, who had lately appeared in Clyde Fitch's comedy *Girls*, onstage at the Daly Theater, New York City had become convinced, in May 1908, that kissing between women should cease. To that end she had undertaken to organize an anti-kissing club, with membership to be confined exclusively to women. Sears aimed at making the movement international and said her object was to confine kissing to its "natural" province or sphere. Said Sears; "I never thought kissing required regulation until called upon to distribute kisses by the bushel in *Girls*. Since then I have been making a quiet investigation, and I find my belief that kissing is baneful, and a sure means of spreading microbes, is sustained by the evidence of many medical men. If for no more than an aid to public health, my anti-kissing club should succeed. Then there is the other material reason that few women are sincere when they exchange kisses. I believe that kissing among themselves tends to make hypocrites of women for women kiss and kiss and then turn and backbite." Sears invited all women interested in the movement to write to her and offer suggestions for the practical establishment of the club. She had written on the subject to President Theodore Roosevelt, Governor Charles Evans Hughes of New York State, Mayor McClellan of New York City, and other public men, "and she expects to preside soon over a meeting in Daly's theater at which the anti-kissing campaign will be open to public discussion."[48]

In May 1910 an anti-kissing organization sprang up in Chicago with the somewhat grandiose name of World's Health Organization. It started its campaign against osculation by urging the school authorities to forbid kissing in the hope that the "pernicious habit" would die out with the present generation. The movement also suggested that young people wear buttons on which were printed the words "Kiss Not" and when anyone tried to start something in the osculatory line the young lady would only have to call attention to the admonition on the button. An editor (in Albert Lea, Minnesota) declared; "It may be possible to start such a crusade in the Windy City but not in Albert Lea. And we are glad it is so. Are none of the joys of heaven to be left on earth?"[49]

More details emerged a few days later. For one thing the society was headquartered in Cincinnati and not Chicago. The president of the group was Mrs. L. Rechtin, who sent out the following appeal; "It has been estimated that one person in every seven is infected with consumption. Who offers to greet you with a kiss? Is it an infected person? Who wants to kiss the little folks? Is it an infected person? You may not be able to answer these questions but you can join the W. H. O. [World's Health Organization] and protect yourself and your friends." She continued by declaring; "If you have the welfare of your country at stake; if you prize your own health; if you care for the health of your relatives; if you have seen a love one weakened by consumption; if you want to protect the babies; if you want to do the world a little good before you die, join the club. The motto is 'Kiss Not.' We have a club button bearing this motto, 'Kiss Not.'" If one of those buttons could be put upon the bib of every newborn baby and worn until the child was 80 years old, Rechtin speculated; "there would be more old people than there are today. Kissing friends in greeting and parting, kissing the baby by well-meaning but infected relatives are the means of spreading consumption faster than any known scientific remedy can check it." In conclusion Rechtin admonished; "Why not stop kissing. It is a time honored custom and one person cannot stop it. It is only in unity that sufficient strength can be gained to convince the civilized world that kissing is unhealthful."[50]

At the end of May 1910 it was noted that the anti-kissing crusade had arrived in Los Angeles, in the person of Mrs. Rechtin, head of the World's Health Organization, who was appealing to local physicians in Los Angeles to interest them in her cause of "No Kissing." To that point, it was said, she had taken for granted their acceptance of the task she would place before them. She had sent them all circulars explaining her 'no kiss' club, with a request that each of the medical men canvass the city for members. Said a journalist; "The medicos who received these circulars in their mail Saturday afternoon were highly edified and not a little amused. Several of them at once announced their intention to enlist under Mrs. Rechtin's banner and to wear the club button, which is neat and not gaudy, containing no emblem, but displaying in bold-faced lettering the club motto, 'Kiss Not.'" To join the club and obtain one of these buttons just two things were necessary – that the applicant sign a pledge to refrain from kissing or being kissed and that the individual pay five cents for the badge. The pledge was worded as follows; "In order to encourage good health and lessen the spread of consumption I desire to join the World's Health Organization, and hereby pledge myself to discourage the custom of kissing on the lips whenever it is in my power." In her communications to Los Angeles physicians Mrs. Rechtin painted a terrifying picture of the danger lurking in the simplest osculation and beseeched them to put a stop to the spread of disease by discouraging the kissing habit. She especially decried the practice of kissing infants and the doctors were reported to agree with her that it was bad for the baby and should be discouraged. "Few of them, however, believe the danger to adults perilous enough to necessitate total abstinence in the matter of labial bliss, though one and all advise discretion in the matter," stated a reporter. Rechtin resided in Cincinnati and her organization, said the journalist "is reported to have made considerable progress there. Now she hopes to extend its influence over the entire county."[51]

Less than 10 days later a report was published that pledge cards for Rechtin's group were being circulated in Huntington, Indiana, and at Hammond, Indiana. A couple of days after that an editorial cartoon spoofed the World's Health Organization by depicting a meeting of the group with very few members assembled and all of those being old and unattractive.[52]

When she was interviewed in Cincinnati on June 18, 1910, Rechtin said that she would keep on struggling until she obtained an abatement of that "awful menace-kissing." In every part of the world, she declared, there were deaths every day that could be cited as coming from kisses and that kissing had come to be not merely a popular salute but a terrible evil that must be stamped out. Furthermore, she said her efforts had led many to forego "oscillatory pleasures." Asserted Rechtin; "People should remember that kissing is merely the habit of centuries. There was a time when all the world kissed everybody they met. There was a time when kissing was quite the thing, but that day has passed. I think that kissing should be done away with entirely." She continued by declaring; "Every member of our organization has been sent buttons to wear showing their aversion to the practice, and the first work of the organization will be in little parties which women have at their homes, and which they invariably soil by kisses. It is essential to the welfare of the people of the nation to do away with this, and I am hoping to have anti-kiss pledges worn by every schoolgirl and every schoolboy in the country before very long."[53]

The World's Health Organization was headquartered at 1723 E. McMillan Street in Cincinnati, Ohio, which was the residence of Rechtin. She said to a journalist; "Why not stop kissing? Of course it is a time honored custom, but is that a reason for continuing with it, when we know it is a menace to health and to life itself? Just wear one of our buttons and you will be immune from all who would try to kiss you." She was reported to be the wife of a "well-known business man" and the mother of two children – boys, whom she never kissed. "The kissing of children and babies by well-meaning but infected relatives and friends is the means of spreading consumption and other diseases faster than science can check them," explained Rechtin. There were no fees or dues for the organization, observed the reporter, all one had to do was to sign the pledge, which bound one to discourage the practice of kissing on the lips, but not on the cheeks. The reporter also remarked that the pledge made one go forth and discourage kissing whenever in your power but that it did not specifically state that the member do no kissing herself.[54]

At the end of July 1910 a journalist observed that; "After years of sporadic crusading a non-kissing organization had been started in Cincinnati that is meeting with surprising success. In that city, according to the president of the society, more than a thousand men, women and children had pledged themselves to abstain from the practice, and the membership roll is steadily on the increase. Supporters of the movement are so ambitious as to prophesy that within a year or two they will have members in every city in the Union." Mrs. John Rechtin was described herein as about 35 years old who, long before her marriage, was "diametrically opposed" to promiscuous kissing. She began to preach her doctrine to her husband, won him over to her way of thinking and then started on her friends with such success that the WHO was founded and she was elected its first president. It was reported that Rechtin was then devoting her attention to the conversion of the fair sex, particularly the young women of Cincinnati, who were about to become brides. If one signed her group's pledge and returned it he or she was furnished with "an attractive button" inscribed with the words "I won't kiss." Said Rechtin: "The custom of kissing a bride on her wedding day is a most dangerous one. To stamp out this evil at once would be to accomplish the impossible, but we have made the start and are much encouraged." She added; "Seventy-five perspective brides have joined the organization this month. On their wedding day they will wear the button of the society." According to the journalist the anti-kissing leaders had mapped out a long campaign and when it ended kissing would be a lost art, they hoped. Soon they would try and make members of the public speakers and signers – of everybody "whose success in life depends on healthy vocal codes." These leaders pledged that in August fathers and mothers would be urged not to kiss their babies while in September teachers would implore their pupils to abjure kissing. In October, believing the less kissing the less hazardous the work of street cleaners and laundresses, so the WHO planned to seek members on the highways and in the laundries. In November women belonging to church clubs, card clubs, and literary clubs were to be asked to join and to wear their buttons and badges at the meetings of their own clubs. Rechtin enthused; "And in December, with its Christmas weddings, we shall turn our attention to lovers. 'My life for just one kiss' sounds thrilling in romance and poetry. But disillusion is found in the hospitals, whence lovers follow one another to the grave in a few short months." According to the reporter the organization headed by Rechtin was known in all the principal cities and arrangements were being made for the establishment of hundreds of branch offices. However, that reporter noted; "In New York,

Philadelphia, and other cities of the east, the non-kiss idea has not met with the favor with which it has been greeted by the people of Cincinnati."[55]

One New York City society woman who commented on the WHO and who was not keen on the idea was Mrs. Belle de Rivera, president of the New York City Federation. She declared; "I think the agitation is extremely silly and in poor taste. Everyone knows a great deal of harm may be done by the promiscuous kissing of children. The fact is so well understood it seems silly to try and organize it. I feel certain New York clubwomen will not join in any such foolish, sensational agitation."[56]

In July 1910 a reporter interviewed Dr. Harvey W. Wiley, chief of the Bureau of Chemistry of the Department of Agriculture in Washington, D.C. He was described as probably knowing as much about disease germs of various kinds as any other man in the country. Wiley told the journalist that he had yet to see a single instance in which a life had been wrecked or shortened as a direct result of disease germs transmitted from a diseased person to a healthy one by the kissing route. Told about Rechtin's Cincinnati organization it caused Wiley to wonder what was the matter with the woman; "A society for the prevention of kissing is nothing less than a society for the prevention of pleasure." When told that society was gaining new members "by the hundreds" Wiley smiled in surprise and replied; "Just imagine a kissless courtship. Can you contemplate a more uninteresting predicament? I certainly would like to get one peep at the members of an organization which approves of such a thing."[57]

Two days after the Wiley interview a journalist by the name of Mary Whiteman said; "Nearly 5,000 members have been enrolled and branches are being established in every large city of the country," referring to the Rechtin organization. In speaking of her work the president of the World's Health Organization asserted; "Physicians all over the country are encouraging the work. I get hundreds of letters each day. One lady has started a branch in Chihuahua, Mexico. The society is growing fast in Denver, where there are thousands of sufferers from tuberculosis. We are confining our efforts at present entirely to the work against kissing at public functions and the promiscuous kissing of babies. Here is where the most harm is done." And, she added; "It is impossible to get sweethearts to realize that they must not kiss each other on the lips. I know of one instance in a suburb of this city where a young woman is a suffered from tuberculosis. The young man who called on her was well and strong. He became infected during the courtship, and our investigation shows that the infection was caused by kissing. They both died before the date set for the wedding. The deaths occurred only two weeks apart." No article about Rechtin's group every mentioned the name of any other officer of the organization. In fact, no specific name of any other member was ever mentioned or quoted in any article. Exact numbers of members was never given out in any article.[58]

In February 1911 Imogene Rechtin was still leading her organization. At that time she declared; "The work of the World's Health Organization is to show the people that the health of our nation demands that we protect ourselves. Do not kiss sick people. In the case of smallpox the disease shows quickly after infection has taken place, but in consumption it does not; therefore do not kiss anyone." Rechtin continued; "You are not sure by looking at a person whether he has consumption or not. He may not know it himself…We must be more active, more earnest, go to the source of supply and stop passing the disease from one to another with our mouths."[59]

The organization was mentioned in an editorial that appeared on March 16, 1911, wherein it said the World's Health Organization was waging a "bitter war against kissing." Said the editor; "Judging by the facial features of the presidentess of the cult appearing in the public prints, she is immune without wearing the ['Kiss Not'] button." And that was that last that was heard about the organization and Rechtin.[60]

In November 1910 a report from Minnesota said that "Osculate? Osculate? was said to be the "official yell" of the anti-kissing society that had been formed among the coeds of the University of Minnesota. Mystery was said to surround the organization but members said the club was started to protect babies from promiscuous kissing and the transmission of germs from the lips of elders.[61]

Dr. George W. Bowling was a dentist in Lindsay Oklahoma who had in mind a plan to promulgate a bill to make osculation a crime under the law. Bowling was the author of a plan for a nation-wide anti-kissing campaign. He had incorporated a society to combat the kissing habit. The movement was said to have begun on March 28, 1912 and, said a reporter, it already had a state-wide hold. The dentist declared his association had a membership, in July 1912, of more than 700 and was "constantly growing." Bowling called kissing the "greatest crime" in the calendar of hygienic neglect. He declared; "Kissing, I have to admit, is a pleasant pastime. It is a national game at which we all like to play sometimes and no strict rule can as yet be laid down against it. Still, I must maintain, kissing is the most dangerous thing in the world." He continued by stating; "Homes have been wrecked, nations destroyed, thrones overturned, and all because of the kiss; still that reason or implied reason, is not mine. I am enthusiastic upon the subject simply from a sanitary or hygienic standpoint, and I think that the Legislature should pass a law making it compulsory to teach oral hygiene in the public schools." It was to aid in getting such a bill passed by the Legislature that had moved Bowling and a few others to incorporate the Oral-Hygiene Association and it was one of the association's principles to see that such a law was passed. Most of his proposal dealt literally with oral hygiene, how to care for the teeth, the throat, and so forth; "which are directly connected with kisses." Bowling asserted; "I believe that when people are educated better they will eliminate a great part of the present habit of kissing…Kissing as I look at it is a national crime and should be made such by the laws. I understand, however that such an act would be ridiculed and would be impossible. Still it is a crime just the same. The most dangerous diseases are transferred more frequently by kissing than by any other method. Tuberculosis is the most frequently transferred in this manner." The dentist went on to assert; "I am not a crank on this subject. I myself kiss a few people now and then and like to do it. But I am careful and that is what others should be. Children should be guarded very, very carefully." Other members of the Oklahoma State Dental Association did not agree with Bowling. According to a journalist; "Dr. Bowling says he was 'kicked out' of the State Professional Association because he founded the Anti-Kissing League, and so far the association has refused to reinstate him.[62]

Not many anti-kissing clubs emerged after 1912. Their heyday was apparently over. There were a couple, though. In March 1919 it was reported that "No more kissing" was the motto of Nu Epsilon Sigma, a secret society organized by three girls at Lawrence College in Appleton, Wisconsin. Those charter members were Esther Baldwin, Winifred Harvey, and Ada Burt. Another eight girls had joined since the formation of the group but their names were not given. According to a reporter; "Seeing two fellows grip hands in greeting after an absence of a few years and then settle into a calm conversation without osculatory displays of affection gave the girls an inspiration. They decided if the boys could be perfectly happy with those greetings, why not the girls, and so do away with the perpetual hug and kiss." The journalist added; "Effects of the nonkissing club on Lawrence College will be felt over the campus. Each group of bubbly girls will be severely criticised by the members if any demonstration of lip-smacking affection is made in public or private corners of the campus."[63]

Young women of Sayre Pennsylvania, in an effort to prevent the spread of influenza, organized a society in January 1920, the members of which were sworn to refrain from being kissed until the danger of the flu epidemic was past. Reportedly the organization had already gained members i Waverly, New York and in Athens, Pennsylvania.[64]

Pictured here are three of the founding members, in July 1902, of a society called the "Kiss Shunners" that was set up at Northwestern University in Evanston Illinois.

HUSBANDS WEARY AND BACHELORS WARY DECREE AGAINST THE KISS

Some of Oakland's Choicest Bits of Masculinity Timidly Form Anti-Osculation Society, Content to Live and Die Unthrilled by Fond Embrace, Fearful That Red Lips May Be the Ambush of Fork-Tailed Microbes

An Oakland California anti-kissing society received a fair amount of publicity in April 1903. Pictures here are two of the group;s officers, Dr. Frank Huis and E. Fritsch. This group was said to be composed of many profession men such as doctors and lawyers.

SAYS SHE'LL NEVER REST UNTIL KISSING IS NO MORE

Cincinnati Woman Declares She's Going to Keep Right on Fighting Dread Peril.

This 1910 photo shows Mrs. Rechtin, founder and president of the anti-kissing society called the World's Health Organization.

Ch. 6. Rules, Regulations, and Laws.

Another outcome of the anti-kissing agitation were attempts, at various levels of government or society to impose rules, regulations or laws on the practice and thus control kissing, limit kissing, or abolish it altogether. Needless to say, such efforts had no chance of being successful. In the case of organizations opposed to the practice they tended to be formed in the earlier parts of the time period covered by this book; while in the case of rules, laws, and so forth, those tended to emerge in the later parts of the time period. Boards of Health in various jurisdictions often tried to regulate the practice of osculation in some fashion. Those attempts are included in chapter one.

In May 1887 the Park Commissioners of Harlem Park in Baltimore made kissing and hugging in the park a misdemeanor with the penalty for a violation of the rule being a fine of from $5 to $25. That ban on kissing and hugging in the city of Baltimore's parks remained in place for over 20 years. The ban was finally lifted in September 1909.[1]

At a date that fell between the establishment of the ban on kissing and hugging in Baltimore parks, and the ban being lifted, a report was published in July 1893 that stated the Maryland city's anti-kissing law had been declared unconstitutional by the court.[2]

In Montreal Canada in July 1890 there came before the Recorder in that city what was described as a "peculiar" case. Some ladies from England had arrived in Montreal to visit "one of its most respectable and well-connected citizens." After dinner one evening the group took a walk in the park. One of the couples was engaged to be married and wandered away from the rest of the party. When the rest of the party got home they received a message from the police station that the young couple had been arrested and were lodged in cells. The friends went to the station and bailed the couple out; they had been caught kissing in the street. When the couple came before the Recorder for their trial the judge fined the young Englishman $15 and treated him to a lecture on the immorality of kissing in public places, the defendant having admitted to the offense. The Recorder said that the English people had to live up to their standard of morality of which they bragged so much. They were fond of reproaching the French – the Recorder was a Francophone – with the laxity of their morals while they themselves pretended to be very rigid. "At all events, public parks were not the place for kissing and in future, if he wanted to indulge in this weakness, he must do so at home," noted a reporter. When the Recorder asked counsel for the woman what her defense was her lawyer said the woman was "quite prostrated" and preferred to receive the judgment of the court rather than to make any defense. The Recorder therefore fined her $10.[3]

 An article that appeared in print on May 24, 1893, speculated that the city of Boston might be ready to launch a crusade against kissing in the city parks. According to the chairman of the park commissioners if the example of Baltimore girls and boys was taken to any extent the same or similar steps would be taken by the park commissioners to put a stop to the practice of kissing in the parks to their city. Yet it was admitted that the park policemen had never entered a complaint in regard to indiscriminate kissing going on in any of the city parks. Park Commission Chairman Kendricken was asked if he and his colleagues intended to follow the lead of Baltimore in that respect. He stated; "The commissioners have not given the matter any attention as yet, but there is very little doubt in my mind that the time will come before very long when we shall be obliged to." Kendricken added; "It is only fair to the park commissioners to say that they would not allow any hugging or kissing to be carried on in the parks if they could prevent it." The reporter then asked the chairman if he would allow a young man to show affection for his sister in a shady nook in Franklin Park. Replied the chairman; "No. If he was so fond of her he would have to make it apparent somewhere else."[4]

 It was noted in June 1894 that the old blue laws of Connecticut and Massachusetts that prohibited kissing on Sundays had never been repealed but had been allowed to fall into "innocuous desuetude." The law against kissing on Sundays had not been enforced since early colonial times.[5]

 Representative Fow of Philadelphia wanted to prohibit kissing the bible in Pennsylvania as part of the administering of oaths, at the beginning of 1895. Commented an editor; "Unless Mr. Fow can show that temporal disease emanates from a spiritual kiss, or that the bible is not worth kissing, then we say

stick to the old form. In fact the bible is not kissed but simple pressed to the lips of those who love and

fear its admonitions." Less than two months later, though, another article stated; "The microbe

agitation has abolished 'kissing the book' in Pennsylvania courts."[6]

According to an account in a Kansas newspaper in August 1895 the legal status of the kiss has been

decided in a Georgia case. Mr. Martin was arrested for kissing his wife on the street. It seemed that

Martin and his wife met on the street several days earlier and he kissed his wife not thinking it was

against the law for a man to kiss his wife. However, two young men testified it was more than that as

"Martin warmly embraced his wife on divers section of Peters Street for a distance of several blocks,

and that the performance created disturbance and disorder in the locality of Peters and Fair Streets, so

sensational did it become. The couple fairly reveled in the performance of bidding each other a long

farewell, the festivities being prolonged for such a length of time that a policeman arrived on the scene

and arrested the affectionate couple, complaints having seen made to him by W. F. Westerly, a

storekeeper, and others of the conduct of the man and woman." Officer Phillips said it had been

reported to him that the couple had been hugging and kissing in a store and that they were made to

leave by the proprietor who said he didn't want any such conduct in his place of business. After

hearing the evidence the court said that the disorderly conduct charge had not exactly been established

in his mind, the court not being able to see anything particularly harmful with a man kissing his wife on

the street or elsewhere, although it might not be "etiquette." Since the court could see nothing

disorderly or immoral in a man kissing and hugging his wife he dismissed the case. It was a result that

pleased the Kansas editor because he concluded; "The decision was sound law, and with the law on its

side, and the strong tide of human tendency in its favor, the uncarbolized kiss, the smack and the lalli-

gagging gurgle must survive and the only thing left for aestheticism, pathology and the anti-kissing

societies is to go and soak their respective heads."[7]

Near the end of 1897 The United States Treasury Department announced it had resuscitated an old and long-forgotten rule, which said that passengers arriving on ocean steams could not greet their waiting friends until their luggage had been inspected and passed. Commented a reporter; "This is practically a law against kissing, and will doubtless meet with much opposition from ocean voyagers." When a steamship arrived at Hoboken, New Jersey late in December there was a great rush forward of friends who embraced the returning travelers. The 50 policemen on hand, reportedly, could to nothing to enforce the new rule. Four officials of the United States Customs Service were on the pier when the ship arrived, including Special Treasure Agent Smith of Boston. They agreed that the reunions were very inconvenient. A reporter declared; "Kissing, being bad for business, will no longer be tolerated at the steamship piers here or elsewhere in the United States. That's what the officials say."[8]

In a different account a journalist wrote that; "There is the fiercest kind of a strife going on in the custom house. The cause of it is a crusade that is to be made against kissing. The crusade is said to be against the indiscriminate and long drawn out kissing that takes place whenever a passenger steamship comes into port from foreign countries." Those travelers who were returning from Europe each had from two to a dozen or more friends on the pier to meet them when they came in and their friends taken altogether, amounted sometimes to 2,000 or 3,000 people. "Each friend wants to kiss and hug the newly arrived exile, and as every hug and every kiss takes up a minute or more at least it is usually an hour or more before the kissing and hugging are finished." And, concluded the reporter; "Nobody thinks of the baggage until the kissing and hugging have been finished. A delay of from an hour to two hours is consequent." He insisted that the old and then resuscitated treasury department rule "Is likely to be enforced."[9]

Also late in December 1897 a news story began by satirically stating; "No promiscuous kissing is allowed in New Jersey. Those who are entitled to kiss each other must take out licenses. All others must be unkissed." The anti-kissing crusade began a few days earlier in Englewood, New Jersey when a Miss Emma Marshall was fined $10 for kissing an "unknown" man. Jokingly, the reporter continued;

"An official kisser-catcher is to be appointed at Englewood, it is said…The law against kissing prevails also at Hoboken, adding one more to the disadvantages of that city as a place of residence." George C. Schwenck was described as acting as unofficial kisser-catcher and he arrested a couple and brought them before the Court of General Sessions. They were identified as Henry and Amelia De Place – they were husband and wife. Judge Hudspeth ordered the jury to acquit the prisoners on the ground that the crime was not fully proven. The court officers then released the couple and let them go, "to the great disappointment of the unofficial kisser-catcher."[10]

A different newspaper that covered the New Jersey story started its account by declaring; "To be kissed is to be guilty of disorderly conduct in Englewood, N. J., if one be a girl and kissed by a young man at the door of one's apartment under an apartment where two spinsters, not so young, live above." Emma Marshall was kissed by John Markham. As a result Emma was summoned to the Recorder's Court, charged with the crime of disorderly conduct and fined $10. When asked her response to the affair Emma shrugged her shoulders and said the whole thing was absurd. Her parents had recently sent her to the area to learn stenography and typewriting in New York City but advised her to live in Englewood where the parents had acquaintances and where the cost of room and board was not as expensive as it was in New York. Emma went to Englewood and took a room in the apartment of Mr. and Mrs. William Hopper. Later she went to a dance at the Pavilion with her hosts where she met Markham. Mrs. Hopper asked him to call on Emma, and he did. He called often. Miss Maria Van Wyck and Miss Carrie Van Wyck, who lived in the apartment above Emma noticed his visits and on the evening of December 23 they heard his kisses. In court they testified to those facts but Markham said in court, in his anxiety to defend Emma, that she was persecuted because she was envied by the sisters. He said; "Miss Carrie Van Wyck asked me to take her to the dance at the Pavilion. I replied that I was tired. But I took Emma to the dance, and Carrie has been angry ever since that night." Markham told a reporter; "I have kissed many girls and not one was ever summoned to court."[11]

Marshall's lawyer, Norman L. Rowe of Jersey City stated; "These charges are too absurd. I will not even take the trouble to make a defense." And he did not make a defense. When he was summing up the charges the judge spoke of the goodwill that should unite neighbors, of the mutual concessions that they should make in order to live in happiness; then he fined Marshall $10. After the trial was over a reporter visited Recorder Ernest T. Fellowes and said to him; "So it appears that you have punished Miss Marshall for no other reason than that she was kissed by a popular young man in the village." Replied Fellowes; "At 10 o'clock at night, to the intense annoyance of other tenants in the apartment house." James Terhune, Englewood Police Chief, was asked the same question by the reporter. He replied; "No, Miss Marshall was not punished for having been kissed. No sane man believes that she was." When the chief was asked what she was punished for the lawman declared; "disorderly conduct." Then the journalist asked what that offense consisted of. To which Terhune replied; "She was kissed in the hallway of the house where she lives. Yes, that is all. No, there were some remarks." Asked to elaborate on that statement the police chief said that Markham had said to Emma; "Come, let me take another kiss." Reportedly, the police chief blushed as he repeated that remark. Carrie Van Wyck told the journalist' "I do not care for Johnnie Markham, but I care about preserving respectability in a house where my sister and I have to live. It is not respectable for people, whether they be married or engaged, to kiss each other in the hall of an apartment house. We have effectually prevented the recurrence of such a disgraceful scene, I hope." The Van Wyck sisters were described as dressmakers and they claimed they were cousins of New York's mayor-elect, Robert Van Wyck.[12]

At the beginning of 1898 a different journalist mused over the question of how kissing should be done in Englewood, New Jersey. To answer that question the newsman called on city Mayor Ernest T. Fellowes [also Recorder]. Said the reporter; "He has interpreted public opinion to be against kissing in general and the surprise which followed his decision [to fine Emma $10] made it seem necessary to let him elaborate his ideas somewhat." When Fellowes was asked if it was true he fired a woman $10 for kissing a man in his town the mayor replied; "It is true that I fined a young woman for a breach of the peace." Wondering if kissing was a breach of the peace in Englewood, the reporter was told; "Under certain circumstances we judge it to be so." Asked what circumstances made the act of kissing reprehensible he was told by Fellowes; "Well, we have an ordinance which declares that disorderly conduct may consist of an overt act of boisterous behavior." Did that mean, wondered the journalist, that a man could not kiss his wife good-bye on the doorstep of their home? "Certainly not," was the reply. "A man kissing his wife is a very different matter from the kissing of two young people." The next question the newsman posed was to wonder if it was only a misdemeanor when the couple kissing were unmarried. "I should be absurd to make such restrictions or try to," said the mayor, annoyed. "Certainly when two young people are betrothed and honest in their intentions no one would think of molesting their quiet love-making." Would you allow two such young people to kiss on the doorstep then, he wondered? "Yes, certainly," or over the garden gate, "Ye-es." Or on the street? "Well, I can't say as to that. It would hardly be thought a decent necessity to carry love-making into the street...Or on the stairs of an apartment-house."[13]

Fellowes added; "I fined her for disorderly conduct. You see we have to look at the motive of the deed. The motive is everything. The journalist continued his relentless needling of the mayor/recorder by wondering if it did not take considerable psychic powers to discover motives with accuracy. "See here. Here is a man who spends most of his time loafing and drinking and bragging on street corners of his conquests. Is he a fit man to sit on the stairs of an apartment-house making love to a girl," replied the mayor. Then it was a fatherly interest you took in the girl, wondered the newsman? "No, I can't be a father to every girl in the village. I have no desire to be a censor of public morals. You've got the wrong idea again," responded Fellowes. "Don't you know there is a class of men, butchers, barbers, bakers, bartenders that go with young girls and then malign their character? I mean to put a stop to their villainous business." The mayor added; "It seems to me that it is patent when a young woman is receiving numerous callers and bestowing her favors on all of them that her motives are not good." Countered the reporter; "But she comes from the country where kissing is not so strictly accounted for and where, as she says, they play 'snap and catch 'em' and other kissing games at their church sociable, kissing perhaps a dozen men in one night." Fumed Fellowes; "It's awful. It isn't decent. Don't they draw the line somewhere?" Then the reporter wondered if Emma, fresh from the rural districts, was ignorant of the social restriction of Englewood. "She may be; no doubt she is. But she must have some inner refinement, some innate sense of propriety that teaches her not to be so indiscriminate with her favors," replied the mayor. The reporter wondered if that meant not to be a flirt. Said Fellowes; "Not to associate with degraded characters – by Jove! We've got to draw the line somewhere. This man boasts of his conquests publicly." Then the reporter raised an issue that no other account had done to that date. He asked why the Recorder had fined the girl and stigmatized her, but had not fined the man. "She encouraged him to come to her house, and he went there and made a racket. It was a breach of the peace. They were scandalizing the house. I hoped to give her a strong lesson, a warning to save her from wrong-doing," declared Fellowes. When the reporter called on Emma Marshall she said to him; "I meant no harm. I have kissed lots of boys. No, I'm not engaged to either Doc Clements [former boyfriend] or Johnnie Markham. I don't believe Doc ever talked bad about me and if Johnnie did he's a scoundrel. I liked them both and – yes – I have kissed them both."[14]

According to an August 1899 news item the Blue Laws were being revived in some parts of Connecticut. In the town of Winsted, no man was permitted to kiss his wife or sweetheart on Sundays. Remarked an editor; "Think of it, Sunday sparking and no kissing…To think that the law prohibits this little bit of paradise is a bewildering idea." A little earlier that year another newspaper editor observed, in a general sense; "It is as difficult to enforce a prohibitory law against kissing as one against tippling. Neither are harmless and both are dangerous, public censorship being the only bar."[15]

On October 25, 1899 at New Haven, Connecticut, Stephen Lawrence of the Yale Law School became, reportedly, the first Yale undergraduate in 50 years to be sentenced to jail. Lawrence was that morning sentenced to 15 days' imprisonment for the crime of kissing a girl. Fairness was imposed in this case as the judge also sentenced the girl involved to 15 days' imprisonment. Lawrence had immediately appealed and the pair were both out on bail. On the evening of October 24, Lawrence took May

Carroll, a shop girl, out for dinner. He was 22 and she was 18. After the meal as they left the

restaurant he leaned over and kissed her. Standing outside the restaurant door and a witness to the

entire incident was policeman Winchell, who declared; "In this State it offends the law to kiss in

public." Winchell promptly arrested Lawrence and Carroll and took both to the station house.

Lawrence called his friends and had them both bailed out so they did not have to spend the night in jail.

On the morning of October 25 the pair appeared in the city court before Judge Erwin C. Dow, who

listened carefully to the testimony of Winchell. The general statute gave to the judge the discretion of

administering a fine of from $10 to $100 or of imprisoning each of them for up to 30 days "for the

crime of kissing in public, even if the girl kissed does not object."[16]

The couple were due to appear in Superior Court in New Haven on November 10, 1899, in order to

have their appeal heard. However, neither showed up in court that day and so Lawrence forfeited the

$300 he had posted to have the two of them released on bail. When neither answered the judge's call

that day he ordered the bonds to be forfeited. The authorities, it was reported, were content with the

bonds and that the couple would not be arrested and jailed. Lawrence was said to have acted in this

matter on the advice of his father, a "leading" New York lawyer. Since the time of his arrest Lawrence

had not missed a day of classes at Yale. Faculty at the school had declined to interfere in the matter

although Lawrence was the only student there who ever received a jail sentence.[17]

There had been so much kissing at church entertainments in the community of Winthrop,

Massachusetts that the town board tabooed it, in December 1900. Town Constable Jenkins had been

notified to enforce the local law against it. The board declared that kissing bred disease. However, the

girls of Winthrop were reportedly displeased, noted a journalist; "They say their kisses are not

inoculated with microbes, and that they'll continue kissing. The law is a pretty severe jolt for the boys,

but they will stand by the girls."[18]

Thomas Sweeney said, on the stand in court in July 1901, that he did not kiss Amelia Amind. If he did kiss her, he said, he was not looking and he could not remember having embraced the woman and then hugging her on a public street. The incident took place in Richmond Virginia and policeman Kelleher, however, said he was a witness to the kissing episode. It shocked the bluecoat to such an extent that he arrested both, on charges of disorderly conduct. In court the pair were convicted with Sweeney being fined $3 while Amind was fined $10. Sweeney was a 63-year-old laborer and said he was not averse to kissing members of the fair sex when they did not object. Amind was 38 and she did not deny that she appreciated a good kiss and she was not ashamed to kiss in public. She did not deny the accusation. Asked if he was opposed to kissing Officer Kelleher declared; "I am. I never was kissed except by my mother and sister."[19]

In June 1902 officials of the Pennsylvania Railroad Company issued orders instructing their representatives to prohibit kissing at the Chicago depots of the company. That prompted reporters to canvass other Chicago area railroads to assess their attitude to the situation. Said C. A. Goodnow, general manager of the Chicago Rock Island and Pacific Railroad; "No indeed, such an order is not likely to be issued in Chicago as there are no conditions here that would justify the prohibition of kissing. But the Jersey City station of the Pennsylvania handles enormous crowds of suburban passengers, and it may be that there have been complains from some passengers that they have been annoyed by effusive or too prolonger greetings and farewell." He added; "The order may justly apply there. Where it is necessary to load or unload trains within three or four minutes every measure must be adopted that will facilitate handling of passengers. The Rock Island has found no serious trouble from demonstrations of affection on the part of passengers." A. P. Morrison was assistant to the passenger traffic manager of the Atchison, Topeka and Santa Fe Railroad and he exclaimed; "What, cut off kissing? Not on your life! There isn't enough of it in the world, anyway. Passengers on our line can hug and kiss as much as they please; no one will ever stop them at the Dearborn street station. We have never found any trouble from that sort of thing and never expect to find any.[20]

The formal notice from the Pennsylvania Railroad Company was dated New York City, June 12, 1902 and was put out over the signature of P. Abercrombie, Superintendent of the Pennsylvania RR Company. It declared; "All trainmen, gatemen and ticket examiners in charge of the Jersey City exits will stop all persons from exchanging kisses upon the arrival and departure of trains in this station. This order must be rigidly enforced." Remarked an editor; "Was ever greater tyranny attempted? The American people have always been extremely hostile to anything approaching sumptuary laws, but no sumptuary law ever attempted anything so outrageous as this. Railroad men are commanded to prevent the mother from kissing her babe, the husband his wife, the sweet girl graduate her dearest girlfriend." The editor continued; "But if kissing can be prohibited by a railroad company, why may not handshaking and the 'good-bye' that must be said." He concluded; "The Pennsylvania railroad has invaded the constitutional rights of the American citizen. The Constitution guarantees to every citizen the right to life, liberty and the pursuit of happiness. If kissing is not life, liberty and the pursuit of happiness, what is?"[21]

About one month after that, near the end of July 1902, it was reported that the officials of the New York Central Railroad were going to make, and enforce, a rule against kissing in train sheds or stations or on car platforms. A newsman speculated that it would be interested to watch, when they began to enforce that rule. He added; "The objection to this time-honored expression of emotion is that it is a hindrance to traffic and takes too much time. Rich-throwing has been stopped, and it is thought that the prohibition of kissing will still further expedite matters." In conclusion he wrote; "No, kissing is not the only hindrance to traffic on railroads. Farewell conversations take a good deal more time than osculation…No, this blue-law business on railroads is not likely to make life pleasant for the railroad man."[22]

With respect to that proposed New York Central Railroad ban a journalist reported; "The Central officers are considering the advisability of issuing an order that all rice-throwing be prohibited in the train shed of their road, and now the ban on kissing is to be promulgated. The company, it is said, wants it understood that it does not care so much about kissing, but that it must be regulated. It may be done in the waiting rooms, in carriages and on the streets, but in the train shed and on car platforms, it declares, the custom is a nuisance and a hindrance to traffic." Remarked train depot gatekeeper Dennis O'Brien; "It has always been a nuisance. Bridal parties come in her just in time to catch the train. Then they stand around and kiss and giggle, until the like of it you never saw."[23]

One month after that, late in August 1902, there was said to remain a strong feeling against the New York Central's proposed new rules that it was still proposing to introduce. Those proposals still had had been promulgated but at a recent meeting of the officers of the railroad Chauncey Depew, president of the line, suggested that tunnel collisions and other matters might perhaps have been traced to these little amenities. A journalist noted that it was not known if he meant those remarks as a joke or if he meant them seriously. And, he added; "The way of the newly-wed and the too soon parted is to be made hard and spartanlike, relieved of either greenness, mellowness or mushiness. Padlocks are to be metaphorically put on lips and the old slipper and rice dealers will be robbed of their principle source of revenue." As to when those proposed measures might be introduced, the reporter observed that the officials of the line spoke "evasively" about the issue.[24]

Apparently, not much came from the rules proposed by the railroads. Early in August 1902 a single-sentence item declared: "The efforts of the railroads to forbid kissing at the depots have been unsuccessful." At the end of September an editorial cartoon appeared in a Boston newspaper lampooning what would happen if the New York Central implemented its proposal to ban kissing on various parts of its properties, which inferred that the proposals had still not been implemented.[25]

December 1, 1902, marked the start of one of the more well-publicized efforts to rein in kissing. On that date in Richmond Virginia, in the Virginia House of Delegates, Dr. R. B. Ware, a practicing physician, introduced a bill to make "promiscuous kissing" a misdemeanor in his state. His proposed bill read, in part, as follows; "Whereas, Kissing has been decided by the medical profession to be a medium by which contagious and infectious diseases are transmitted from one person to another, therefore be it enacted by the general assembly of Virginia that it shall be unlawful for any person to kiss unless he can prove by his family physician that he hasn't any contagious or infectious disease." Violators of the proposed law would be fined not less than $1 nor more than $5 for each offense.[26]

When a reporter summed up, on December 2, the session of the House of Delegates he stated that it had been brief and of little importance. A few bills were introduced, none of which were of much interest, "and one or two of them rather on the order of freak legislation, notably a bill of Mr. Ware's to prevent kissing. This is a measure designed to be serious and based on hygienic lines but which has been the subject of merriment and jest among the other members." That proposed bill read, in this account, as follows; "Whereas, kissing has been decided by the medical profession to be a medium by which contagious and infectious diseases are transmitted from one person to another; and whereas the prohibiting of such an offence will be a great preventive to the spreading of such diseases as pulmonary tuberculosis, diphtheria and many other dangerous diseases; Therefore, Be it enacted by the General Assembly of Virginia (1) that it shall be unlawful for any person to kiss another unless he can prove by his family physician that he has not an infectious or contagious disease. (2) If his physician testifies that the defendant has weak lungs, he shall be found guilty of a misdemeanor and the same penalty shall be imposed as if he had some infectious or contagious disease. (3) Any person violating the provisions if this act shall be deemed guilty of a misdemeanor and fined not less than one dollar nor more than five dollars for each offence." The bill was sent to the Committee on General Laws. Doctor Ware was from Amherst Virginia.[27]

The merriment over the bill extended state-wide. On December 4 a Richmond newspaper published snippets of editorial comments from around Virginia. An editor with a Norfolk newspaper wrote; "Why not offer a bill providing the James River shall flow uphill…Take something like that that is reasonably easy to accomplish. But this: Ah, Dr. Ware: We would advise you – have a care." A newsman from Fredericksburg stated: "The Legislature has before it a bill that will sleep the sleep of death. It is a proposition to fine people for kissing and its patron is Dr. Ware, of Amherst County. We only wish to say that wouldn't like to be-Ware." An editor on a Newport News paper declared" "He may get his bill passed, but some kissing will be un-a-Ware," while an editor on a different Newport News newspaper said; "At any rate, when Dr. Ware wants another job, we think we can promise him one. There will be a pace waiting for him among the exhibits in the freak department of the Jamestown Exposition."[28]

An editor with a Richmond Virginia newspaper remarked; "Mr. Johns S. Wise and Mr. Ware are getting more editorial space in our Virginia exchanges than any other two men. They are outshining President Roosevelt. Very wrathful sentences are aimed at the former, while the latter is laughed at good-humoredly, because of his proposition to enact a law regulating kissing." He continued; "From the newspaper matter printed we are surprised to know how much Virginia editors know about kissing. They have discussed it from every standpoint – scientific, educational, social, political, and financial."[29]

Editorial comment continued to fill newspaper across the state of Virginia and then across the United States. From the *Fredericksburg Star*; "That anti-kissing bill seems to be meeting with opposition everywhere. Even the Baltimore physicians declare that no Virginian lives who is able to stop kissing." From the *Norfolk Ledger*; "Out in Iowa a judge has decided that a farmer may kiss a neighbor's daughter provided he had been acquainted with her five years and she doesn't object – but in Virginia under the Ware law, even such a protracted and torturing probation as that wouldn't count, without a doctor's certificate." A poem was delivered by an editor on a Newport News paper; "Dear Dr. Ware, I do declare,/ You'd make me forego bliss;/ The lover fond will now despond/ At prospects of no kiss." From an editor with the *Boston Globe*; "The bill introduced in the Virginia House of Delegates to prohibit promiscuous kissing will hardly become a law. There are too many bachelors and married men, not to mention widowers among the members of the Legislature." From the *Florida Times-Union*; "The Virginia Legislature should, by a unanimous vote, defeat the Ware bill providing for certificated kissing. The measure is a reflection on the gallantry of Virginia and casts undeserved obloquy upon ever pair of lips in the Old Dominion. It should be killed by a majority so overwhelming that there shall hereafter be no manner of doubt as to how Virginia stands on such a soul-blasting proposition."[30]

An editorial cartoon appeared on December 7 that wondered who would ever testify if Ware's bill became law. Dr. R. B. Ware, who had already been the object of humorous attacks from editorial writers and essayists throughout Virginia and the rest of the United States, was then serving his second term in the Virginia House of Delegates from Amherst County. He was a member of the Board of Health of his county and a graduate of the Medical College of Virginia, at Richmond. He had also attended William and Mary College where he obtained his academic education. Commented a journalist; "From the nature of the measure, the impression has prevailed that Dr. Ware is a sedate old gentleman who, looking back upon the follies of youth with an eye and soul devoid of sentiment, has sought to put a legal curb in the mouths of the love-sick swains to prevent them from an over-indulgence in kissing. On the contrary he is a young man just 29 years of age, and is the father of five bright children." When a reporter asked Ware how the bill, if it became law, would be put into practical operation the physician replied; "I never expect it to become a law. I have asked the committee to indefinitely postpone its consideration. My purpose was to bring the attention of the public to the dangers of indiscriminate kissing and I thought that the plan of introducing a measure in the Virginia Legislature would be the best means to that end." Ware believed the custom of kissing was more prevalent in the country than in the cities. He said; "My attention to the dangers of promiscuous kissing was attracted by the fact that a young woman in advanced stages of consumption kissed one of my children without thinking of the serious consequences that might result from this evidence of affection and while I know that my bill cannot be made operative, I am sure that any agitation of the question through the press will direct the attention of the public to this evil, and make people afflicted with contagious diseases more careful about kissing others." Richmond City Coroner Taylor gave his opinion of the matter. He said he would favor Ware's bill provided it was amended to make it punishable by a fine of $10 for kissing the Bible used in the court of Police Justice John Crutchfield. "There's something for the microbe fiends to shoot at," said Taylor. "I understand they're making Bibles now with aluminum covers for swearing purposes, so they can be scoured. I think they ought to send that one at Crutchfield's court out to the crematorium and have it parboiled." Ware insisted he felt satisfied he had accomplished his mission of laying the matter before the public – attracting its attention – and he was then content to let the measure remained in the pigeonhole of the committee to which it had been referred. The Ware proposal spawned the following poem; "Whenever there's temptation / For sweetest osculation / With maiden meditation / Fancy Free. Please give consideration / To Virginia legislation / And there'll be some hesitation / Don't you see. For if you are dyspeptic / consumptive, epileptic / And haven't antiseptic / Near at hand. When you kiss your Evalina / Even in paying Philopena / Twill be a misdemeanor / In the land."[31]

When the *Chattanooga Times* brought up Ware's proposal the editor declared; "Of course the measure will not pass, but all the same the man ought to be shunted into the James River for proposing a thing the funny men and paragraphers will be writing about to the thorough disgust of the reading public for months to come."[32]

Later in December the editor of a Richmond Virginia newspaper observed; "The fame of Dr. Ware, such as it is, is still growing in extent. His now famous anti-kissing bill, offered some time ago in the Virginia Legislature, continued to be a fruitful subject for the paragraph writers all over the country. Some of the dignified journals are discussing the bill and ridiculing its author with really more seriousness than the subject calls for." One of those papers, he said, was the *New Orleans Picayune*. It reported on the bill and noted that it was the only bill Dr. Ware had ever introduced "except by request." That newspaper went on to editorialize; "This doctor belongs to that class of medical madmen who want to change the laws of nature and regulate the physical life of the human race according to their insane and arbitrary whims." He continued on by stating; "Fortunately, the number of these insane theorists is small and they will never be permitted to carry out their murderous designs any more than the anti-kissing man will be allowed to interfere with love-making in the Old Dominion." To end the piece the Richmond editor asserted; "The Doctor, with the assistance of the newspapers, has certainly advertised his theory as well as himself but we doubt if the theory or the advertising of the same had reduced the number of kisses in Virginia or anywhere else."[33]

Still later in December 1902, and as the result of the widespread discussion of the Ware anti-kissing bill in the Legislature, Virginia State Senator McIlwaine of Petersburg Virginia offered a bill prohibiting the kissing of the Bible in the administration of oaths before the courts. The author of the bill declared he had taken that stance "for sanitary reasons." His bill read; "Be it enacted by the General Assembly of Virginia, that the practice of kissing the Bible upon the administration of oaths in the courts of this Commonwealth and by all officers charged with the duty of administering oaths be and the same is prohibited. The sanctity of every oath presented by law is declared to be as great and the penalty of false swearing the same as if this act had not been passed."[34]

Near the end of January 1903 the Virginia Senate refused to pass McIlwane's Bible anti-kissing bill. After much discussion in the Senate it was defeated by a vote – in a Senate session – of 16 to 11. Senator Clayton wanted to offer an amendment requiring merely the placing of hands upon the Bible in administering the oaths. McIlwaine said he simply wanted "to stop the filthy practice of kissing the Bible." While there was then no law in Virginia that required anyone taking an oath to kiss the Bible many did not know that, and thought they had to kiss the Bible. McIlwaine had earlier read a newspaper clipping in which the writer recommended the abolishing of that custom.[35]

When the *Atlanta Constitution* offered its opinion on the Ware proposal the editor discussed the bill at length and said, among other things; "The presumption of the law stepping in to prevent two spirits rushing together in clinging, resounding osculation! Certified kissing, forsooth! Virginia chivalry has been dealt a scientific slap by the mere introduction of such a monstrous bill and if its author stands for re-election – well, we hope he will stand for re-election."[36]

In February 1903 the Ware bill was still getting media coverage even though it was effectively dead and buried in a forgotten pigeonhole in the Virginia Legislature. An editor with a Kentucky paper declared; "The West Virginia Legislature is trying to pass a law prohibiting the young people from kissing in public. Well, it would be a good law, and let 'em abolish it, for a kiss before a crowd is absurd, and is about on a par with cold soup."[37]

A Louisiana newspaper editor offered his thoughts on the Ware bill by stating, in April 1903; "We are very much opposed in this anti-kissing business. In this microbe age the extra smart say you get yellow fever and smallpox and quinsy and rheumatism from kissing a pretty woman. In thunder tones we denounce this as slander on women. There is no more danger in kissing a woman than in kissing the sunlight." He added; "And we simply say to the sisters, here stands a man who fears no diabolical microbe. Think of a legislature passing a law forbidding kissing! It would give us great pleasure not only to evade such a law, but to break it squarely in the middle and maul the legislators with the ravelled ends."[38]

Almost one year later, in January 1904 the Ware bill got its apparently last mention in print. It was reported at that time that Ware's proposal was not introduced as a joke "but in dead, serious earnest, and based his objection to promiscuous contacts of lips largely on the researches of Reynal Fere, the distinguished French scientist, who maintains that infectious diseases are transmitted from one human organism to another by this method of displaying affection almost in as great a proportion as typhoid is implanted by drinking of water or milk laden with the germs of that disease." The newsman declared that Fere approved of the law proposed by Ware and that that it should become a general law throughout the United States. Fere said kissing was unknown in New Zealand. Men and women in that country, he insisted, rubbed noses when they wished to show their feelings for each other.[39]

Minnesota State Senator Hiler Horton of St. Paul introduced a bill in January 1903 into his Legislature that would prohibit "promiscuous kissing" unless the kissers possessed physicians' certificates of good health. The bill also "gravely" declared that as any person having a weak heart was liable to suffer from severe shock such a person should be deprived of kissed. The penalty fixed by the bill for those convicted of violating it was a fine that ranged from $1 to $5. Violation of the bill was a misdemeanor. It stated that the certificate of a physician declaring a person to have a weak heart "shall constitute a bar to kissing."[40]

It was reported in early February 1903 that another legislature was seeking "fame by the anti-kiss bill route." The Honorable Barnes of the Tennessee general assembly went a step further by introducing a bill that absolutely prohibiting kissing by persons between the ages of 16 and 45 years of age in public or private, unless they were married – to each other. Violation of the proposed act meant a fine ranging from $5 to $50 and/or from one to 12 months' imprisonment. Commented a newspaper editor; "The reason for so drastic an enactment is not given but its introduction shows the love of notoriety even in small matters."[41]

Members, though, of the Tennessee Legislature took their revenge on Representative T. I. Barnes of the Tennessee House of Representatives. On February 10 he found himself, by law, prohibited from kissing in that state. A reporter observed; "For Mr. Barnes in a fit of originality and excessive humor perpetrated on the Tennessee Legislature a bill prohibiting kissing in this State. The legislators, knowing what a good thing it was, were not inclined to pass it." The bill slumbered alone until some legislative humorist suggested that if Barnes wanted to be "held, restrained, and prevented from the osculation aforesaid" then they ought to accommodate him. So they solemnly passed the bill proposed by Barnes with the proviso that it apply only to Representative Barnes, of Lauderdale. Reportedly, Barnes was then trying to get the Tennessee governor to veto that bill.[42]

Also early in February 1903, the North Carolina Senate passed a bill to do away with kissing the Bible in the administering of oaths in that State. The Judiciary Committee offered a substitute for Senator Godwin's bill to prohibit kissing the Bible. The substitute measure, instead of prohibiting kissing the Bible, simply abolished the necessity of kissing the book. Godwin had proposed his bill because of the fear of microbes on the Bible. The only thing stricken out of the existing bill from the code was "and he shall kiss the Holy Gospel." Most people then did not kiss the book, said Godwin, but ladies and children obeyed the judge when he said "Kiss the book." Mr. Hicks of Granville appealed to the Senate not to destroy that old tradition and that the courthouse kiss was not the kiss of affection and the witness was not expected to take half the book in his mouth. Hicks declared that in his county there was a "white supremacy" Bible, "the judge having ordered one Bible for colored people and one for white." Mr. Beasley of Munroe said he favored the tradition but he "wanted the landmarks clean." If a man really obeyed the judge, he said, he would have to violate the rule of personal cleanliness. He did not think it possible to keep a courthouse Bible clean.[43]

Still in early February 1903 there appeared a brief editorial remark with respect to yet another state that, however briefly, had gotten on the anti-kiss bandwagon. Said the newsman; "The member who introduced the anti-kissing bill in the Minnesota legislature is said to be so homely that his own dog barks at him when he sees him. The law, if made, would certainly work no hardship on him."[44]

Reportedly, in August 1903 from every boathouse on the Charles River in Boston, protests erupted against the recent anti-kissing rule imposed by the park police of Boston. A mass meeting to protest the decision was scheduled to be held at Frost's boathouse. Many canoe owners were said to be awaiting the result of the trial of Mr. Peterson and Miss Smith and of the agitation caused by their arrest. "It is earnestly hoped by the large majority of the canoe owners that the offensive rules will be withdrawn, or at least modified so as to be less stringent and not interfere with the rights claimed by the canoe owners," said a journalist. The conservative element among the canoe owners believe that their favorite pastime has received a severe blow through the arrest made by the park police, and one from which it will not readily recover. "These people claim that the notoriety caused by the Peterson-Smith case will cause many to shun the river who otherwise would frequent the Charles, and they look upon this arrest as placing a stigma upon the sport as conducted all along the picturesque banks of the river," noted the reporter. With respect to the other side of the argument the newsman remarked; "the park commissioners have received a number of letters since the arrest of the young couple praising the new rules and referring to the necessity of a sterner moral code among canoeists." The by then famous canoe kissing case continued to be a hot topic.[45]

Superintendent Habberly of the Boston Metropolitan Police was the man in charge of the park police. When a Boston newspaper reporter went to interview him he was reluctant to talk and refused to allow his photograph to be taken. He was described as being married and about 30 years old. Habberly supervised the seven park police "who are the guardians of the morals of the Charles." The journalist reported; "In vain I tried to coax from him some definition of a kiss proper and a kiss improper. He is sorry to have to refuse his photograph to a lady, but he wasn't at all sorry to decline to tell her whether he objected to kissing on general principles or only as inspired by the picturesque and romantic surroundings of a leafy shore, a shady spot, a dainty canoe and a charming girl on an ideal summer's day." He told the newswoman he could not discuss it and he declined to say how he felt about kissing generally.[46]

A few days after the initial report about kissing on the Charles was published another story emerged to relate that canoeing on the Charles River was doomed for the year as manifested by the sparse number of canoeists on the river, on August 21. Warren M. Ryan had been canoeing on the Charles River for 17 years and said; "The river is spoiled forever. Habberly has driven away the best people, and only hoodlums remain. Persons who lay out money on canoes and fittings do not come up her to indulge in disgraceful conduct." Reportedly there was a movement afoot then to remove Superintendent Habberly from his position. Besides the no kissing rule in the park it was also against park police rules for a couple to recline in a canoe (even if they did so separately in opposite ends of the canoe) and it was also a rule violation for a couple to stop their canoe at a riverbank, regardless of what they did when they were stopped.[47]

Later in 1903 a journalist remarked that there were a few foreign places where kissing was indeed a crime. He mentioned Cherson [Kherson] in Russia which had a local ordinance that provided that every man who was caught kissing a woman in a public thoroughfare was to be fined 15 rubles (about

$11.25). If the man was caught with his arm around his girlfriend a policeman took him before a judge who fined him $8.25. Kissing in public was also reported to be forbidden in Milan Italy where the man, if caught kissing his girlfriend in public, was fined six lire.[48]

At the end of October 1903 it was reported that Wisconsin's war against kissing had broken out in a new quarter. It had started in Janesville where the city council tried in vain to pass a measure making the janitors in public schools special officers to arrest any young people found kissing "so loud and so long on the school steps as to keep people residing in the neighborhood awake." Next, Waukesha began its attack on courting couples. First the faculty of Carroll College took action and made it an offense worthy of expulsion for a college student to be found "loving" a girl in the college grounds. In addition the city council had instructed officers to stop the use of high school and district school steps by courting couples. The Carroll College action was, reportedly, due to a report made by the police officers that there was too much kissing at that institution. Recently that same faculty had forbidden the playing of football.[49]

Henceforth from November 20, 1903, Zion City, Illinois, was to be kissless. The leader of that city "Elijah II" laid down that edict. One young man of that city had already been caught. A few evenings earlier the man had hosted a party during which he kissed somebody there who was a guest. That information was passed on to the authorities and the host of that party was forbidden to give any more parties.[50]

Councilman John. W. Q. M. Miller of Colonial Beach Virginia was vigorously waging a campaign, in November 1903, for the passage of a city ordinance prohibiting kissing and hugging in public. At the last meeting of the town council he introduced the following resolution; "Resolved, that every man or woman caught hugging or kissing another man or woman on the streets, shall be fined not less than $1 and not more than $5." That resolution was not looked upon with favor by fellow councilmen wrote a newsman, "and it was unceremoniously tabled without discussion."[51]

A ban on kissing was reportedly put in place in Atlantic City, New Jersey in September 1904. Signs were said to have been posted on the beaches. The reporter remarked that no such ban existed in New York on Coney Island; "Here they'll not send you up for life for kissing your own wife or, indeed, the girl to whom you've whispered foolish words of love. At Coney they encourage rather than disparage."[52]

Magistrate Whitman in McConnellsburg Pennsylvania was called upon in June 1907 to pass on the question as to whether or not kissing in public amounted to disorderly conduct. The court decided that it did not, if the girl was willing. James F. Higgins, a clerk by profession, was the victim of that test case. He was standing on the street in a doorway one evening with three girls, one of whom he was kissing and embracing when policeman Stapleton came along and told Higgins to "beat it." Higgins did not like the idea and refused, whereupon he was locked up on a charge of disorderly conduct. When Higgins was arraigned the Court asked what he had done. The policeman replied that he was found kissing a girl on the street. When Whitman asked if that was all, the reply from the officer was that was the only misbehavior. Declared Whitman; "I guess this young man was merely saying good night to his lady friend and I don't see anything wrong in that. I will discharge the defendant."[53]

Beginning in July 1907 a kiss at Coney Island, New York, would thereafter cost the perpetrator and the recipient $10 each or 10 days in jail. According to a journalist "it is part of the response to the general anti-kissing campaign then underway in America." Nineteen-year-old Rosalie Miller was with "her sweetheart" Benjamin Burg and when they were at Coney Island he kissed her. New York Police Department Detective Gleason caught them in the act and took the pair to the police station where they were charged with disorderly conduct and locked up. Then they were convicted in court and fined $10 each. The reporter commented, with respect to the kiss and the arrest and the charge by writing; "Local Dogberrys incited to action by the diatribes of the Western preacher on the melting inferno of welded lips, have decided that the erstwhile paradise for love-lorn youth and maidens shall take the lead in the reform. They have weighed and considered the kiss...and pronounced it disorderly conduct."

Dogberry was a character created by William Shakespeare for his play *Much Ado About Nothing*. That character was described as a "self-satisfied night constable" with an inflated view of his own importance as the leader of a group of comically bumbling police watchmen.[54]

According to a June 1909 report New York City then had an "official anti-kissing" campaign that was ongoing; "It's official, too – that is to say, it proceeds from and is being engineered and enforced by the municipal authorities." It was said that nobody knew just who inspired that campaign nor was it known who suggested it. Police Commissioner Theodore Bingham, New York's top cop, emphatically denied that the idea came from him. New York City Mayor George McClellan also denied that he was responsible. "Anyhow, the anti-kissing crusade is on. The cops are arresting couples caught kissing everywhere they find them; nor does it appear to make any difference whether the couple possess a legal license to osculate or not – that is to say, the mere fact that the publicly kissing couples happen to be duly married…" didn't let them off, explained the journalist.[55]

Kissing was under the ban in Atlanta Georgia, as of August 1909, or so it was reported; "It's unhealthy and embarrassing to those not taking part in the exercise. A few months ago they convicted and fined a traveling man who kissed his wife on the street as he arrived home from a trip." The journalist continued; "And now they have called out the police and the electric light company to put a stop to reckless osculation in the public parks. The electric light company is to erect lights every now and then in the parks so that the kissing squad may catch and arrest the awful violators of the law." And, it was also noted that; "People who live near the parks say that they are driven from their verandas every pleasant night by the wholesale love-making under their very noses. So the word has gone forth, 'no kissing goes.'"[56]

An article appeared in April 1910 that explained the kissing situation with respect to railway stations in France. A new prohibition was to be posted in the stations on the railroad lines managed by the French state. That notice declared, in white lettering on a blue background; "Kissing strictly forbidden." That prohibition was not then in effect and the notices still had to be posted but the inspectors of the state railways were behind the measure and had strongly recommended that it be adopted. It was planned to forbid kissing upon the platforms and in the waiting rooms and upon the steps of the carriages of the state railways. Purportedly it was a step to be taken in an attempt to reduce or eliminate the delays in travel that were said to happen frequently because of kissing.[57]

In Chicago osculation became forbidden at the marriage license office, as of August 1911. Lewis C. Legner had drawn the line on kissing in front of his window. A big sign bearing the works "No Kissing Here" appeared above his window one day in August. Explained the clerk; "Kissing and cooing is going to be stopped in front of this window. The great majority of prospective brides and bridegrooms are dignified and sedate. They seem to prefer to cherish their love in silence, and although I frequently notice an exchange of long glances as they are handed their clearance papers to matrimony there is no other manifestation." Legner added; "Some couple, however, seem to forget everything when their eyes fall on a license. I cannot explain it unless it is the power of suggestion. It is not uncommon for a man to kiss a girl as both look at their license." The marriage license clerk went on to comment' "I was walking through Lincoln park the other evening about sunset. Scattered through the park on almost every bench was a pair of cooing sweethearts. I caught several of them kissing, but they seemed to care little about it. Many of them, I know, will appear later at the marriage license window. Kissing has its place, but the public park, the bathing beach and the marriage license window are not the places for it." In conclusion Legner fumed; "Promiscuous kissing leads to the divorce court. I do not believe in sending people to prison for kissing, but I do believe in sounding a warning. That is why I decided to begin here and draw the line even on the betrothed."[58]

Spooning (kissing and cuddling) in the parks of the nation's capital received the official okay of Major Richard Sylvester, Superintendent of Police of Washington, D.C., in April 1912. A reporter asked the chief of police is there was any law prohibiting spooning in the parks of the city. Sylvester replied; "Well, that depends on what you mean by spooning. If you mean hugging and kissing then spooning is permissible. But it must not become too brazen. I should advise the lovers to seek the secrecy of the tree shadows and the unfrequented paths, for if they make their spooning too public it may be repulsive to some." Added Sylvester; "I do not believe that there is any one in the city who is opposed to lovers spooning in the parks, so long as they do not make a public spectacle of their loving. If the spooners go too far, it is within the province of the policeman, if he sees fit, to arrest the lovers on a charge of disorderly conduct."[59]

On June 18, 1912 it was announced that the Milwaukee Physicians' Association was going to prepare a bill for the next sitting of the Wisconsin Legislature that; "intended to stop the practice of kissing and stopping the habit as a blot on civilization and a menace to health and decency," wrote a reporter. That action was decided upon at a meeting held by the physicians on June 17 during which a dozen or more papers were read on the subject; "A substitute for the practice offered was that of rubbing noses or foreheads this being held more decent by the physicians."[60]

When a reporter on another newspaper looked at the Milwaukee physicians and their proposed action he declared; "The annual silly season agitation against the kiss is now on. Neither political conventions nor third-term candidates can obscure this news in the month of rose and moons – honeymoons." According to this account a dozen doctors read papers on the subject of kissing at that meeting wherein they decided a prepare   a bill for the next Wisconsin legislature to regulate the practice. As well, a series of lectures were being prepared to be delivered to the public to educate them in order to secure support for their proposed bill. Those doctors declared that promiscuous kissing had to stop. A reporter with a New York City newspaper took the clippings of the story to Dr. Eugenia Hancock, of New York City, for her comment. She said; "Of course it's perfect nonsense to suggest that rubbing noses or any other form of caress will ever take the place of the kiss between two people who really care for each other." Hancock added; "I do not believe in promiscuous kissing, but I don't see how it can be stopped by law…a blue law even more impossible of enforcement than the old New England one, which forbade a man to kiss his wife on Sunday. That was enacted in the name of religion, but some of our modern extremists attempt just as silly things in the name of health." Then the reporter asked Hancock if she was opposed to promiscuous kissing how she would check it if not by law. "By education in the dangers of the practice. It is perfectly true that death often lurks in a kiss, or at least serious disease. One of Queen Victoria's daughters insisted on kissing her little son on the lips when he was lying ill of diphtheria" she replied. She caught the disease and died. The ordinary cold or cough is readily transmitted in a kiss, which is doubtless one reason why these ailments seem to go in epidemics." Hancock went on to explain that blood diseases had often been transmitted by kissing; "Less serious but unpleasant and painful distempers affecting the gums and teeth are communicated in the same way. Nor is actual disease necessary to make kissing dangerous." She elaborated; "I know of a case in my own practice where a beautiful baby boy, only a few months old, visibly pined and dwindled under the constant kissing of his grandmother. She was not actually ill, but she was an old woman with a number of decayed teeth. The carbonic acid gas from her breath actually poisoned her grandson." When that grandmother returned to her home in the West her grandson immediately began to recover; "More and more mothers are making it a rule of the nursery that no visitor shall be allowed to kiss their children on the mouth. The little ones are taught to turn the cheek to affectionate callers." In Hancock's view; "It's such an excellent idea to bring up children to be sparing of the direct mouth-to-mouth caress. If this be done, and then if the girls and boys be taught the physical reasons for it, as they grow older, the result will be a finer reserve and dignity between our young men and women than exists at present." Hancock continued by stating; "The old sentimental ideal was that the girl should save her first kiss for the man she married. And it seems to me that's rather fine and not at all impossible." She concluded; "As for the 'society kiss,' exchanged at every meeting by women who scarcely know each other, that's utterly gushing and insincere and useless. It's cheapening the coinage again. The women themselves know it's just a form, that it means nothing in the way of sincere and deep affection, yet what other way have they left of greeting their real friends?"[61]

That proposal by the Milwaukee Physicians' Association to produce a bill for the Wisconsin Legislature to regulate kissing in some way provoked a number of editorials that pointed out how difficult such an undertaking would be and how impossible and silly it all was. One editorial cartoon published in a New York City paper showed nine very old, ancient men sitting around at a meeting of the Anti-Kissing Board.[62]

In August 1912 a ban on kissing on some of the riverboats cruising on the Potomac River in Washington, D.C. was announced. The rules that went into effect applied to the steamboats "St. Johns" and "Charles Macalester" and prohibited kissing, embracing, and the use of phrases such as "baby doll," "dearie," and "honey boy" on those vessels. In general, spooning of all kinds was banned. However, holding hands, as long as it was done on the upper deck, was still permitted. An official of a steamship line declared; "We don't mind a fellow holding his girl's hand just a bit, or he may even put his arms lightly around her, but we must now prohibit the rest, especially the soul-kissing." He added; "Some couples do not seem to care who is watching. I have seen as many as three and four couples within a few feet of each other, all of them caressing to beat the band and heedless of the presence of others." That official went on to state; "We must maintain certain standards of decorum, and if the free-for-all lovemaking continues it will be a question of time until our patronage would dwindle, and only the spooning couples would take the trips down the river." For many years those two steamboats had made nightly trips down the Potomac and, said a reporter, there had always been more or less spooning aboard and there had been no guard watching out for such behavior and nobody seemed to care. He admitted that no one seemed to know why the sudden change in attitude and the introduction of the new rules, finding himself puzzled over the matter. Concluded the journalist; "All that, however, is beside the issue." The rules are made, and watchmen now patrol the decks commanding innocent couple to 'break away.' The reverberant sound of a wholesome kiss sends the watchman scurrying to that part of the deck from which it emanates."[63]

Neenah Wisconsin Police Chief James Brown declared, on August 13, 1912, kissing and spooning around the railway depots had become too promiscuous and too frequent. Officers of his police force were instructed to stop all kissing at those railroad depots.[64]

Also in August 1912 the committee on elementary schools of the New Orleans School Board issued instructions to the superintendent of schools to warn teachers of the dangers that lurked in osculation and to advise them against practicing it in greeting their pupils. The action was taken, reportedly, after the consideration of a letter from the Louisiana Anti-Tuberculosis League, condemning kissing as a dangerous medium for the transmission of germs.[65]

A month later, in September 1912 an announcement was made that the Bavarian railways had placed a ban on kissing on its trains, platforms, and other premises of the company. The decree issued by the railways was reportedly due to the innocent behavior of a man and his wife who boarded a train after a cycling tour. The woman, who was fatigued, laid her head on her husband's shoulder and he placed his arm around her. The other passengers on the train car did not like that and summoned the conductor. They "accused the couple of kissing" and asked the conductor to make them behave themselves. The husband later complained to the authorities of the line about the action of the conductor in interfering with him. He denied the kissing charge but the officials apparently assumed he was guilty and issued the decree to prohibit kissing in the future.[66]

The Montgomery Alabama School Board put into effect on February 1, 1913, a rule prohibiting kissing among the pupils of the public schools. The ruling was said to have been an outcome of the anti-tuberculosis campaign then underway in the area.[67]

Early in May 1914, Miss Margaret Warner was arrested in Zion City, Illinois, under that city's anti-kissing law. She was alleged to have embraced Mr. Simons, a cashier in a Zion City bank. No outcome of the case was reported.[68]

Ruth Stonehouse, the Essanay Studios actress, declared in January 1915 in favor of the one-foot kiss in film scenes. The Board of Censors had recently put a ban on film kisses that lasted longer than three feel of film but Stonehouse went them one better and said that three feet was entirely too long for a kiss to last. Said Stonehouse; "It is sometimes necessary for actresses to kiss in portraying love-scenes. It is not a personal matter, but one of carrying out the activity of the play. The actress, in kissing, is not doing it as herself, but as the character she is representing. As she must be completely wrapped up in this character, the kiss is entirely impersonal." Stonehouse added; "I think that one foot if film is plenty for any kiss, as it is not the kiss in itself that is significant. That is merely the symbol for the emotion of love, and it is the emotion and not the act that the player wishes to express. If the actress understand the character and the art of expression, she can convey the idea of a love scene to the spectator without the prolonged kissing, upon which unskilled actresses sometimes rely to express emotion." Very roughly, a three-foot screen kiss lasted two seconds while the one-foot kiss elapsed in two-thirds of one second.[69]

In February 1915 it was reported that; "The mayor of Chicago has refused to forbid young men and women here from meeting in the public dance halls, and he has called down upon his head the denunciation of those who make a business of supervising the morals of the people, by refusing to put a ban on kissing."[70]

In Seattle Washington in November 13, 1915, county prison Superintendent Hally placed an official ban on the kissing of women prisoners by visitors. A few months earlier he served notice that no more kissing would be allowed in the visitors' lobby of the men's section following the discovery that illegal drugs in various forms were being transferred from visitors to prisoners by the lip-to-lip route. A similar discovery had just been made, he said, in the women's area, with the result the ban on kissing was extended to the female prisoners.[71]

A man had a right to spank his wife if she refused to kiss him. That was in substance, said a reporter, the opinion handed down on August 12, 1916 by Magistrate Steers in Brooklyn, New York, where Mrs. Charles Becker appeared to press a charge of assault against her husband. "I wanted to kiss her Judge," Becker told the court. "I wanted to love her and I threw an arm around her and told her so. She didn't like it and pushed my arm off. I again tried to be affectionate and she slapped my face." Becker added; "Then, Your Honor, I picked her up, placed her over my knee and spanked her" Judge Steers dismissed the charge against Becker.[72]

Joseph Littlefield of New York City was the varsity crew manager and coach at the Massachusetts Institute of Technology in Cambridge. In March 1917 he issued a new set of rules for his oarsmen. Kissing and hugging for one week before any of the season's races was forbidden to the crew men. The oarsmen complained about the edict but in vain. Their girlfriends were also talking mutiny but Littlefield was reported to be adamant in his position although he admitted the rule did not affect himself.[73]

Lake Elsinore California was said, in May 1918, of having the distinction of being the first Southern California city to adopt Riverside California's "famous anti-kissing ordinance." By a unanimous vote the trustees, On May 9, expressed themselves in favor of the law and it was to come up for its first reading on May 13. Reverend Robert J. Coyne, pastor of Grace Methodist Church of Lake Elsinore and Dr. Milbank Johnson of Los Angeles addressed the trustees and argued in favor of the passage of the anti-spooning measure.[74]

Long Beach California was another city in that state that attempted to make kissing in public a misdemeanor. It, in fact, enacted such an ordinance but on November 16, 1918, Superior Court Judge Frank A. Willis ruled that Long Beach had acted arbitrarily and in violation of the constitution. That decision was rendered in a case appealed from the police court in Long Beach by a man who was arrested for an alleged violation of what was known there as the "anti-kissing ordinance." Late in December 1918 the city of Long Beach lifted the ban it had placed on kissing in public. Heretofore it was a violation of a city ordinance and all the participants were subject to a fine, especially if the embrace was within public view. According to a reporter, who failed to mention that the measure had been declared unconstitutional; "The city commissioners adopted the anti-kissing ordinance as a war time measure and now that hostilities have ceased, repealed it."[75]

A news story published on May 4, 1919, noted that following the repeal of Riverside California's "famous" anti-kissing ordinance that prohibited men and women from kissing each other publicly,

Riverside Mayor Horace Porter issued an official city proclamation denying his administration was "too puritanical" and stating that he favored "legitimate lovemaking." While there was no lid on lovemaking in Riverside, as of May 3, the mayor, a former pastor, let it be known that a "frowning eye" would be cast upon people who sought to take advantage of the privilege and toy with the affections of "Riverside's fair daughters." That proclamation stated; "Love-making is a perfectly natural and normal phenomenon. I should certainly hate to see any city law which would interfere with legitimate love…I'm in favor of dancing if it is conducted in the proper manner."[76]

According to a January 2, 1920 account kissing in public was forbidden in Japan, it was also taboo in motion pictures. The police censors of Tokyo had, in the previous six months, removed 2,350 kisses from the films that had entered the country, according to a report from the *North China Daily News* of Shanghai. Said the report; "Curiously enough, the objectionable films mostly came from America, where some old laws against kissing still are in existence."[77]

In the community of Georgetown Texas, in September 1920, Mayor Sharpe was said to have caused to be passed what was termed "the most drastic anti-spooning ordinance in America." The community was a college town, home to Southwestern University. Supporters of the new measure declared; "Youth cannot study and spoon at the same time" while opponents said; "Youth can't study and not spoon." The latter was the opinion of not just students but also many others who did not like blue laws. Sharpe's ordinance read" "Be it ordained…that any man who shall by word, motion, wink, sign, action, or by any other means, encourage any woman to become acquainted with him, without then and there having been properly introduced previously, shall be guilty of flirting and upon conviction, thereof shall be fined not less than $50 nor more than $300. That any man or any woman, not then and there husband and wife, or not then and there engaged to be wed, or not then and there related to each other by blood within the third degree, who shall…be found kissing, holding hands or in any other manner fondling the other, shall be deemed guilty of love-making and each or either, upon conviction thereof, shall be fined in any sum not less than $50 and not more than $300." Added his comment was Sheriff

Tom Rogan who enthused; "And by crickey I'll enforce that there law to the letter."[78]

During that same mouth in Spain a severe reprimand and a warning not to let the misdemeanor occur

again was administered to a visitor to Madrid who, when he assisted his wife into a cab at the door of

his hotel kissed her good-bye. A policeman on duty nearly witnessed the event and remonstrated with

the man, threatening to take him to the police station. When the visitor dared him to take him to the

station the officer did just that. The police captain lectured the man and pointed out that he had

committed a serious offense against the laws of Madrid which forbid a man to kiss any women while in

the streets of the city, with or without her consent. However, the police captain let the visitor off with a

warning. A Spanish newspaper commented on the case by noting; "the worst kind of prostitution and

libertinage are permitted under the very noses of the police of Madrid without any effort to stop them,

but a respectable man may be dragged through the streets to a police station for kissing his wife."[79]

A very brief news item that appeared on February 14, 1922, announced that Chicago railroad officials

would abolish kissing at the railroad gates of that city.[80]

OFFICIAL KISS - CATCHERS WANTED FOR NEW JERSEY.

Husband and Wife Are Arrested for Saluting Each Other, but Are Discharged for Lack of Evidence.

IT COST THE LARGE SUM OF $10 EACH FOR KISSES AT RETAIL IN ENGLEWOOD.

Puncherbocker dressed for New Jersey.

The Englewood Anti-Kissing Mask.

These sketches from late in 1897 spoof the recent arrest of two set of people in highly publicized cases that involved the punishment of those doing the kissing.

In 1915 actor Ruth Stonehouse offered her thoughts on how long a kiss should last on the silver screen, in response to regulations imposed by a censor board. She favored a maximum length of two-thirds of a second, less than the length mandated by censors.

Notes.

Chapter 1.

1. "Kissing." *Boston Sunday Globe*, January 26, 1902.

2. "Laws against kissing." *Intelligencer* (Anderson, SC), September 30, 1915.

3. J. Armoy Know. "An essay on kissing." *Syracuse Herald*, October 11, 1891; No title. *Daily Comet* (Baton Rouge, LA), April 20, 1854.

4. "No public kissing allowed in Japan." *Washington Times*, September 9, 1920.

5. "Local intelligence." *Vermont Phoenix* (Brattleboro), February 18, 1860.

6. No title. *Bloomfield Times* (New Bloomfield, PA), October 14, 1873.

7. "Dismalisms." *Cincinnati Daily Press*, March 30, 1860.

8. "The friendship of women." *Wheeling Daily Intelligencer* (WV), May 31, 1866.

9. "Personal recollections." *Jackson Standard* (OH), June 30, 1870.

10. "Ledger lines." *Public Ledger* (Memphis, TN), May 9, 1876.

11. "Kissing in the street." *Elk County Advocate* (Ridgway, PA), June 4, 1869.

Chapter 2.

1. No title. *New Orleans Republican*, January 10, 1875.

2. "Don't kiss the baby." *Helena Weekly Herald* (MT), February 18, 1875.

3. No title. *Salt Lake Herald*, January 5, 1883.

4. "Don't kiss the babies." *St. Paul Globe*, February 5, 1884.

5. "The osculation problem." *St. Paul Globe*, March 1, 1885.

6. "The dangers of kissing." *Postville Review* (IA), September 25, 1886.

7. "Daily blob." *Abbeville Press and Banner* (SC), August 9, 1885.

8. "Dangers of kissing," *Butler Weekly Times* (PA), March 30, 1887.

9. "Decline of the kiss," *Gazette* (Fort Worth, TX), August 26, 1889.

10. "Gen. Sherman on kissing." *Boston Sunday Globe*, November 16, 1890.

11. "Kisses and microbes." *Burlington Evening Gazette* (IA), November 22, 1890.

12. "Hygiene for the home." *Seattle Post-Intelligencer*, June 25, 1891.

13. "Crusade against kissing." *Helena Independent* (MT), February 14, 1893.

14. "The extinction of the kiss." *Newberry Herald and News* (SC), February 15, 1893.

15. No title. *Greenfield Adair County Democrat* (IA), February 23, 1893.

16. "Unregulated kissing." *Boston Globe*, March 21, 1893.

17. "No more kissing." *San Francisco Call*, November 29, 1893.

18. "Destroying bacteria by labial explosions." *Austin Weekly Statesman* (TX), November 30, 1893.

19. No title. *Evening Bulletin* (Maysville, KY), July 18, 1894.

20. "The ubiquitous microbe." *Scranton Tribune* (PA), September 7, 1894.

21. "Departures in social usage." *Virginia Enterprise* (MN), October 5, 1894.

22. "In babyland." *San Francisco Call*, March 10, 1895.

23. "The carbolized kiss." *Wichita Eagle*." August 13, 1895.

24. "Kissing hygienically unhealthy." *Canton Times* (MS), September 27, 1895.

25. "That bacillus in a kiss." *Indianapolis Sun*, November 4, 1896.

26. "How cruel." *Cedar Rapids Evening Gazette* (IA), November 10, 1896.

27. "Disinfected kisses." *Evening Star* (Washington), November 14, 1896.

28. "Kissing not unfashionable." *Yakima Herald* (WA), November 26, 1896.

29. "Did not give up kissing." *Des Moines News* (IA), September 3, 1987.

30. "The dangers of kissing." *Progressive Farmer* (Winston, NC), October 26, 1897.

31. "New York Stricken." *St. Paul Globe*, December 23, 1898.

32. "It smacks of opposition." *Anaconda Standard* (MT), September 26, 1899.

33. Leon Noel. "Medical notes." *St. Paul Globe*, December 2, 1900.

34. Ibid.

35. "Danger of kissing the sick." *Arizona Republican* (Phoenix), January 17, 1901.

36. "Death in his kiss." *Minneapolis Journal*, April 2, 1901.

37. "Comments of the press." *Dubuque Telegraph Herald* (IA), October 26, 1902.

38. "Bryan paragraphs." *Crittenden Press* (Marion KY), November 6, 1902; No title. *Washington Standard (Olympia, WA), November 7, 1902.*

39. "Kissing is still safe." *Seattle Star*, November 8, 1902.

40. "Those wicked microbes again." *Indianapolis Journal*, December 7, 1902.

41. "Is handshaking dangerous?" *Salt Lake Herald*, December 23, 1902.

42. "The art of throwing kisses." *Sun* (NY), September 27, 1903.

43. "Danger in shaking hands." *State Center Enterprise* (IA), January 21, 1904.

44. "Says thou shalt not kiss." *Minneapolis Journal*, January 22, 1904.

45. Nixola Greeley-Smith. "Take your kisses boiled." *Evening World* (NY), January 25, 1904.

46. "Ban on kissing." *Janesville Gazette* (WI), May 12, 1904; "Board of Health to denounce kissing." *Racine Journal* (WI), May 12, 1904.

47. "No germs, he says, in kisses." *Boston Post*, June 10, 1904.

48. "In 1954." *Camden Chronicle* (TN), June 10, 1904.

49. "Discovers a new peril in kissing." *St. Louis Republic*, October 23, 1904.

50. "Kisses and the law." *Spokane Press*, May 16, 1905.

51. "What will the poor girl do?" *Los Angeles Herald*, May 17, 1905.

52. "New ban on kisses." *Clinch Valley News* (Jeffersonville, VA), November 10, 1905.

53. "Heartless scientists." *Barbour County Index* (Medicine Lodge, KS), December 20, 1905.

54. "Robbing school of charm." *Elkhart Daily Review* (IN), August 9, 1906.

55. "Kissing in school tabooed by Indiana Board of Health action." *Rock Island Argus* (IL), August 10, 1906.

56. "War on kissing." *Bedford Democrat* (IN), August 17, 1906.

57. "Feels European ridicule." *New York Tribune*, August 27, 1906.

58. "No kisses worries Hoosiers." *Des Moines Daily News* (IA), August 28, 1906.

59. "The non-osculant Hoosier." *Arizona Republican* (Phoenix), September 11, 1906.

60. No title. *Goodwin's Weekly* (Salt Lake City), September 29, 1906.

61. "A ban on kissing." *Plymouth Tribune* (IN), October 25 1906.

62. "Condemns kissing of invalids." *San Francisco Call*, October 19, 1906.

63. "Ban on kissing games." *Washington Herald*, November 11, 1906.

64. "Chasing the kissing bug out of Malden." Boston Sunday Post, November 18, 1906.

65. "Mesa." *Arizona Republican* (Phoenix), January 29, 1907.

66. "Peril lurks in kisses." *Los Angeles Herald*, March 14, 1907.

67. Ibid.

68. "Cupid wins and doctors put no ban on kissing." *Evening World* (NY), June 7, 1907.

69. "Don't kiss the babies." *Norfolk Weekly News-Journal* (NE), June 7, 1907.

70. "The habit of kissing." *Montour American* (Danville, PA), June 13, 1907.

71. "Awful germs lurk in schoolboy kiss." *Washington Times*, July 4, 1907.

72. "Ban on kissing games." *Norfolk Weekly News-Journal* (NE), July 5, 1907.

73. "Beware the kiss of death." *Boston Sunday Post*, July 7, 1907.

74. "Don't kiss the baby or he will be sick." *Albuquerque Evening Citizen*, July 23, 1907.

75. Ibid.

76. "Anti-kissing female is headed for Zion." *Salt Lake Tribune*, July 26, 1907.

77. "The kiss that kills." *Clifton Record* (TX), January 3, 1908.

78. "Kissing games." *Ogden Standard* (UT), May 22, 1908.

79. "Anti-kissing crusade advocated by physicians." *Plymouth Tribune* (IN), June 11, 1908.

80. "The microbe's safe graft." *Spokane Press*, November 9, 1908.

81. "On kissing." *Staunton Spectator and Vindicator* (VA), November 27, 1908.

82. "A ban on kissing." *Bode Bugle* (IA), May 28, 1909.

83. "Seattle man believes in no kissing." *Spokane Press*, August 27, 1909.

84. "Who's afraid." *Washington Standard* (Olympia, WA), January 14, 1910.

85. Lue F. Vernon. "Iowa against kissing." *Washington Standard* (Olympia, WA), August 12, 1910.

86. "Don't kiss me warning." *Bennington Evening Banner* (VT), November 20, 1909.

87. Ad. *San Francisco Call*, November 25, 1909.

88. "School board puts a ban on kissing." *Seattle Star*, November 27, 1909.

89. "Will it ever be stopped." *Herald and News* (Newberry, SC), May 13, 1910.

90. "The risk of kissing." *Boston Post*, July 12, 1910.

91. "Advises wife to make her husband fumigate beard for each kiss." *Seattle Star*, October 26, 1910.

92. "Is kissing healthful? Should it be abolished?" *Judith Gap Journal* (MT), April 14, 1911.

93. "State board adopts unique anti-kissing poster." *Indianapolis Star*, May 28, 1911.

94. "Wants barbers to study medicine." *Boston Post*, March 18, 1912.

95. "How to keep baby cool in the summer." *Tacoma Times*, July 17, 1912.

96. "If you must kiss, be sure and boil 'em." *El Paso Herald*, November 30, 1912.

97. "Blocks ban on kissing." *Chickasha Daily Express* (OK), August 26, 1913.

98. "Grip causes ban on kissing." *Sun* (NY), December 21, 1915.

99. "Warns against kissing evil," *Washington Herald*, December 22, 1915.

100. "Grip germs entrenched throughout Middle West." *Daily Gate City* (Keokuk, IA), December 23, 1915.

101. "Naughty mistletoe." *Canton News* (OH), December 29, 1915.

102. "A kissless city in New Jersey." *Day Book* (Chicago), December 30, 1915.

103. "No more kissing girls." *Day Book* (Chicago), December 30, 1915.

104. "Kissing will not be under ban in El Paso." *El Paso Herald*, January 8, 1916.

105. "Mayor Young will not issue proclamation against kissing." *Arizona Republican* (Phoenix),

January 16, 1916.

106. "Germs in kisses? Forget 'em says this Boston physician." *Boston Sunday Post*, May 14, 1916.

107. "State board of health places ban on kissing." *Bridgeport Evening Farmer* (CT), July 27, 1916.

108. "Ban on kissing to stop sore throat epidemic." *Topeka State Journal* (KS), March 13, 1917.

109. "Better babies is Tacoma's slogan." *Tacoma Times* (WA), May 1, 1917.

110. "Health board puts ban on kissing." *Challis Messenger* (ID), September 25, 1918.

111. "Ban on kissing." *Oakland City Journal* (CA), January 23, 1920.

112. "Would ban baby kisses as breeders of disease." *Washington Times*, October 14, 1920.

113. "Beware the cold kiss." *Evening World* (NY), June 9, 1921.

114. "Blame blisters on kissing." *Logan Republican* (UT), September 29, 1921.

Chapter 3.

1. "The kiss hygienic: guaranteed innocuous." *New York Tribune*, September 12, 1909.

2. "The kiss hygienic." *Colfax Gazette* (WA), December 17, 1909.

3. "Kiss through silk gauze." *Virginia Enterprise* (MN), April 22, 1910.

4. "Kissing is now perfectly safe." *Ogden Standard* (UT), April 30, 1910.

5. "Antiseptic kissing introduced by Professor Harry Butler." *New York Tribune*, May 15, 1910.

6. Ibid.

7. Ibid.

8. Ibid.

9. "Here we have something to kill germs and make kissing safe." *Muskogee Times Democrat* (OK), February 16, 1912.

10. "Class opposed to sanitary kiss." *Washington Times*, May 25, 1912.

11. "The sanitary kiss." *Pioneer Express* (Pembina, ND), October 30, 1914.

12. "The sanitary kiss." *East Liverpool Evening Review* (OH), March 10, 1915.

13. "No more kisses, little girls, pat-pat in proper thing." *Reno Evening Gazette*, July 24, 1915.

14. "Ah ha! Now it is the pat-pat that will succeed the old time kiss." *Plymouth Times* (OH), September 3, 1915.

15. "Truth will out, doctor." *Altoona Mirror* (PA), September 18, 1915.

16. "Sanitary kiss rule is much modified." *New Castle News* (PA), December 22, 1919.

17. "New Castle old-fashioned when it comes to adopting the latest sanitary kiss." *New Castle News* (PA), February 6, 1919.

Chapter 4.

1. "The kissing question." *Eaton Democrat* (OH), May 26, 1881.

2. "The whispering gallery." *Wheeling Intelligencer* (WV), June 6, 1885.

3. "Kissing is doomed." *Democratic Press* (Ravenna, OH), January 7, 1886.

4. No title. *Hazel Green Herald* (KY), February 10, 1886.

5. No title. *Kern County Californian* (Bakersfield, CA), September 21, 1889.

6. "All about kisses." *St. Paul Globe*, November 3, 1889.

7. "Anti-kissing societies for women." *Lock Haven Express* (PA), November 26, 1889.

8. J. Armoy Knox. "An essay on kissing." *Syracuse Herald*, October 11, 1891.

9. "Personal and pertinent." *New York World*, February 23, 1893.

10. "Society's fads." *Marshall County Independent* (Plymouth, IN), May 3, 1895.

11. "Concerning stage kisses." *Evening Star* (Washington), December 19, 1882.

12. No title. Burlington Hawk Eye (IA), April 11, 1889.

13. No title. *Daily Morning Astorian* (Astoria, OR), June 13, 1889; No title. *Keowee Courier* (Pickens, SC), July 11, 1889.

14. "A war over kissing games." *Evening Star* (Washington), January 20, 1890.

15. "Two men get on board." *Pittsburgh Dispatch*, February 20, 1890; "For the babies' sake." *Pittsburgh Dispatch*, June 6, 1890.

16. "Enough of kissing." *Evening Star* (Washington), September 13, 1890.

17. "Of kisses and kissing." *New York Tribune*, June 17, 1891.

18. "Against kissing picnics." *Washington Standard* (Olympia, WA), July 17, 1891.

19. "Osculations." *Fort Wayne News* (IN), December 1, 1894.

20. No title. *Juniata Sentinel and Republican* (Mifflintown, PA), June 30, 1897.

21. "Says kissing isn't nice." *Boston Post*, March 6, 1899.

22. No title. *Breckinridge News* (Cloverport, KY), March 15, 1899.

23. "Miss Lindley on kissing." *Sun* (NY), May 9, 1899.

24. "Kissing forbidden." *Indianapolis Journal*, November 20, 1899.

25. "How, whom, when to kiss." *Comet* (Johnson City, TN), November 8, 1900.

26. "Priest puts ban on kissing parties." *New York World*, December 11, 1900.

27. "War on kissing declared." *Logansport Reporter* (IN), December 28, 1900.

28. Lavinia Hart. "If you kiss, use an antiseptic daily." *New York World*, December 28, 1900.

29. Ibid.

30. "They refuse to swear off." *Minneapolis Journal*, January 1, 1901.

31. "How about this girls?" *Anaconda Standard* (MT), January 1, 1901.

32. No title. *Williamsport Warren Republican* (IN), January 3, 1901.

33. "Aldermen in danger." *Kalispell Bee* (MT), January 8, 1901.

34. "Anti-kissing crusade." *Watchman and Southron* (Sumter, SC), January 9, 1901.

35. "No time for such nonsense." *Minneapolis Journal*, January 15, 1901.

36. "A question of privilege." *Guthrie Daily Leader* (OK), January 11, 1901.

37. "Kissing." *Columbia Herald* (TN), February 15, 1901.

38. "Morbid fear." *Indianapolis Journal*, February 24, 1901.

39. "He has never kissed a woman." *Minneapolis Journal*, April 25, 1901.

40. "Women wild to wed man who never kissed one of them." *St. Louis Republic*, April 28, 1901.

41. No title. *Boston Globe*, April 30, 1901.

42. "Women might have kissed Prof. Crook." *St. Louis Republic*, April 28, 1901.

43. "Crook not a wonder." *Jamestown Weekly Alert* (ND), May 23, 1901; "Crook, the unkissed."

    Pascagoula Democrat-Star, (MS), May 24, 1901.

44. "Kissing and non-kissing families." *Virginia Enterprise* (MN), August 23, 1901.

45. Byron Williams. "Philosophical observations." *Jennings Daily Record* (LA), December 12, 1902.

46. "Teachers dislike kissing." *Guthrie Daily Leader* (OK), September 16, 1904.

47. "Must never kiss in public." *Deseret Evening News* (Salt Lake), October 13, 1906.

48. Ibid.

49. Susan W. Ball. "Womans world." *Terre Haute Saturday Spectator* (IN), October 20, 1906.

50. "The spice." *Manning Times* (SC), April 24, 1907.

51. "Lovers' kisses sacred and natural impulse, says woman physician." *Washington Times*, July 19,

    1907.

52. "Kissing devil." *Manning Times* (SC), July 24, 1907.

53. "Kisses and cash to doom the nation." *Bisbee Review* (AZ), July 31, 1907.

54. "Wants anti-kiss law." *Evening Bulletin* (Honolulu), August 10, 1907.

55. "Would abolish kissing." *New York Tribune*, February 1, 1909.

56. "Quit your kissing." *Rock Island Argus* (IL), February 18, 1909.

57. "Women laugh at minister's war against kissing." *Evening World* (NY), February 23, 1909.

58. "Chat about women." *Omaha Daily Bee*, January 30, 1910.

59. "Praise work of societies." *Syracuse Post*, March 9, 1910.

60. Nixola Greeley-Smith. "Anti-kissing crusade all nonsense." *Evening World* (NY), November 10,

    1911.

61. "Dr. Wiley favors kissing." *Virginia Enterprise* (MN), August 2, 1912.

62. "Pray for husband." *Syracuse Herald*, September 2, 1912.

63. "Queen Ena inaugurates anti-kissing crusade." *Washington Times*, March 27, 1914.

64. No title. *Hopkinsville Kentuckian*, August 12, 1915.

65. "Kissing in public places." *Biloxi Daily Herald* (MS), August 30, 1915.

66. "Columbia girls approve kissing." *Bridgeport Evening Farmer* (CT), March 30, 1916.

67. Nixola Greeley-Smith. "If Princeton were only nearer New York." *Evening World* (NY), April 1, 1916.

68. Betty Brown. "Is it wrong to kiss in the park?" *Arizona Republican* (Phoenix), June 11, 1919.

69. "Kissing." *Rock Island Argus* (IL), April 3, 1920.

70. "Law enforcement." *Topeka State Journal* (KS), November 15, 1920.

71. Frederick J. Haskin. "The Haskin letter." *Great Falls Tribune* (MT), March 22, 1921.

72. "Too much kissing lowers morals is warning of woman." *Comanche Chief* (TX), January 6, 1922.

73. "Should mates kiss in public?" *Tulsa World*, February 26, 1922.

Chapter 5.

1. No title. *Edgefield Advertiser* (SC), March 2, 1871; No title. *Daily Phoenix* (Columbia, SC), September 9, 1871; No title. *Greenville Advance* (PA), September 30, 1871.

2. "Local paragraphs." *Pascagoula Democratic-Star* (MS), January 23, 1880.

3. "War on kissing brides." *Postville National Advocate* (IA), December 25, 1884.

4. No title. *Atchison Globe* (KS), April 6, 1889.

5. "The kiss has come to stay." *Fort Wayne Gazette* (IN), April 30, 1890; No title. *Brennan Weekly Banner (TX), May 8, 1890.*

6. "Anti-kissing club." *Burlington Gazette* (IA), December 12, 1894.

7. "Kiss all you want to." *Wichita Daily Eagle*, December 14, 1894.

8. No title. *Freeland Tribune* (PA), February 11, 1895.

9. "Anti-kissing." *St. Paul Globe*, May 10, 1895.

10. Ibid.

11. No title. *North Platte Tribune* (NE), December 26, 1894; No title. *Coconino Weekly Sun* (Flagstaff,

AZ), January 3, 1895.

12. No title. Butler Citizen (PA), February 21, 1895; "Some queer clubs." *Kansas City Journal* (MO), April 20, 1895.

13. No title. *Weekly Register* (Point Pleasant, WV), October 13, 1897; No title. *Middleburgh Post* (PA), October 21, 1897; No title. *St. Paul Globe*, October 29, 1897.

14. "Form an anti-kissing club." *St. Paul Globe*, February 13, 1898.

15. "Defends anti-kissing crusade." *Somerset Herald* (PA), February 16, 1898.

16. "She makes war on kissing." *Dubuque Herald* (IA), February 20, 1898.

17. "They object to kissing." *Greensburg Review* (IN), August 9 1899.

18. "Kissing microbe feared." *Davenport Daily Republican* (IA), March 17, 1901.

19. "Men agree not to kiss their wives." *Janesville Gazette* (WI), June 1, 1901; "Anti-kissing club." *Indianapolis Journal*, June 2, 1901.

20. "Anti-kissing society." *Shelbyville Republican* (IN), June 11, 1901.

21. No title. *Richmond Dispatch* (VA), June 11, 1901.

22. "Shun kissing." *Independent* (Honolulu), August 6, 1901.

23. No title. *Cook County Herald* (Grand Marais, MN), August 31, 1901.

24. "In society." *Fort Wayne Journal Gazette* (IN), January 2, 1902.

25. "Crusade against kissing." *St. Paul Globe*, July 14, 1902.

26. "Anti-kissing club." *Stark County Democrat* (Canton, OH), July 15, 1902.

27. "Evanston, Ill., young people start a new order, the kiss shunners." *Boston Post*, July 16, 1902.

28. "They will not osculate." *Arizona Weekly Journal-Miner* (Prescott), July 23, 1902.

29. "United order of kiss shunners is no more." *St. Paul Globe*, July 23, 1902.

30. No title. *Cook County Herald* (Grand Marais, MN), September 27, 1902.

31. "Anti-kissers break vows." *Bismarck Tribune* (ND), June 17, 1903.

32. "Got engaged and broke up the anti-kissing society." *Seattle Star*, July 2, 1903.

33. "They shun kissing." *Butler Weekly Times* (MO), January 15, 1903.

34. "Husbands weary and bachelors wary decree against the kiss." *San Francisco Call*, April 5, 1903.

35. "Is kissing harmful?" *Kokomo Tribune* (IN), December 23, 1903.

36. Ibid.

37. "Anti-osculation society." *Jamestown Weekly Alert* (ND), December 24, 1903.

38. "Young man founded an antikissing society." *Tacoma Times* (WA), February 1, 1904.

39. "Unnecessary precautions." *Kinsley Graphic* (Kansas), March 4, 1904.

40. No title. *Alexandria Gazette* (VA), September 19, 1904.

41. "Anti-kissing club." *San Francisco Call*, October 9, 1904.

42. "Girls form anti-kissing club." *Salt Lake Tribune*, October 3, 1904.

43. "Women agree not to kiss." *Evening Star* (DC), December 12, 1904.

44. No title. *Elyria Reporter* (OH), February 20, 1906.

45. "Anti-kissing club is formed by girls." *Minneapolis Journal*, March 4, 1906.

46. "Anti-kissers." *Defiance Express* (OH), March 6, 1906.

47. "Kisses full of germs." *Columbian* (Bloomsburg, PA), February 13, 1908.

48. "Anti-kissing club." *News* (Frederick, VA), May 8, 1908.

49. No title. *Albert Lea Evening Tribune* (MN), May 23, 1910.

50. "New club starts with 'kiss not' as a war cry." *Spokane Press* (WA), May 26, 1910.

51. "Begins crusade against kissing." *Los Angeles Herald*, May 30, 1910.

52. "Pledge cards for anti-kissing league." *New Ulm Review* (MN), June 8, 1910; "Every town has its anti-kiss enthusiast." *Monett Times* (MO), June 10, 1910.

53. "Says she'll never rest until kissing is no more." *Evening Star* (Washington), June 19, 1910.

54. "Illness and bliss both lie in kiss." *Indianapolis Sun*, June 22, 1910.

55. "A non-kissing organization." *Evening Star* (Washington), July 31, 1910.

56. "To kiss or not to kiss." *San Francisco Call*, July 31, 1910.

57. "Wiley is very wise." *Ocala Evening Star* (FL), July 5, 1910.

58. Mary Gwynn Whiteman. "Social." *Daily Ardmoreite* (Ardmore, OK), July 7, 1910.

59. "Wages war on kissing." *Portsmouth Times* (OH), February 25, 1911.

60. "Needs no button." *Princeton Union* (MN), March 16, 1911.

61. "Ban on kissing." *Plymouth Tribune* (IN), November 10, 1910.

62. "Dentist in war against kissing." *Indianapolis Star*, July 6, 1912.

63. "Miss Baldwin is a charter member of non-kissing club." *Escanaba Press* (MI), March 11, 1919.

64. "Young women form anti-kissing society." *Hanover Evening Sun* (PA), January 27, 1920.

Chapter 6.

1. No title. Omaha Daily Bee, May 16, 1887; "Special mention." Livingstone Enterprise (MT), June 25, 1887; "Ban on park kissing lifted." Carbondale Free Press (IL), September 29, 1909.

2. No title. *Alton Telegraph* (PA), July 3, 1893.

3. "No kissing in the park." *Indianapolis Journal*, July 15, 1890.

4. "Stolen sweets beware." *Boston Globe*, May 24, 1893.

5. "Ancient laws." *San Francisco Call*, June 18, 1894.

6. No title. *Columbian* (Bloomsburg, PA), January 18, 1895; "People and things." *Omaha Daily Bee*, February 27, 1895.

7. "The carbolized kiss." *Wichita Eagle*, August 13, 1895.

8. "Forbids kissing." *Boston Post*, December 24, 1897.

9. "Crusade against kissing." *Kansas City Journal* (MO), December 25, 1897.

10. "Official kiss catchers wanted for New Jersey." *New York World*, December 30, 1897.

11. "She was fined for kissing." *Evening Times* (Washington), December 29, 1897.

12. Ibid.

13. "Kissing laws in New Jersey." *New York World*, January 2, 1898.

14. Ibid.

15. "Nancy Leg on freaks and the day's doings." *Seattle Post-Intelligencer*, August 27, 1899; "The

dangers and damages of kissing." *Wichita Eagle*, March 5, 1899.

16. "For kissing in public." *Indianapolis Journal*, October 26, 1899.

17. "High-priced osculation." *Evening Times* (Washington), November 10, 1899.

18. "Law against kissing." *Indianapolis Sun*, December 20, 1900.

19. "Find kissing costly." *Richmond Planet* (VA), July 20, 1901.

20. "That kissing business." *Albuquerque Citizen*, June 20, 1902.

21. "The tyranny of the P.R.R. Co." *Deseret Evening News* (Salt Lake), June 17, 1902.

22. "A rule against kissing." *Evening Times* (Washington), July 25, 1902.

23. "Stop kissing." *Boston Globe*, July 24, 1902.

24. "Proposes kissing ban." *St. Paul Globe*, August 24, 1902.

25. "The ballad of the rail." *Goodwin's Weekly* (Salt Lake), August 2, 1902; "If railroad managers are

to prohibit kissing at train gates." *Boston Sunday Post*, September 28, 1902.

26. "Asks law against kissing." *Cedar Rapids Evening Gazette* (IA), December 2, 1902.

27. "Anti-kissing bill." *Richmond Dispatch* (VA), December 2, 1902.

28. "Dr. Ware's anti-kissing bill." *Times* (Richmond, VA), December 4, 1902.

29. "Ware and wise." *Richmond Dispatch* (VA), December 4, 1902.

30. "Dr. Ware's anti-kissing bill." *Times* (Richmond, VA), December 5, 1902.

31. "Who would testify." *Richmond Dispatch* (VA), December 7, 1902; "Anti-kissing bill." *Richmond

Dispatch* (VA), December 7, 1902.

32. "Dr. Ware's anti-kissing bill." *Times* (Richmond, VA), December 9, 1902.

33. "Dr. Ware is famous." *Times* (Richmond, VA), December 10, 1902.

34. "No more kissing of the Bible." *Lexington Gazette* (KY), December 24, 1902.

35. "Barksdale bill is recommended." *Times* (Richmond, VA), January 23, 1903.

36. "Dr. Ware gets no rest." *Times* (Richmond, VA), December 25, 1902.

37. "Kissing before public." *Hopkinsville Kentuckian*, February 20, 1903.

38. "Anti-kissing law." *Southern Sentinel* (Winnfield LA), April 24, 1903.

39. No title. *St. Paul Globe*, January 21, 1904.

40. "Minnesota law aims to regulate kissing." *Washington Times*, January 30, 1903; "To enforce a germless kiss." *Butler Weekly Times* (MO), February 5, 1903.

41. No title. *Semi-Weekly Journal* (Stanford, KY), February 6, 1903.

42. "Forbidden to kiss." *Newberry Herald and News* (SC), February 13, 1903.

43. "Witnesses need no longer kiss Bible." *Washington Times*, February 7, 1903.

44. No title. *Rock Island Argus* (IL), February 11, 1903.

45. "Canoeists meet to protest against anti-kissing rules tonight." *Boston Post*, August 19, 1903.

46. "Wouldn't talk on kisses." *Boston Post*, August 19, 1903.

47. "Charles River deserted except by children and elderly women." *Boston Post*, August 22, 1903.

48. "Where kissing is a crime." *Monroe City Democrat* (MO), October 8, 1903.

49. "Now Waukesha joins in." *Minneapolis Journal*, October 30, 1903.

50. "Zion City will be kissless henceforth." *St. Paul Globe*, November 21, 1903.

51. "Declared war on kissing." *Free Lance* (Fredericksburg, VA), November 24, 1903.

52. "No ban on kissing at old Coney Island." *Sandusky Star* (OH), September 5, 1904.

53. "Kissing in public not a crime." *Fulton County News* (McConnellsburg, PA), June 20, 1907.

54. "Kiss at Coney? No, say police; it's disorderly." *Washington Times*, July 20, 1907.

55. Clarence Cullen. "Anti-osculation crusade is originated in New York by police." *Evening Star* (Washington), June 19, 1909.

56. "Atlanta leads in reform." *Bamberg Herald* (SC), August 26, 1909.

57. "A ban on kissing." *New York Tribune*, April 17, 1910.

58. "Kissing as a peril." *Baxter Springs News* (KS), August 17, 1911.

59. "Maj. Sylvester puts o.k. on spooning in parks." *Washington Herald*, April 14, 1912.

60. "For law against kissing." *Evening Star* (Washington), June 18, 1912.

61. "Kiss, rub noses or shake hands; which is best." *Evening World* (NY), June 19, 1912.

62. "The anti-kissing board in session." *New York Tribune*, June 23, 1912.

63. "Cruel captains forbid spooning." *Washington Times*, August 12, 1912.

64. "Police put ban on kissing at depot." *Logansport Journal* (IN), August 14, 1912.

65. "Kissing under ban." *Lexington Dispatch* (SC), August 14, 1912.

66. "Must not kiss in trains." *Bridgeport Evening Farmer* (CT), September 26, 1912.

67. "Kissing prohibited." *Washington Times*, February 1, 1913.

68. "Chicago briefs." *Day Book* (Chicago), May 7, 1914.

69. "Photo plays." *Evening Public Ledger* (Philadelphia), January 22, 1915.

70. "Health of city and country." *Washington Herald*, February 11, 1915.

71. "Bans dope kiss in prison." *Kansas City Sun* (MO), November 13, 1915.

72. "Husbands may spank non-kissing wives." *Washington Herald*, August 14, 1916.

73. "Ban on kissing placed by oarsmen by coach." *Evening Public Ledger* (Philadelphia), March 6, 1917.

74. "Elsinore adopts anti-kissing ordinance." *Corona Courier* (CA), May 10, 1918.

75. "Anti-kissing law not constitutional." *Bakersfield Morning Echo* (CA), November 17, 1918; "Ban on kissing lifted at Long Beach, Calif." *El Paso Herald*, December 27, 1918.

76. "Riverside mayor favors legitimate love-making." *Richmond Times-Dispatch* (VA), May 4, 1919.

77. No title. *Maui News* (Wailuku, HI), January 2, 1920.

78. Jack Carberry. "Kissing ban arouses Texas." *Cumberland Evening Times* (MD), September 9, 1920.

79. "Spanish law forbids kissing in public." *Ocala Evening Star* (FL), September 14, 1920.

80. No title. *Columbia Evening Missourian*, February 14, 1922.

Bibliography.

"A ban on kissing." *Plymouth Tribune* (IN), October 25, 1906.

"A ban on kissing." *Bode Bugle* (IA), May 28, 1909.

"A ban on kissing." *New York Tribune*, April 17, 1910.

"A kissless city in New Jersey." *Day Book* (Chicago), December 30, 1915.

"A non-kissing organization." *Evening Star* (Washington), July 31, 1910.

"A question of privilege." *Guthrie Daily Leader* (OK), January 11, 1901.

"A rule against kissing." *Evening Times* (Washington), July 25, 1902.

"A war over kissing games." *Evening Star* (Washington), January 20, 1890.

Ad. *San Francisco Call*, November 25, 1909.

"Advises wife to make her husband fumigate beard for each kiss." *Seattle Star*, October 26, 1910.

"Against kissing picnics." *Washington Standard* (Olympia, WA), July 17, 1891.

"Ah ha! Now it is the pat-pat that will succeed the old time kiss." *Plymouth Times* (OH), September 3, 1915.

"Aldermen in danger." *Kalispell Bee* (MT), January 8, 1901.

"All about kisses." *St. Paul Globe*, November 3, 1889.

"Ancient laws." *San Francisco Call*, June 18, 1894.

"Anti-kissers break vows." *Bismarck Tribune* (ND), June 17, 1903.

"Anti-kissing bill." *Richmond Dispatch* (VA), December 2, 1902.

"Anti-kissing bill." *Richmond Dispatch* (VA), December 7, 1902.

"Anti-kissing club." *Burlington Gazette* (IA), December 12, 1894.

"Anti-kissing club." *Indianapolis Journal*, June 2, 1901.

"Anti-kissing club." *Stark County Democrat* (Canton, OH), July 15, 1902.

"Anti-kissing club." *San Francisco Call*, October 9, 1904.

"Anti-kissing club." *News* (Frederick, VA), May 8, 1908.

"Anti-kissing club is formed by girls." *Minneapolis Journal*, March 4, 1906.

"Anti-kissing crusade advocated by physicians." *Plymouth Tribune* (IN), June 11, 1908.

"Anti-kissing crusade." *Watchman and Southron* (Sumter, SC), January 9, 1901.

"Anti-kissing female is headed for Zion." *Salt Lake Tribune*, July 26, 1907.

"Anti-kissing law." *Southern Sentinel* (Winfield, LA), April 24, 1903.

"Anti-kissing law not constitutional." *Bakersfield Morning Echo* (CA), November 17, 1918.

"Anti-kissing societies for women." *Lock Haven Express* (PA), November 26, 1889.

"Anti-kissing society." *Shelbyville Republican* (IN), June 11, 1901.

"Anti-kissing." *St. Paul Globe*, May 10, 1895.

"Anti-kissing." *Defiance Express* (OH), March 6, 1906.

"Anti-osculation society." *Jamestown Weekly Alert* (ND), December 24, 1903.

"Antiseptic kissing introduced by Professor Harry Butler." *New York Tribune*, May 15, 1910.

"Asks law against kissing." *Cedar Rapids Evening Gazette* (IA), December 2, 1902.

"Atlanta leads in reform." *Bamberg Herald* (SC), August 26, 1909.

"Awful germs lurk in schoolboy kiss." *Washington Times*, July 4, 1907.

Ball, Susan W. "Woman's world." *Terre Haute Saturday Spectator* (IN), October 20, 1906.

"Ban on kissing." *Janesville Gazette* (WI), May 12, 1904.

"Ban on kissing." *Plymouth Tribune* (IN), November 10, 1910.

"Ban on kissing." *Oakland City Journal* (CA), January 23, 1920.

"Ban on kissing games." *Washington Herald*, November 11, 1906.

"Ban on kissing games." *Norfolk Weekly News-Journal* (NE), July 5, 1907.

"Ban on kissing lifted at Long Beach, Calif." *El Paso Herald*, December 27, 1918.

"Ban on kissing placed by oarsmen by coach." *Evening Public Ledger* (Philadelphia), March 6, 1917.

"Ban on kissing to stop sore throat epidemic." *Topeka State Journal* (KS), March 13, 1917.

"Ban on park kissing lifted." *Carbondale Free Press* (IL), September 29, 1909.

"Bans dope kiss in prison." *Kansas City Sun* (MO), November 13, 1915.

"Barksdale bill is recommended." *Times* (Richmond, VA), January 23, 1903.

"Begins crusade against kissing." *Los Angeles Herald*, May 30, 1910.

"Better babies is Tacoma's slogan." *Tacoma Times*, May 1, 1917.

"Beware the cold kiss." *Evening World* (NY), June 9, 1921.

"Beware the kiss of death." *Boston Sunday Post*, July 7, 1907.

"Blame blisters on kissing." *Logan Republican* (UT), September 29, 1921.

"Blocks ban on kissing." *Chickasha Daily Express* (OK), August 26, 1913.

"Board of health to denounce kissing." *Racine Journal* (WI), May 12, 1904.

Brown, Betty. "Is it wrong to kiss in the park?" *Arizona Republican* (Phoenix), June 11, 1919.

"Bryan paragraphs." *Crittenden Press* (Marion, KY), November 6, 1902.

"Canoeists meet to protest against anti-kissing rules tonight." *Boston Post*, August 19, 1903.

Carberry, Jack. "Kissing ban arouses Texas." *Cumberland Evening Times* (MD), September 9, 1920.

"Charles River deserted except by children and elderly women." *Boston Post*, August 22, 1903.

"Chasing the kissing bug out of Malden." *Boston Sunday Post*, November 18, 1906.

"Chat about women." *Omaha Daily Bee*, January 30, 1910.

"Chicago briefs." *Day Book* (Chicago), May 7, 1914.

"Class opposed to sanitary kiss." *Washington Times*, May 25, 1912.

"Columbia girls approve kissing." *Bridgeport Evening Farmer* (CT), March 30, 1916.

"Comments of the press." *Dubuque Telegraph Herald* (IA), October 26, 1902.

"Concerning stage kisses." *Evening Star* (Washington), December 19, 1882.

"Condemns kissing of invalids." *San Francisco Call*, October 19, 1906.

"Crook not a wonder." *Jamestown Weekly Alert* (ND), May 23, 1901.

"Crook, the unkissed." *Pascagoula Democrat-Star* (MS), May 24, 1901.

"Crusade against kissing." *Helena Independent* (MT), February 14, 1893.

"Crusade against kissing." *Kansas City Journal* (MO), December 25, 1897.

"Crusade against kissing." *St. Paul Globe,* July 14, 1902.

Cullen, Clarence. "Anti-osculation crusade is originated in New York by police." *Evening Star* (Washington), June 19, 1909.

"Cupid wins and doctors put no ban on kissing." *Evening World* (NY), June 7, 1907.

"Daily Blob." *Abbeville Press and Banner* (SC), August 9, 1885.

"Danger in shaking hands." *State Center Enterprise* (IA), January 21, 1904.

"Danger of kissing the sick." *Arizona Republican* (Phoenix), January 17, 1901.

"Dangers of kissing." *Butler Weekly Times* (PA), March 30, 1887.

"Death in his kiss." *Minneapolis Journal*, April j2, 1901.

"Declared war on kissing." *Free Lance* (Fredericksburg, VA), November 24, 1903.

"Decline of the kiss." *Gazette* (Forth Worth, TX), August 26, 1889

"Defends anti-kissing crusade." *Somerset Herald* (PA), February 16, 1898.

"Dentist in war against kissing." *Indianapolis Star*, July 6, 1912.

"Departures in social usage." *Virginia Enterprise* (MN), October 5, 1894.

"Destroying bacteria by labial explosions." *Austin Weekly Statesman* (TX), November 30, 1893.

"Did not give up kissing." *Des Moines News* (IA), September 3, 1897.

"Discovers a new peril in kissing." *St. Louis Republic*, October 23, 1904.

"Disinfected kisses." *Evening Star* (Washington), November 14, 1896.

"Dismalisms." *Cincinnati Daily Press*, March 30, 1860.

"Don't kiss baby or he will be sick." *Albuquerque Evening Citizen*, July 23, 1907.

"Don't kiss me warning." *Bennington Evening Banner* (VT), November 20, 1909.

"Don't kiss the babies." *Norfolk Weekly News-Journal* (NE), June 7, 1907.

"Don't kiss the baby." *Helena Weekly Herald* (MT), February 18, 1875.

"Don't kiss the baby." *St. Paul Globe*, February 5, 1884.

"Dr. Ware gets no rest." *Times* (Richmond, VA), December 25, 1902.

"Dr. Ware is famous." *Times* (Richmond, VA), December 10, 1902.

"Dr. Ware's anti-kissing bill." *Times* (Richmond, VA), December 4, 1902.

"Dr. Ware's anti-kissing bill." *Times* (Richmond, VA), December 5, 1902.

"Dr. Ware's anti-kissing bill." *Times* (Richmond, VA), December 9, 1902.

"Dr. Wiley favors kissing." *Virginia Enterprise* (MN), August 2, 1912.

"Elsinore adopts anti-kissing ordinance." *Corona Courier* (CA), May 10, 1918.

"Enough of kissing." *Evening Star* (Washington), September 13, 1890.

"Evanston, Ill., young people start a new order, the kiss shunners." *Boston Post*, July 16, 1902.

"Every town has its anti-kiss enthusiast." *Monett Times* (MO), June 10, 1910.

"Excursion boats. Cruel captains forbid spooning." *Washington Times*, August 12, 1912.

"Feels European ridicule." *New York Tribune*, August 27, 1906.

"Find kissing costly." *Richmond Planet* (VA), July 20, 1901.

"For kissing in public." *Indianapolis Journal*, October 26, 1899.

"For law against kissing." *Evening Star* (Washington), June 18, 1912.

"For the babies' sake." *Pittsburgh Dispatch*, June 6, 1890.

"Forbidden to kiss." *Newberry Herald and News* (SC), February 13, 1903.

"Forbids kissing." *Boston Post*, December 24, 1897.

"Form an anti-kissing club." *St. Paul Globe*, February 13, 1898.

"Gen. Sherman on kissing." *Boston Sunday Globe*, November 16, 1890.

"Germs in kisses? Forget 'em says this Boston physician." *Boston Sunday Post*, May 14, 1916.

"Girls form anti-kissing club." *Salt Lake Tribune*, October 3, 1904.

"Got engaged and broke up the anti-kissing society." *Seattle Star*, July 2, 1903.

Greeley-Smith, Nixola. "Take your kisses boiled." *Evening World* (NY), January 25, 1904.

Greeley-Smith, Nixola. "Anti-kissing crusade all nonsense." *Evening World* (NY), November 10, 1911.

Greeley-Smith, Nixola. "If Princeton were only nearer New York." *Evening World* (NY), April 1, 1916.

"Grip causes ban on kissing." *Sun* (NY), December 21, 1915.

"Grip germs entrenched throughout Middle West." *Daily Gate City* (Keokuk, IA), December 23, 1915.

Hart, Lavinia. "If you kiss, use an antiseptic daily." *New York World*, December 28, 1900.

Haskin, Frederick J. "The Haskin letter." *Great Falls Tribune* (MT), March 22, 1921.

"He has never kissed a woman." *Minneapolis Journal*, April 25, 1901.

"Health board puts ban on kissing." *Challis Messenger* (ID), September 25, 1918.

"Health of city and county." *Washington Herald*, February 11, 1915.

"Heartless scientists." *Barbour County Index* (Medicine Lodge, KS), December 20, 1905.

"Here we have something to kill germs and make kissing safe." *Muskogee Times Democrat* (OK), February 16, 1912.

"High-priced osculation." *Evening Times* (Washington), November 10, 1899.

"How about this girls?" *Anaconda Standard* (MT), January 1, 1901.

"How cruel." *Cedar Rapids Evening Gazette* (IA), November 10, 1896.

"How to keep baby cool in the summer." *Tacoma Times*, July 17, 1912.

"How, whom, when to kiss." *Comet* (Johnson City, TN), November 8, 1900.

"Husbands may spank non-kissing wives." *Washington Herald*, August 14, 1916.

"Husbands weary and bachelors wary decree against the kiss." *San Francisco Call*, April 5, 1903.

"Hygiene for the home." *Seattle Post-Intelligencer*, June 25, 1891.

"If railroad managers are to prohibit kissing at train gates." *Boston Sunday Post*, September 28, 1902.

"If you must kiss, be sure and boil 'em." *El Paso Herald*, November 30, 1912.

"Illness and bliss both lie in kiss." *Indianapolis Sun*, June 22, 1910.

"In 1954." *Camden Chronicle* (TN), June 10, 1904.

"In babyland." *San Francisco Call*, March 10, 1895.

"In society." *Fort Wayne Journal Gazette* (IN), January 2, 1902.

"Is handshaking dangerous?" *Salt Lake Herald*, December 23, 1902.

"Is kissing harmful?" *Kokomo Tribune* (IN), December 23, 1903.

"Is kissing healthful? Should it be abolished?" *Judith Gap Journal* (MT), April 4, 1911.

"It smacks of opposition." *Anaconda Standard* (MT), September 26, 1899.

"Kiss all you want to." *Wichita Daily Eagle*, December 14, 1894.

"Kiss at Coney? No, say police; it's disorderly." *Washington Times*, July 20, 1907.

"Kiss through silk gauze." *Virginia Enterprise* (MN), April 22, 1910.

"Kiss, rub noses or shake hands; which is best." *Evening World* (NY), June 19, 1912.

"Kisses and cash to doom the nation." *Bisbee Review* (AZ), July 31, 1907.

"Kisses and Microbes." *Burlington Evening Gazette* (IA), November 22, 1890.

"Kisses and the law." *Spokane Press*, May 16, 1905.

"Kisses full of germs." *Columbian* (Bloomsburg, PA), February 13, 1908.

"Kissing." *Boston Sunday Globe*, January 26, 1901.

"Kissing." *Columbia Herald* (TN), February 15, 1901.

"Kissing." *Rock Island Argus* (IL), April 3, 1920.

"Kissing and non-kissing families." *Virginia Enterprise* (MN), August 23, 1901.

"Kissing as a peril." *Baxter Springs News* (KS), August 17, 1911.

"Kissing before public." *Hopkinsville Kentuckian*, February 20, 1903.

"Kissing devil." *Manning Times* (SC), July 24, 1907.

"Kissing forbidden." *Indianapolis Journal*, November 20, 1899.

"Kissing games." *Ogden Standard* (UT), May 22, 1908.

"Kissing hygienically unhealthy." *Canton Times* (MS), September 27, 1895.

"Kissing in public not a crime." *Fulton County News* (McConnellsburg, PA), June 20, 1907.

"Kissing in public places." *Biloxi Daily Herald* (MS), August 30, 1915.

"Kissing in schools tabooed by Indiana Board of Health action." *Rock Island Argus* (IL), August 10, 1906.

"Kissing in the street." *Elk County Advocate* (Ridgway, PA), June 4, 1869.

"Kissing is doomed." *Democratic Press* (Ravenna, OH), January 7, 1886.

"Kissing is now perfectly safe." *Ogden Standard* (UT), April 30, 1910.

"Kissing is still safe." *Seattle Star*, November 8, 1902.

"Kissing laws in New Jersey." *New York World*, January 2, 1898.

"Kissing microbe feared." *Davenport Daily Republican* (IA), March 17, 1901.

"Kissing not unfashionable." *Yakima Herald* (WA), November 26, 1896.

"Kissing prohibited." *Washington Times*, February 1, 1913.

"Kissing under ban." *Lexington Dispatch* (SC), August 14, 1912.

"Kissing will not be under ban in El Paso." *El Paso Herald*, January 8, 1916.

Knox, J. Armoy. "An essay on kissing." *Syracuse Herald*, October 11, 1891.

 "Law against kissing" *Indianapolis Sun*, December 20, 1900.

"Law enforcement." *Topeka State Journal* (KS), November 15, 1920.

"Laws against kissing." *Intelligencer* (Anderson, SC), September 30, 1915.

"Ledger lines." *Public Ledger* (Memphis, TN), May 9, 1876.

"Local intelligence." *Vermont Phoenix* (Brattleboro), February 18, 1860.

"Local Paragraphs." *Pascagoula Democratic-Star* (MS), January 23, 1880.

"Lovers' kisses sacred and natural impulse, says woman physician." *Washington Times*, July 19, 1907.

"Maj. Sylvester puts o.k. on spooning in parks." *Washington Herald*, April 14, 1912.

"Mayor Young will not issue proclamation against kissing." *Arizona Republican* (Phoenix), January 16, 1916.

"Men agree not to kiss their wives." *Janesville Gazette* (WI), June 1, 1901.

"Mesa." *Arizona Republican* (Phoenix), January 29, 1907.

"Minnesota law aims to regulate kissing." *Washington Times*, January 30, 1903.

"Miss Baldwin is a charter member of non-kissing club." *Escanaba Press* (MI), March 11, 1919.

"Miss Lindley on kissing." *Sun* (NY), May 9, 1899.

"Morbid fear." *Indianapolis Journal*, February 24, 1901.

"Must never kiss in public." *Deseret Evening News* (Salt Lake), October 13, 1906.

"Must not kiss in trains." *Bridgeport Evening News* (CT), September 26, 1912.

"Nancy Lee on freaks and the day's doings." *Seattle Post-Intelligencer*, August 27, 1899.

"Naughty mistletoe." *Canton News* (OH), December 29, 1915.

"Needs no button." *Princeton Union* (MN), March 16, 1911.

"New ban on kisses." *Clinch Valley News* (Jeffersonville, VA), November 10, 1905.

"New Castle old-fashioned when it comes to adopting the latest sanitary kiss." *New Castle News* (PA), February 6, 1919.

"New club starts with 'kiss not' as a war cry." *Spokane Press*, May 26, 1910.

"New York Stricken." *St. Paul Globe*, December 23, 1898.

"No ban on kissing at old Coney Island." *Sandusky Star* (OH), September 5, 1904.

"No germs, he says, in kisses." *Boston Post*, June 10, 1904.

"No kisses worries Hoosiers." *Des Moines Daily News* (IA), August 28. 1906.

"No kissing in the park." *Indianapolis Journal*, July 15, 1890.

"No more kissing." *San Francisco Call*, November 29, 1893.

"No more kissing girls." *Day Book* (Chicago), December 30, 1915.

"No more kissing of the bible." *Lexington Gazette* (KY), December 24, 1902.

"No more kissing, little girls, pat-pat is proper thing." *Reno Evening Gazette*, July 24, 1915.

"No public kissing allowed in Japan." *Washington Times*, September 9, 1920.

"No time for such nonsense." *Minneapolis Journal*, January 15, 1901.

No title. *Daily Comet* (Baton Rouge, LA), April 20, 1854.

No title. *Edgefield Advertiser* (SC), March 2, 1871.

No title. *Daily Phoenix* (Columbia, SC), September 9, 1871.

No title. *Greenville Advance* (PA), September 30, 1871.

No title. *Bloomfield Times* (New Bloomfield, PA), October 14, 1873.

No title. *New Orleans Republican*, January 10, 1875.

No title. *Salt Lake Herald*, January 5, 1883.

No title. *Hazel Green Herald* (KY), February 10, 1886.

No title. *Omaha Daily Bee*, May 16, 1887.

No title. *Burlington Hawk Eye* (IA), April 11, 1889.

No title. *Daily Morning Astorian* (Astoria, OR), June 13, 1889.

No title. *Keowee Courier* (Pickens, SC), July 11, 1889.

No title. *Kern County Californian* (Bakersfield, CA), September 21, 1889.

No title. *Brenham Weekly Banner* (TX), May 8, 1890.

No title. *Kokomo Tribune* (IN), December 29, 1890.

No title. *Greenfield Adair County Democrat* (IA), February 23, 1893.

No title. *Evening Bulletin* (Maysville, KY), July 18, 1894.

No title. *North Platte Tribune* (NE), December 26, 1894.

No title. *Coconino Weekly Sun* (Flagstaff, AZ), January 3, 1895.

No title. *Columbian* (Bloomsburg, PA), January 18, 1895.

No title. *Freeland Tribune* (PA), February 11, 1895.

No title. *Butler Citizen* (PA), February 21, 1895.

No title. *Juniata Sentinel and Republican* (Mifflintown, PA), June 30, 1897.

No title. *Weekly Register* (Point Pleasant, WV), October 13, 1897.

No title. *Middleburgh Post* (PA), October 21, 1897.

No title. *St. Paul Globe*, October 29, 1897.

No title. *Breckinridge News* (Cloverport, KY), March 15, 1899.

No title. *Williamsport Warren Republican* (IN), January 3, 1901.

No title. *Richmond Dispatch* (VA), June 11, 1901.

No title. *Cook County Herald* (Grand Marais, MN), August 31, 1901.

No title. *Cook County Herald* (Grand Marais, MN), September 27, 1902.

No title. *Washington Standard* (Olympia, WA), November 7, 1902.

No title. *Semi-Weekly Journal* (Stanford, KY), February 6, 1903.

No title. *Rock Island Argus* (IL), February 11, 1903.

No title. *St. Paul Globe*, January 21, 1904.

No title. *Alexandria Gazette* (VA), September 19, 1904.

No title. *Elyria Reporter* (OH), February 20, 1906.

No title. *Goodwin's Weekly* (Salt Lake), September 29, 1906.

No title. *Boston Globe*, April 30, 1910.

No title. *Albert Lea Evening* Tribune (MN), May 23, 1910.

No title. *Hopkinsville Kentuckian*, August 12, 1915.

No title. *Maui News* (Wailuku, HI), January 2, 1920.

No title. *Columbia Evening Missourian*, February 14, 1922.

Noel, Leon. "Medical notes." *St. Paul Globe*, December 2, 1900.

"Now Waukesha joins in." *Minneapolis Journal*, October 30, 1903.

"Of kisses and kissing." *New York Tribune*, June 17, 1891.

"Official kiss catchers wanted for New Jersey." *New York World*, December 30, 1897.

"On kissing." *Staunton Spectator and Vindicator* (VA), November 27, 1908.

"Osculations." *Fort Wayne News* (IN), December 1, 1894.

"People and things." *Omaha Daily Bee*, February 27, 1895.

"Peril lurks in kisses." *Los Angeles Herald*, March 14, 1907.

"Personal and pertinent." *New York World*, February 23, 1893.

"Personal recollections." *Jackson Standard* (OH), June 30, 1870.

"Photo plays." *Evening Public Ledger* (Philadelphia), January 22, 1915.

"Pledge cards for anti-kissing league." *New Ulm Review* (MN), June 8, 1910.

"Police put ban on kissing at depot." *Logansport Journal* (IN), August 14, 1912.

"Praise work of societies." *Syracuse Post*, March 9, 1910.

"Pray for husband." *Syracuse Herald*, September 2, 1912.

"Priest puts ban on kissing parties." *New York World*, December 11, 1900.

"Proposes kissing ban." *St. Paul Globe*, August 24, 1902.

"Queen Ena inaugurates anti-kissing crusade." *Washington Times*, March 27, 1914.

"Quit your kissing." *Rock Island Argus* (IL), February 18, 1909.

"Riverside mayor favors legitimate love-making." *Richmond Times-Dispatch* (VA), May 4, 1919k.

"Robbing school of charm." *Elkhart Daily Review* (IN), August 9, 1906.

"Sanitary kiss rule is much modified." *New Castle News* (PA), December 22, 1919.

"Says kissing isn't nice." *Boston Post*, March 6, 1899.

"Says she'll never rest until kissing is no more." *Evening Star* (Washington), June 19, 1910.

"Says thou shalt not kiss." *Minneapolis Journal*, January 22, 1904.

"School board puts a ban on kissing." *Seattle Star*, November 27, 1909.

"Seattle man believes in no kissing." *Spokane Press*, August 27, 1909.

"She makes war on kissing." *Dubuque Herald* (IA), February 20, 1898.

"She was fined for kissing." *Evening Times* (Washington), December 29, 1897.

"Should mates kiss in public?" *Tulsa World*, February 26, 1922.

"Shun kissing." *Independent* (Honolulu), August 6, 1901.

"Society's fads." *Marshall County Independent* (Plymouth, IN), May 3, 1895.

"Some queer clubs." *Kansas City Journal* (MO), April 20, 1895.

"Spanish law forbids kissing in public." *Ocala Evening Star* (FL), September 14, 1920.

"Special mention." *Livingstone Enterprise* (MT), June 25, 1887.

"State board adopts unique anti-kissing poster." *Indianapolis Star*, May 28, 1911.

"State board of health places ban on kissing." *Bridgeport Evening Farmer* (CT), July 27, 1916.

"Stolen sweets beware." *Boston Globe*, May 24, 1893.

"Stop kissing." *Boston Globe*, July 24, 1902.

"Teachers dislike kissing." *Guthrie Daily Leader* (OK), September 16, 1904.

"That bacillus in a kiss." *Indianapolis Sun*, November 4, 1896.

"That kissing business." *Albuquerque Citizen*, June 20, 1902.

"The anti-kissing board in session." *New York Tribune*, June 23, 1912.

"The art of throwing kisses." *Sun* (NY), September 27, 1903.

"The ballad of the rail." *Goodwin's Weekly* (Salt Lake), August 2, 1902.

"The carbolized kiss." *Wichita Eagle*, August 13, 1895.

"The dangers and damages of kissing." *Wichita Eagle*, March 5, 1899.

"The dangers of kissing." *Postville Review* (IA), September 25, 1886.

"The dangers of kissing." *Progressive Farmer* (Winston, NC), October 26, 1897.

"The extinction of the kiss." *Newberry Herald and News* (SC), February 15, 1893.

"The friendship of women." *Wheeling Daily Intelligencer* (WV), May 31 1866.

"The habit of kissing." *Montour American* (Danville, PA), June 13, 1907.

"The kiss has come to stay." *Fort Wayne Gazette* (IN), April 30, 1890.

"The kiss hygienic." *Colfax Gazette* (WA), December 17, 1909.

"The kiss hygienic: guaranteed innocuous." *New York Tribune*, September 12, 1909.

"The kiss that kills." *Clifton Record* (TX), January 3, 1908.

"The kissing question." *Eaton Democrat* (OH), May 26, 1881.

"The microbe's safe graft." *Spokane Press*, November 9, 1908.

"The non-oscuolant Hoosier." *Arizona Republican* (Phoenix), September 11, 1906.

"The osculatory problem." *St. Paul Globe*, March 1, 1885.

"The rise of kissing." *Boston Post*, July 12, 1910.

"The sanitary kiss." *Pioneer Express* (Pembina, ND), October 30, 1914.

"The sanitary kiss." *East Liverpool Evening Review* (OH), March 10, 1915.

"The spice." *Manning Times* (SC), April 24, 1907.

"The tyranny of the P.R.R. Co." *Deseret Evening News* (Salt Lake), June 17, 1902.

"The ubiquitous microbe." *Scranton Tribune* (PA), September 7, 1894.

"The whispering gallery." *Wheeling Intelligencer* (WV), June 6, 1885.

"They object to kissing." *Greensburg Review* (IN), August 9, 1899.

"They refuse to swear off." *Minneapolis Journal*, January 1, 1901.

"They shun kissing." *Butler Weekly Times* (MO), January 15, 1903.

"They will not osculate." *Arizona Weekly Journal-Miner* (Prescott), July 23, 1902.

"Those wicked microbes again." *Indianapolis Journal*, December 7, 1902.

"To enforce a germless kiss." *Butler Weekly Times* (MO), February 5, 1903.

"To kiss or not to kiss." *San Francisco Call*, July 31, 1910.

"Too much kissing lowers morals is warning of woman." *Comanche Chief* (TX), January 6, 1922.

"Truth will out, doctor." *Altoona mirror* (PA), September 18, 1915.

"Two men get on board." *Pittsburgh Dispatch*, February 20, 1890.

"United order of kiss shunners is no more." *St. Paul Globe*, July 23, 1902.

"Unnecessary precautions." *Kinsley Graphic* (KS), March 4, 1904.

"Unregulated kissing." *Boston Globe*, March 21, 1893.

Vernon, Lue F. "Iowa against kissing." *Washington Standard* (Olympia, WA), August 12, 1910.

"Wages war on kissing." *Portsmouth Times* (OH), February 25, 1911.

"Wants anti-kiss law." *Evening Bulletin* (Honolulu), August 10, 1907.

"Wants barbers to study medicine." *Boston Post*, March 18, 1912.

"War on kissing." *Bedford Democrat* (IN), August 17, 1906.

"War on kissing brides." *Postville National Advocate* (IA), December 25, 1884.

"War on kissing declared." *Logansport Reporter* (IN), December 28, 1890.

"War on kissing declared." *Logansport Reporter* (IN), December 28, 1900.

"Ware and wise." *Richmond Dispatch* (VA), December 4, 1902.

"Warns against kissing evil." *Washington Herald*, December 22, 1915.

"What will the poor girl do?" *Los Angeles Herald*, May 17, 1905.

"Where kissing is a crime." *Monroe City Democrat* (MO), October 8, 1903.

Whiteman, Mary Gwynn. "Social." *Daily Ardmoreite* (Ardmore, OK), July 7, 1910.

"Who would testify." *Richmond Dispatch* (VA), December 7, 1902.

"Who's afraid." *Washington Standard* (Olympia, WA), January 14, 1910.

"Wiley is very wise." *Ocala Evening Star* (FL), July 5, 1910.

"Will it ever be stopped." *Herald and News* (Newberry, SC), May 13, 1910.

Williams, Byron. "Philosophical observations." *Jennings Daily Record* (LA), December 12, 1902.

"Witnesses need no longer kiss Bible." *Washington Times*, February 7, 1903.

"Women agree not to kiss." *Evening Star* (Washington), December 12, 1904.

"Women laugh at minister's war against kissing." *Evening World* (NY), February 23, 1909.

"Women might have kissed Prof. Crook." *St. Louis Republic*, April 28, 1901.

"Women wild to wed man who never kissed one of them." *St. Louis Republic*, April 28, 1901.

"Would abolish kissing." *New York Tribune*, February 1, 1909.

"Would ban baby kisses as breeders of disease." *Washington Times*, October 14, 1920.

"Wouldn't talk on kisses." *Boston Post*, August 19, 1903.

"Young man founded an antikissing society." *Tacoma Times* (WA), February 1, 1904.

"Young women form anti-kissing society." *Hanover Evening Sun* (PA), January 27, 1920.

"Zion City will be kissless henceforth." *St. Paul Globe*, November 21, 1903.